Paramount Pictures

and the People
Who Made Them

Also by I. G. Edmonds

Big U Universal in the Silent Days
Second Sight
Buddhism
Motorcycle Racing for Beginners

Paramount Pictures and the People Who Made Them

I. G. Edmonds and Reiko Mimura

SAN DIEGO • NEW YORK
A. S. BARNES & COMPANY, INC.
IN LONDON:
THE TANTIVY PRESS

Paramount Pictures and the People Who Made Them
text copyright ©1980 by I. G. Edmonds and Reiko Mimura
A. S. Barnes and Co., Inc.

The Tantivy Press
Magdalen House
136-148 Tooley Street
London, SE1 2TT, England

First Edition
Manufactured in the United States of America
For information write to A. S. Barnes and Company, Inc.,
P.O. Box 3051, San Diego, CA 92038

Library of Congress Cataloging in Publication Data

Edmonds, I G
  Paramount Pictures and the people who made them

  Includes indexes.
  1. Paramount Pictures Corporation. I. Mimura, Reiko
joint author. II. Title.
PN1999.P3E3   384′.8′0979494   78-75304
ISBN 0-498-02322-2

1 2 3 4 5 6 7 8 9 84 83 82 81 80

Dedication

Once again to Oliver Dernberger
with the deepest thanks for his indispensable help these many years.

Acknowledgments

All scenes from films used in this book were originally copyrighted between 1913 and 1967 by the Famous Players Film Company, Jesse L. Lasky Feature Play Company, Famous Players-Lasky Corporation, Paramount-Publix Corporation, Paramount Pictures Inc., Paramount Pictures Corporation, Paramount-Artcraft, or Realart Corporation. On many of the earlier films there is no record of copyright renewal.

Other credits include *My Friend Irma*, copyright 1949 by Hall Wallis Productions; *The Heiress*, copyright 1948 by Liberty Productions; *Strange Love of Martha Ivers*, copyright 1946, Hall Wallis Productions; *The Stooge*, copyright 1953, Hall Wallis Productions; *Tarzan's Greatest Adventure*, copyright 1959, Solar Film Productions; and *Last Train From Gun Hill*, copyright 1958, Hal Wallis, Joseph Hazen. All rights are reserved in every case.

Most of the photographs are from the authors' collections, assembled in almost 50 years of collecting. For assistance on the others the authors are deeply indebted to Oliver Dernberger; Malcolm Willets, and Leonard Brown of Collector's Bookstore; Milton Luboviski of Larry Edmonds Bookstore; and the library staff of the Academy of Motion Picture Arts and Sciences.

Contents

Paramount Pictures

and the People
Who Made Them

Introduction-A Mountain and Stars

William Wadsworth Hodkinson was seeking a name for a company he was organizing to distribute feature motion pictures. He happened to pass a building displaying a sign reading "Paramount Apartments."

"Paramount! That's it," Wadsworth said to himself.

Later he sat down to draw a sketch of a trademark logo for his new name. The slender, prematurely bald film salesman loved mountains. So he began with the outline of a mountain. Something was lacking. Hodkinson ringed the peak with stars. He liked that and took the design to an artist for refinement. The designer added "Paramount Pictures," and a famous logo was born.

In time the majestic mountain with its stars became one of the most famous trademarks in the entertainment world and a symbol to conjure with in the world of high finance. Then an astute publicity man coined a slogan to go with the trademark: "If it's a Paramount Picture, it's the best show in town."

Paramount did not always offer the best show in town, but it happened so often that no one could really quarrel with the slogan. From its founding in 1914 until the big studio system crumbled in the 1950s and 1960s, Paramount produced many memorable films, including all-time classics such as *The Ten Commandments, Peter Pan, Wings, The Covered Wagon, Sunset Boulevard, Lost Weekend, The Godfather,* and others.

And Paramount had the stars, too. Metro-Goldwyn-Mayer claimed to have more stars than there were in heaven, but Leo the Lion never had the gall to boast that he had more stars than Paramount. Looking back over the years we find Mary Pickford, Fatty Arbuckle, William Farnum, Minnie Maddern Fiske, Douglas Fairbanks, William S. Hart, Eddie Cantor, Clara Bow, Wallace Reid, Adolphe Menjou, Wallace Beery, Gary Cooper, Ronald Colman, Shirley Temple, Bing Crosby, Ethel Merman, Bob Hope, Ray Milland, Mae West, John Wayne, Dorothy Lamour, Richard Dix, Jack Holt, Nancy Carroll, Buddy Rogers, Richard Arlen, George Bancroft, Maurice Chevalier, Jeanette MacDonald, W. C. Fields, Charles Farrell, Lon Chaney, Sr., Thomas Meighan, Betty Compson,

Wings, 1927, was the first aviation epic. This classic picture was directed by William Wellman. *Copyright 1927 by Paramount Pictures, Inc.*

Louise Brooks, Valentino, Marlene Dietrich, Pola Negri, Gloria Swanson, William Holden, Barbara Stanwyck, Marlon Brando, Kirk Douglas, Burt Lancaster, Carole Lombard, Cary Grant, Clark Gable, Harold Lloyd, George Raft, John Barrymore, and a legion of others, including cockeyed old Ben Turpin.

If some of these names are unfamiliar or are remembered as those of character actors or actresses, let us assure you that everyone of them—at one time or another—was a star in every sense of the word.

Paramount had an outstanding record as a filmmaker. No critic today, seeing these old films at a museum or at a silent movie house, can adequately judge their quality. An old film, like an old book, must be judged in the framework of its own time. A better opinion of any old film comes from the critics of its period. The critics and the moviegoers of the silent period agreed that Paramount dominated the film industry from 1914 until the rise of Metro-Goldwyn-Mayer in 1924. Even then Paramount remained a major force in the industry.

Its films alone are not the whole story. Not so well known to the general public, after Carl Laemmle and William Fox broke the film trust, Paramount began to shape the industry's business and financial development. Paramount blazed new trails in distribution, exploitation, and control of exhibition.

After Adolph Zukor became head of Paramount he set out to become the John D. Rockefeller of the movies. He hoped to monopolize the film industry as Rockefeller dominated the oil industry.

In fighting for his place in the entertainment world, Zukor waged some titanic battles with both his friends and his foes. Some he won, and some he lost. Among the losses was a major one with the United States government that took away Paramount's theaters. But in the end Zukor survived all his contemporaries, both as a major figure in the entertainment world and in the length of his life. When he died in the 1970s he was still "Mr. Paramount."

The story of Paramount's pictures and the people who made them begins properly in Ogden, Utah, in 1909. At that time a young telegrapher for the Union Pacific Railroad saw his first motion picture. It was a scratched print of a six-year-old film called *The Great Train Robbery*. The film was made in 1903 by Edwin S. Porter for the Edison company.

1

Iris in on Hodkinson

There might not have been a Paramount Pictures company at all if the theater owner in Ogden, Utah, had swept his floors. William Wadsworth Hodkinson let a friend finally persuade him to see a "galloping tintype." He loved the movie but hated the squalor and stale air in the showhouse.

Films at this time were being shown in converted stores. Exhibitors painted the windows black, hung a plaster-coated sheet at one end, and put a projector at the other. The seats were kitchen chairs. A ticket office was set up outside. There was no provision for ventilation. The place was usually stifling with the odor of unwashed bodies and tobacco smoke. The floor was filthy. Tobacco chewers and snuff dippers used it in lieu of spittoons. Drunks often interfered with the entertainment.

Hodkinson politely pointed out to the manager that business would increase if he cleaned up the place and threw out the riffraff. He was told in less polite language to mind his own business. At this time no one expected movies to be more than a passing fad. They would never replace live stage shows. Each producer and exhibitor was out to get as much as possible before the rainbow faded. Actors considered films merely a means of earning eating money during the time they were "at liberty" between stage engagements.

Hodkinson persisted in his belief that movie houses would be much more profitable if they cleaned up and catered to the family trade. Carl Laemmle in Chicago had the same idea, but Hodkinson did not know that.

Hodkinson persuaded friends to help finance him to start his own house. In 1909 one could open a movie theater for about $1200 to $1500. This was no small sum at a time when a common laborer made a dollar a day or less. However, profits were high. A house could return from $50 to $200 a week, depending upon its location. Smaller towns, naturally, had less trade. This meant that a theater owner could recoup his investment in a few weeks.

Since Thomas Alva Edison controlled the patents on movie projectors, it was not easy to start a new house. The motion picture trust that Edison had formed wanted to keep down competition. Fortunately, Hodkinson asked for a license just at the right moment. Carl Laemmle, Pat Powers, and William Fox—independent theater owners—had defied

W.W. Hodkinson, founder of Paramount Pictures.

the trust when Jeremiah J. Kennedy, head of the Motion Picture Patents Company (the Edison trust), demanded that every theater pay a $2–a–week license fee above the usual rental cost of trust films.

The rebel independents began making their own films, working in odd places to avoid trust efforts to bring them to court for infringing Edison's patents.

The original theater owner in Ogden refused to pay the license fee and bought independent films. The redoubtable J. J. Kennedy was pleased to set up a rival and okayed Hodkinson's application for a license. Kennedy hoped that Hodkinson would run the other theater owner out of business. This would save Kennedy the cost of going to court to sue the rebel for using Edison machines to show "outlaw" films.

Hodkinson's policy of a clean, family theater prospered. He put in ceiling fans for the summer and wood-burning heaters for the winter. Bouncers threw out drunks who tried to advise the handsome screen hero or who made suggestive remarks about the pretty heroines. Another source of trouble was the refusal of some male customers to remove their hats. When this obscured the view of a person in back, the offended one sometimes grabbed the brim and pulled the hat down over the contrary customer's ears, which naturally resulted in a fight.

Despite his troubles, Hodkinson's house was a success. He expanded into others both in Ogden and in Salt Lake City. His success soon brought him again to the attention of Jeremiah J. Kennedy, who now headed the General Film Company. General Film was formed by the Motion Picture Patents Company to distribute movies made by its licensed producers.

Kennedy invited the young man from Utah to join General Films. Hodkinson agreed and became head of the trust's exchange office in San Francisco.

It was a happy choice both for General Films and for Hodkinson. The young man was a born salesman. In addition, as an exhibitor himself, he understood the theater owner's problems.

Exhibitors had a lot of legitimate complaints against exchanges. They often were shipped old, scratched prints that broke repeatedly during projection. Often unauthorized substitutions were made. In one case Hodkinson received an erotic film entirely unsuited to his family audience. He could not show the film but had to pay the exchange for it or lose his franchise to use their pictures.

Hodkinson changed all this. Working first with the General Film exchange in Salt Lake City and then in San Francisco, Hodkinson gave exhibitors a square deal. He traveled, visiting theaters. He listened to complaints and did something about them. As a result, his exchanges greatly increased their business.

These were trying days for General Film Company. The independents were fighting the company with antitrust suits. At the same time, the independents were making better pictures in many cases. The two-reelers that General Film preferred were not long enough to develop character and tell a well-rounded story. The longer feature films were cutting into the company's business.

By 1914 Hodkinson was ready to go into business for himself. He now knew the business thoroughly. He could see the coming collapse of General Film. Zukor had established his Famous Players in Famous Plays in 1912 and in one year's time had rated himself among the most important film companies. Then in the beginning of 1914 the new Lasky Feature Play Company released its first film, *The Squawman*, based upon a hit play. The Lasky film had gone over big with theater owners. Likewise, Hobart Bosworth and Oliver Morosco were turning out superior films.

Hodkinson had no desire to make films himself. He was a salesman of films—and a very good one. He wanted to become the middle man, the wholesaler of motion pictures. To this end he conceived Paramount Pictures.

Hodkinson explained his ideas in talks with financiers as he struggled to raise capital to get Paramount started.

"Motion pictures have always been made by independent producers. Even those allied with General Film Company are independent in that they do their own financing and production and then release through the trust company," Hodkinson explained.

"Many of these producers works on a shoestring. They all have to pay heavy interest penalties on the money they borrow. My idea is for Paramount Pictures to be a film *financing* and *distribution* company. We act as middlemen between the studios and the theaters. We advance the studios the money to make their films, assuring them a profit. Then we

take the films and make our profit from the exhibitors. We can do this through straight rental fees or by taking a percentage of the gross."

"Isn't that what film exchanges are doing today?" he was asked.

"Film exchanges only distribute film," Hodkinson explained. "We *finance* films in addition to distribution. Financing ties the producer to us.

Dustin Farnum comforts Red Wing after she shoots Billy Elmer (on floor) to save Farnum in *The Squaw Man*. This was the first feature picture made in Hollywood. *Copyright 1914 by Jesse L. Lasky Feature Play Company.*

Movie pioneer Hobart Bosworth, after learning the ropes with
Selig, formed his own company. Here he is with his wife Adele
Farrington in *The Country Mouse*, released by Hodkinson in
1914. *Copyright 1914 by W.W. Hodkinson.*

"As you will recall, I have always been interested in quality. When I was running exchanges for General Film, I sold the poorer films at a discount and charged more for the quality ones. This was at a time when the industry was charging a flat price for both good and bad. I found that exhibitors were glad to pay extra when they got extra quality.

"Now I am interested in Paramount's dealing only with quality pictures—and my experience has shown that we can get quality prices for them." When he was asked where he was going to get this extra quality, Hodkinson told about Lasky, Zukor, Morosco, and Bosworth.

"All four companies are turning out superior products," Hodkinson went on. "Lasky is making 30 pictures a year. Zukor is turning out 50. Bosworth and Morosco are making about 25 each. That gives us nearly two films a week to distribute."

The bankers to whom he made his presentation wanted to know how much money would be involved. "An average feature film costs from $20,000 to $35,000," he replied.

"You are talking about us putting in $3.5 million?"

"No," Hodkinson explained. "Lasky put $20,000 into *The Squaw Man*. Shooting—money spending—began in December 1913. The picture was released February 15, 1914, at which time Goldfish, Lasky's salesman, had collected $60,000 from states' righters."

States' righters were exchange men who bought the rights to exploit a film within a given territory. S. A. Lynch, for example, bought films for a large section of the South. Louis B. Mayer, later the renowned head of Metro-Goldwyn-Mayer, made his first big killing in film by buying the Massachusetts states' rights to Griffith's *Birth of a Nation*.

The money men were interested and agreed to finance Hodkinson if he could indeed get quality production arranged. Hodkinson had no trouble getting Oliver Morosco to agree. Bosworth had left the company bearing his name due to a disagreement on policy. He was forming Pallas Pictures and was eager to solve his financial and distribution problems easily. Hodkinson next talked to Jesse L. Lasky and his partner-salesman Samuel Goldfish. Lasky also agreed to sign a contract to distribute through Paramount Pictures. Lasky had only released a dozen pictures but had scheduled an annual output of 30.

Hodkinson found Zukor harder to deal with. The head of Famous Players wanted a finger in the Paramount pie. Hodkinson refused.

"The motion picture industry is three separate operations," he said. "Each requires its own experts to operate successfully. In my view, producers should make films. Exhibitors should show them. The distributor—which is what Paramount will be—is the middleman between the two."

Zukor was adamant. "I will not bring Famous Players into Paramount unless I can own stock in the company," he said.

Hodkinson told his associates that Zukor was out to get control of Paramount. He broke off negotiations, and his backers withdrew their support. Paramount Pictures was back to being just a picture of a mountain ringed with stars.

Oliver Morosco Photoplay Company was the second firm approached by Hodkinson to join Paramount Pictures. This early Morosco film is *His Sweetheart* with Geroge Beban. Blanche Schwed is the child on the block of ice. *Copyright 1914 by Oliver Morosco.*

Hodkinson was still not beaten. He approached a group of states' rights exchange owners. They were Raymond Pawley of Philadelphia, W. L. Sherry of New York, and Walter Greene and Hiram Abrams of Boston. Later James Steele, representing Rowland and Clark of Pittsburgh, joined them. Richard Rowland, as head of Metro Pictures was to make quite an impression upon the industry. He was responsible for *The Four Horsemen of the Apocalypse*, which brought Rudolph Valentino to attention, and went on to head First National, a formidable Paramount competitor in the 1920s. Abrams eventually headed United Artists.

Adolph Zukor was Mr. Paramount for more than sixty years.

But at this time they were all film salesmen eager to find an assured source of films for their trade territories. Hodkinson now went back to Zukor. He pointed out that Paramount Pictures was going ahead. It had exclusive rights with the most important states' rights distributors in the major cities of the East and intended to move into the Midwest and Southwest as soon as the company was organized. Zukor could expect to be shut out of these markets if he did not join the new company.

Zukor had a Napoleonic complex. He was a compulsive leader, not a follower. But he was also a highly intelligent man. He did not show his anger at being pushed but kept quietly negotiating. His resentment was shoved aside in the name of good business. But it would surface another day.

Hodkinson needed Zukor as much as Zukor needed the new Paramount Pictures. Stock in Paramount had been split among the five founders, each taking 20 percent. Hodkinson went back to his partners. They agreed to let Zukor buy 10 percent of the stock. With each of them holding 18 percent, they thought they could control Zukor. But they did not know Zukor and his compulsion to rule everything he touched.

In joining Paramount the producers did not become a part of the company, except for Zukor's 10 percent. Each production company signed a 25-year contract with Paramount. This called for Paramount to advance up to $35,000 to each company for production of a five-reel film. Additional advances would be made to cover the cost of making the positive prints and to advertise in trade journals. This was expected not to exceed $40,000 in total. Paramount in turn farmed out the films to exhibitors on a percentage deal. Sixty-five percent of the gross went to Paramount, and 35 percent went to the exhibitor.

In this way Paramount handled all the financing for both sides. The producers, of course, shared in the Paramount profits in addition to the money advanced for production.

Benjamin Hampton broke down the average balance sheet for a Paramount–released film of this period in this manner:

Gross total rentals, average for this period, received from exhibitors		$100,000
Minus Paramount's charge for distribution.		−35,000
	Total	65,000

Paramount's deduction for negative costs advanced to producer, average		25,000
Plus Paramount's deduction for positive and trade costs advanced to producer, average.		+ 10,000
	Total	35,000

This $35,000 subtracted from the $65,000 left from the average original $100,000 after deduction of Paramount's $35,000 share, left an average $30,000 profit for the producer.

This assured a producer like Lasky a profit of close to $1 million a year *with no risk* and with no other investment than the real estate and equipment he owned. Zukor's profit, since he made more pictures, netted about 1.5 million.

In this day of $100 million grosses, this sounds like a very small return, but it must be remembered that theater admission prices were about 10 cents in those days. In addition, the producer was free of the heavy interest he had to pay on money borrowed from banks to finance pictures. Because the movies were not considered a solid business, this interest rate was as much as 40 percent in some cases.

In addition to these figures, which were only domestic sales, each film brought in an addition $10,000 or more from foreign sales, which were handled separately. Thus Paramount Pictures was a good deal for all concerned. These figures were correct only for part of 1914 and 1915. The high quality of Paramount–released films and Hodkinson's reputation of being a square dealer brought in other theater owners. Profits increased every year.

This did not keep the partners from fighting. The reasons for the trouble have been obscured by different stories. The Zukor forces said that Hodkinson tried to stifle them by refusing to in-crease the allowance per film. Hodkinson blamed Adolph Zukor's greed and ambition.

There was no question about Zukor's intentions to run Hodkinson out of Paramount. About two years after Paramount was formed Benjamin B. Hampton warned Hodkinson of this. Hodkinson did not believe Zukor could win. "But if he does," Hodkinson said, "then I'll leave the company and start again."

By 1917 Hodkinson was out of Paramount, but details of how it was done were not revealed until 1923 when the Federal Trade Commission held hearings on antitrust charges against Paramount. Walter E. Greene, who was one of the founders of Paramount, testified at hearings in New York that Zukor called a secret meeting at the Hotel Astor with Hiram Abrams, James Steele, and himself. He made a very "generous" offer for enough of their stock to give him 50 percent of Paramount stock. He did not get the stock, but he did get their promise to vote with him to unseat Hodkinson. This was done, and Hiram Abrams was given the presidency of Paramount, succeeding Hodkinson, for his part in supporting Zukor.

Lasky, Bosworth, and Morosco did not figure in the unseating of Hodkinson because they did not own any stock. Unfortunately for Zukor, Hiram Abrams did not act as a Zukor rubber stamp. Still determined to gain full control, Zukor set out to buy more Paramount stock. This was not easy to obtain. It was not sold on the stock market. It was all owned by a handful of men. But Zukor was patient. Sooner or later one or all of them would be short of cash. Zukor would be there with an offer for their stock that could not be denied.

2

Close-Up—Mr. Zukor

Adolph was a small man, about 5 feet, 5 inches. He was slender, quiet, and very dignified. When he was in his seventies, Cecil B. DeMille said that he still called him "Mr. Zukor." In their early associations, all the others were Cecil and Jesse and Ben, but everyone of them called him "Mr. Zukor." He was never close to any of them.

Zukor was born in 1873 in Ricse, Hungary. His parents died when he was very young, and he was raised by relatives. Deciding Hungary held little for him, Adolph immigrated to the United States in 1889. He drifted into the fur business. He prospered and in 1903 visited a friend to see why the friend could not repay money Zukor had advanced to him to get into the nickelodeon business.

This was a peepshow box that Edison had put on the market. You dropped a coin in a slot, peeked through a viewer, and saw a *picture* that actually *moved*! Zukor was enthralled. He took an interest in the penny arcade. Later he branched out by becoming a partner in "Hale's Tour." This was a railroad car set up to rock while a moving painting created the illusion of traveling. It was a failure.

In the meantime, moving pictures advanced from peepshow boxes to shows projected on screens. Zukor was eager to get into this business, but the trust that grew up around Edison's patents discouraged newcomers to their business. Zukor made several unsuccessful attempts to get a license. Then he finally got in to see Jeremiah J. Kennedy, who was the working head of the trust.

Zukor explained carefully that he believed that moving pictures could be made more than an amusement for the lower class of people. "If we can make longer film, starring famous players in famous plays," Zukor told the stony faced Kennedy, "we can bring the New York stage to towns and cities outside of New York at prices everyone can afford to pay."

He got no further. Kennedy cut him off short. "Mr. Zukor," the film head said, "we are not interested in longer films. And we certainly are not interested in paying the salaries Broadway stars would ask. Two-reel films make money. There is no point in making anything longer."

Zukor was not a man who gave up easy. He investigated the situation in the film world. He found that a number of people were bucking the film trust by making pictures and selling them. One of these offered to take Zukor in as a partner.

This man was Edwin S. Porter. Porter had formerly worked for Edison and had made the famous *The Great Train Robbery* for Edison in 1903. Later he left Edison and set up independent production until his former boss went to court and stopped his operations. Now Porter was back in business. He had to keep moving to prevent Edison's investigators from catching up with him. However, he was turning out films and selling them to theaters around the country at 9 cents a foot. He assured Zukor that profits were about 100 percent, which made it worth the risk of court action by Edison.

Zukor was impressed by Porter and amused by Porter's stories of his troubles. While working for Edison, Porter was sent on a tour to demonstrate the new Edison projector. The shows were put on in darkrooms and in carnival tents. At first Porter could not convince people that there really were moving pictures inside the tent. He finally cut a hole in the tent and let people take a peek inside to show them that his sign was not a hoax.

Another time he encountered opposition to moving pictures as being "the devil's work." He countered this by billing himself as Thomas A. Edison, Jr. Edison was so famous as the inventor of electric lights and a machine that talked that the public thought such a man's son must be trustworthy.

Zukor left with a strong impression of Porter but did not want to become involved in something that would get him sued. However, his meeting with Porter did get him into the theater business after all. Shortly after this Porter informed Zukor that Zukor's idea of famous players in famous plays had already been done in France. A young producer named Louis Mercanton had persuaded the famous Sarah Bernhardt to let him film her stage success *Queen Elizabeth*.

Zukor wanted to know why the film had never been shown in the United States. "It is too long," Porter told him. "It runs four reels. The trust will not license anyone to show a film that long."

Zukor's investigations disclosed that Mercanton had tried to sell the Bernhardt film on the American market. He found no takers. Zukor arranged a bank loan and bought the American rights. The price was said to have been $35,000. It appears, however, that Zukor only put up $20,000. The remaining $15,000 was to be paid if the picture turned a profit.

Zukor now had his first "famous play with a famous player." But getting it exhibited turned out to be something else. He again applied to the trust for a license. Again he was refused. He turned to the independent states' rights distributors. He was told that no audience would sit through a film that long. Another told him that it would be a financial disaster despite Berhardt's name. The picture was exactly twice the length of the two-reeler. This meant that an exhibitor would have to take in twice the box office return to make the same amount of money. Double the cost of admissions? It would be suicide.

Another had a more pertinent point. "After you get out of the bigger cities, who in hell ever heard of Bernhardt?"

Zukor was growing desperate when he met his savior, Daniel Frohman. Movie historians dismiss Frohman with a line or two, indicating that he lent his name to Zukor's enterprise for its prestige value.

It so happens that without Frohman there never would have been a Famous Players Company. Zukor would have been whipped before he started. Historians who tell us that it was the prestige of Sarah Bernhardt, the most famous actress of her day, that broke down the resistance of high-class actors, actresses, and audiences to the motion picture just have not dug deeply enough into the records.

Daniel Frohman was the brother of the more famous Charles Frohman. He was born in 1851, the son of a peddler who later owned a soap factory. Young Daniel started out as a messenger for Horace Greeley, editor of the New York *Tribune*, and later worked in advertising for different newspapers. This brought him into contact with show business. Then from 1874 to 1878 Daniel was the advance man for a famous minstrel troupe. He later became manager and finally owner of his own theater, the Lyceum, in New York. In the years that followed some of the most famous stars of the day worked for Frohman.

Frohman was 61 years old and the victim of several play failures when 39-year-old Adolph Zukor came to see him. Zukor knew that Frohman was a good friend of Sarah Bernhardt. He told the play producer his troubles.

Frohman replied, "I have never seen a motion picture. From reports I've gotten of them, I said

The "divine" Sarah Bernhardt mourns for Lou Tellegen in *Queen Elizabeth*, the French-made film that launched Adolph Zukor's motion picture career.

that I never would. But if the Divine Sarah is in one, it cannot possibly be bad. Why don't we take a look at the film? Unless it is a complete atrocity, I think we may be able to find a place for you to show it."

The picture, based upon one of Bernhardt's stage successes, was nothing more than a photographed stage play. Frohman, who was always entranced by Bernhardt, offered Zukor the Lyceum Theater for the New York premiere. Frohman was not making any sacrifices. There was no play scheduled, and the theater was dark.

The film was a success in the New York showing, but even so Zukor could not get it booked anywhere else. He finally hired Al Lichtman, a supersalesman type, to take the print on a road show tour. Lichtman ignored movie houses. He went only to legitimate theaters. He showed them photographs of the large crowds in front of the Lyceum in New York. He produced glowing letters of testimonials from prominent actors who had seen the film. He pointed out that he had with him a projector and a screen. Nothing was needed except the theater manager's cooperation to bring this outstanding performance to the manager's city.

The Lichtman road show went over well in the larger cities and towns. Zukor turned a sizable profit. But much more important for films in general, Zukor had moved them out of dark, dirty storefronts into high society. After the acceptance of Bernhardt, actors and actresses began to look with greater favor upon moving pictures. Up to this time, when forced to work in film (generally for D. W. Griffith) they disguised themselves and took assumed names.

This change was due entirely to Zukor's stubbornness and faith in going ahead with the purchase of *Queen Elizabeth* in the face of opposition. However, Paramount publicity persons in later years tried to gain him more credit than he deserved. When Bernhardt died in 1923 they put out a story that it was Zukor who persuaded her to make the film for him. She is supposed to have gratefully told him, "This is my one chance for immortality!"

It was, of course, Louis Mercanton who made the film. As for the often-quoted line about immortality, what the great French actress said was, "Now you have put me in pickle for all time!"

After the success of *Queen Elizabeth*, Zukor told Frohman about his ambitions to make more films like this one. "Famous Players in Famous Plays, I want to call the company," he told Frohman.

Frohman encouraged him, but turned down an offer to become a partner. Frohman did agree to accept a director of production position with Famous Players, if and when Zukor could get it launched. He would be on a salary retainer and would demand no stock in the company. Frohman would arrange for the rights to the famous plays and would persuade the famous players to appear in them. In addition, Zukor could use Frohman's name for its prestige value as "Daniel Frohman Presents . . ." above the title of each picture.

Financing was no problem for Zukor. He paid back the loan on *Queen Elizabeth* so promptly that his credit was good. Two days after their talk, Frohman told Zukor that he could assure him James O'Neill in *The Count of Monte Cristo*, the swashbuckling story by Alexander Dumas, as the first of the Famous Players in Famous Plays.

"And I happen to control the dramatic rights to *The Prisoner of Zenda*," Frohman went on. "As soon as James K. Hackett is free, I can get him to star for you. I gave Hackett his start. He will do the film for me."

At this point Zukor faced only one obstacle to putting his dream into operation. This was the motion picture trust and its control of cameras. Zukor again went to see Jeremiah J. Kennedy. He thought that his success with *Queen Elizabeth* would break down Kennedy's refusal to grant him a General Film license. Kennedy refused to see him.

Zukor went back to see Daniel Frohman. He explained the trouble. "Kennedy runs General Film," Zukor said. "He is also the president of the Motion Picture Patents Company that controls General Film Company. However, both companies are based upon Thomas A. Edison's patents, and Edison really has the biggest voice in the companies if he wants to use it. Edison could cause Kennedy to change his mind and grant us a license."

"Have you talked to Edison?" Frohman asked.

"I do not know Mr. Edison," Zukor replied. "Hundreds of people are constantly besieging him for all kinds of favors. I would be just another nuisance. But you are a very famous man. He would listen to you."

"I don't know Mr. Edison either," Frohman protested.

PARAMOUNT

DANIEL FROHMAN
Presents

The powerful drama
By
CLYDE·FITCH

"THE
STRAIGHT ROAD"
with
GLADYS HANSON
In Four Parts of Motion Pictures

Clyde Fitch's great human
drama of a submerged
soul's conflict and triumph.
Released Nov. 12th

Daniel Frohman's name was used for its prestige value to "present" Famous Players' films. This one, *The Straight Road,* was released in November 1914. *Copyright 1914 by Famous Players Film Company.*

29

"Then he must be the only person of consequence in the world that you do not know," Zukor said. "You should get to know him."

Frohman was still doubtful, but he agreed to try. He badly needed the money Zukor promised to pay him. Edison was so busy that it took two weeks to get the appointment. Edison's laboratory was then at Menlo Park, New Jersey.

In his autobiography, *Daniel Frohman Presents,* Frohman wrote: "I explained the situation to him. He seemed to doubt that he could help us. He said that he had only certain rights in the company and could be outvoted. I stuck to my point and explained how important this new movement was in behalf of elevating the standards of motion pictures. It would improve the character of the entire industry."

Unknown to Frohman, Edison had a poor opinion of the future of moving pictures. He had not even bothered to patent his inventions in Europe. He thought they would be a passing fad.

However, he agreed to give Frohman a letter to Kennedy. It was a polite note asking Kennedy to consider Zukor's proposition. There was nothing in it to indicate Edison's own interest or desire to help Zukor. Frohman saw at once that Kennedy would recognize it for what it was—an attempt of Edison's to be nice to someone who was bothering him. The letter was worthless for what Frohman and Zukor wanted it for.

Frohman wanted a stronger letter. He did not know how to go about getting it. Fortunately, Edison was inclined to chat awhile and began asking Frohman questions about the theater. He mentioned that when he first began making short films for his nickelodeon he used many stage people.

"It is a mistake to say that Bernhardt is the first actress of fame to appear in films," Edison said. "We had May Irwin in a sequence from *The Widow Jones*."

Frohman agreed. Although he kept it to himself, he knew that comedienne May Irwin was hardly in Bernhardt's league. The sequence from *The Widow Jones* became famous as *The Kiss*. It was nothing more than a brief flash showing a matronly woman of the Marie Dressler type being kissed by a handsome man who coveted her rich farm.

In the course of the conversation, Frohman mentioned that he was working as an office boy for the New York *Tribune* when Edison was married. He recalled for the inventor a story that appeared in the paper about it. After the wedding ceremony Edison had gone back to his laboratory for a few minutes. He got interested in his work and forgot about the wedding entirely. The wedding guests, waiting for the wedding dinner to begin, could not understand what had happened to him. Finally the best man went to search and informed the surprised inventor that he was supposed to be escorting his bride to dinner. (It has been claimed that the newspaper story about this was the germ that gave O. Henry the idea for his story *The Romance of a Busy Broker,* in which a harried businessman forgot that he had been married the day before and proposed to his bride again.)

Edison laughed heartily at the recollection. He explained that his mind was disturbed at the time because the owners of an important firm were trying to prevent him from marketing an invention they thought would harm their business. Edison had been trying to convince the company's managers that the invention would help instead of hurt them. He did not say which of his many inventions this was. Frohman, seeing a perfect opening for his own plea, did not bother to inquire.

"Mr. Edison!" Frohman cried. "You were in exactly the same position then that I am now. Mr. Zukor and I also have an idea that can uplift our profession, but your men stand in our way just as those businessmen stood in yours. You are the only one who can help us!"

Edison thought for a moment. Then he slapped his leg. "By Jingo, you are right," he said. "I'll do it!"

He went to his desk and quickly scratched out two letters to each of his top officials in the patents company. According to Frohman, the letters were "somewhat mandatory in tone."

Now that he had what he came for, Frohman was ready to go, but Edison insisted on taking the producer back to the laboratory to show him his latest invention. It was talking pictures. It was no more than an attempt to hook an Edison phonograph to a movie projector. The results were not good, and Frohman was not impressed.

Zukor was jubilant when Frohman returned with the letters. He had them photographed so he could have copies when the originals were sent to the film executives.

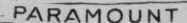

May Irwin is famous in movie history as the lady of *The Kiss,* an
early Edison film. In *Mrs. Black Is Back,* the cast also included
Elmer Barth, left, and Charles Lane. *Copyright 1914 by Paramount
Pictures, Inc.*

Three days later Adolph Zukor had his license to use Edison machines, and Famous Players in Famous Plays (later shortened to the Famous Players Film Company) was in business. Zukor handled financing and overall supervision. Frohman was in charge of getting plays and persuading talent to join them. Edwin S. Porter came on board as cameraman-director, and Hugh Ford, a stage director, was the second director.

True to his promise, Frohman got James O'Neill to star in *The Count of Monte Cristo.* James was the father of the famous dramatist Eugene O'Neill, who wrote *Anna Christie* and other plays. Eugene in turn was the father of Oona O'Neill, who was Charlie Chaplin's devoted wife in the comedian's declining years. James O'Neill was famous for his bombastic acting and his equally bombastic drinking.

Fortunately for Zukor, O'Neill had played the role so many times that he could stagger through it blind

The Count of Monte Cristo was Famous Players Film Company's first production. The star, James O'Neill, is shown here being dragged to the dungeon. *Copyright 1913 by Famous Players Film Company.*

drunk. Edwin S. Porter used the regular painted stage scenery and flats to give the film a photographed stage play appearance.

The story condensed Alexander Dumas' famous novel into four major parts. The first dealt with the framing of Edmond Dantes by four men. He was accused of trying to help restore Napoleon to the throne of France and was arrested at his wedding. He spent years in a dungeon. Then an old man in an adjoining cell tunneled into Dantes' cell in a futile attempt to escape. This man died after telling Dantes of a treasure he had buried on the island of Monte Cristo.

As the man's body is placed in a sack to be thrown into the sea by the guards, Dantes manages to substitute himself for the corpse and escapes. He finds the treasure and goes to Paris under the name of the Count of Monte Cristo. One by one he finds and ruins each of the men who caused his downfall.

As soon as the film was finished, Zukor found that Selig had filmed the same story with Hobart Bosworth as Dantes. Selig's film was released first. Zukor held up his version for later release, but even then it did not do well because of the Bosworth film. Bosworth was a better screen actor and did a better job.

Zukor's next film was also arranged by Frohman. It was *The Prisoner of Zenda,* based upon a novel by Anthony Hope (Hawkins). Frohman recognized the dramatic possibilities when the novel was first published. He cabled Hope in England, but the author had given dramatic rights to Edward Rose, a playwright. Although Rose had a dozen other offers from managers wanting to stage the play, he accepted Frohman's offer because the American producer had once bought a one-act play from Rose when the British writer was down on his luck.

The play was a huge success with E. H. Sothern in the dual role. After Sothern took the play on tour, Frohman restaged it in New York with James K. Hackett.

Hackett had been a teenage student in an academy near the Lyceum theater. He used to come every day to sit in the balcony and watch Sothern in *The Prisoner of Zenda.* Frohman was so amused by the boy's hero worship that he took Hackett on as a juvenile. Later Hackett took over Sothern's role in the play.

In time Hackett became his own manager. In 1907 he bought a play called *A Fool and a Girl* written by a young actor. The play, despite having Elsie Ferguson in the lead, flopped on tryout. The author, after two more years of failures, got a job at Biograph and became D. W. Griffith.

Anyway, Hackett owed his start in show business to Frohman. He was delighted to repay his debt by appearing in a screen version of *The Prisoner of Zenda* for his old friend.

The Prisoner of Zenda is a foolproof script. It has been filmed three times and has been a hit every time. The Hackett version was first. Then the Rex Ingram version in 1922 made a star of Ramon Novarro in the villain role. In the sound period Ronald Colman did a splendid job in David O. Selznick's remake.

The story line is about a scandal that once involved a visiting lady and the king of Ruritania. Ever after, at various periods, one of the lady's male descendents would be born looking exactly like the king's side of the family. Rudolf Rassendyll was one of these.

Hearing that Rudolf V is to be crowned the new king of Ruritania, Rassendyll visits Ruritania. He meets the king, and they are look-alikes. Then when Black Michael, trying to prevent the coronation, kidnaps the king, the prime minister gets Rassendyll to impersonate the monarch at the ceremony.

Rudolf V is engaged to the beautiful Princess Flavia. She and Rassendyll fall in love, but this does not prevent the honorable Rassendyll from swimming the moat to rescue the real king. Flavia prefers Rassendyll, because he has a more kindly nature than the king. But the two lovers give each other up in the name of duty. Rassendyll returns to England. Thereafter, every year on the anniversary of their parting, he receives a rose and a note reading, "Rudolf, Flavia, always."

A movie like this could hardly fail in 1913. It was released as the Famous Players Film Company's first presentation because of the hold up on release of O'Neill's *The Count of Monte Cristo*. It did well, and Famous Players was in business.

Zukor needed more stars. It was here that Daniel Frohman again proved his worth to the new company. He knew everyone in the theatrical business. His prestige overcame stars' reluctance. He scored a real triumph in persuading Minnie Maddern Fiske to appear in her great success, *Tess of the D'Urbervilles*, a play based upon Thomas Hardy's famous novel.

The actress was the wife of Harrison Gray Fiske of the *Dramatic Mirror*. This paper was devoted primarily to the stage, but Frohman pointed out to Zukor that Fiske would not dare refuse to give a good review to his wife.

Tess had gone to work for blind Mrs. D'Urberville but was seduced by the son, Alec. Disgusted with him and herself, Tess returns home. Her child is born sickly, dies, and is refused a Christian burial. Tess goes to another town to work as a milkmaid where she meets Angel Clare. She tells him about Alec D'Urberville, and Clare leaves for Brazil. Brokenhearted, Tess moves from one menial job to another until she meets Alec again. She hates him but is finally persuaded to go live with him. Angel, returning from abroad, goes to seek Tess and finds her with Alec. Tess tells Angel that he is too late. A short time later, Angel finds Tess fleeing. She has stabbed and killed Alec. Tess is caught by the police and executed.

Famous Players lived up to its name when Daniel Frohman persuaded Minnie Maddern Fiske to star in *Tess of the D'Urbervilles*. Raymond Boundel played the male lead. Edwin S. Porter directed. *Copyright 1913 by Famous Players Film Company.*

33

This grim story was Minnie Fiske's greatest triumph. John Strang said of her performance: "The person who sees *Tess* for the first time is so moved by the tragedy that he takes little account of the actress's art, an involuntary tribute that he pays to her spontaneity and naturalness." The scene where she pleads with Angel not to leave her after he learns of her indiscretion with Alec was especially praised for its dramatic intensity.

Marie Doro in *The Morals of Marcus* is the story of a surprised young man who finds himself guardian of a young girl who was raised in an Eastern harem. *Copyright 1915 by Famous Players Film Company.*

Minnie Fiske was "born" in the theater. Her father and mother were strolling players. She played her first part—a ghost in *MacBeth*—when she was three. She was 46 years old when she played Tess for Zukor. She was very "well preserved," as the expression went in those days, but even so she did not look like a young girl. This was one of the flaws in Zukor's dream of Famous Players in Famous Plays. By the time an actress or actor got really famous, he or she was generally up in years. The greatly magnified image on the screen also magnified the signs of age which were not visible to a theater audience. Zukor and Frohman quickly realized this and began looking for younger "famous players."

But before this happened, Zukor faced a financial crisis. The need to withhold his first film because Selig beat him to the screen with *The Count of Monte Cristo* caused a delay in Zukor's expected cash flow. The second film, *The Prisoner of Zenda*, depleted his treasury, and money was not yet coming in from its distribution when he went into *Tess of the D'Urbervilles*.

Going to see Zukor one day, Frohman found the young producer in a very worried state. He had difficulty getting Zukor to talk about his troubles. When he finally did find out what was worrying Zukor, Frohman said, "I'll see what I can do about it."

Zukor took no notice, because he considered it just a polite remark. He knew that Frohman had had a series of money-losing plays and was not in good financial condition. As for himself, Zukor had borrowed all the money he could get on his personal notes. If he got anymore, he would have to lose control of his company.

The next day he was surprised when Frohman came in and laid a check for $50,000 on his desk. "Where did you get that?" he asked in wonderment.

"Never mind," Frohman replied. "It is not an investment in the company. It is a personal loan. Pay me back when you can."

This story shows how important Frohman was to Famous Players in the early days. Frohman knew only too well how many show people ended their days in abject poverty. When he started making big money, the first thing he did was to put $50,000 in high-grade bonds. These were placed back as his insurance against old age poverty. They were not to be touched for anything. But when he saw Zukor's dejection, Frohman took the risk of losing his long-cherished nest egg to help a friend.

On another occasion Frohman used his own money to help the Famous Players. Frohman was visiting his brother, the more famous Charles Frohman. Charles was complaining about badly needing $25,000. Daniel rushed out and borrowed the money that afternoon. He came back and put the check in front of Charles.

Charles Frohman eyed it suspiciously. "I know you," he said. "What must I do in return?"

"I want the motion picture rights to your plays," Daniel said.

"Done!" Charles cried and grabbed the check as if he thought his crazy brother might take it back. Charles Frohman never had much faith in film. He told Daniel that he was crazy for joining Zukor in the first place.

Daniel replied that Charles might change his mind if he would only see a movie. Charles said with disgust that Daniel would never get him into a movie house. However, when the first of the plays Daniel got from Charles was filmed, he did permit Daniel to take him to see it. The film featured lovely Marie Doro in *The Morals of Marcus*. Charles admitted reluctantly that perhaps films had something to offer after all.

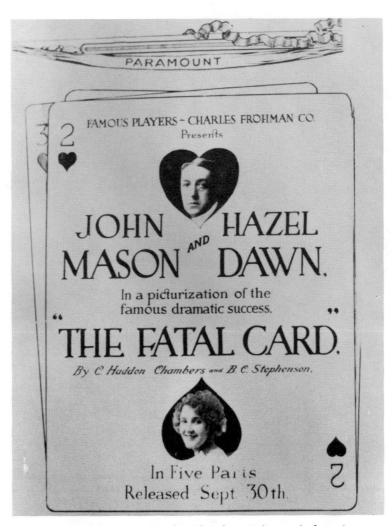

The Fatal Card was one of the first films Zukor made from the Charles Frohman material. Frohman insisted that his name be used as one of the "presenters." *Copyright 1915 by Famous Players Film Company and Charles Frohman.*

3

The Barnyard Players

In 1884 a baby was born in Warsaw, Poland. In time so many legends would be attached to his borrowed name that much of the truth about him would be buried so deeply that it would never be known. One story claims that where ordinary babies cry, "Waa, waa," this one got the words mixed up and they came out backward.

History does not seem to have recorded what this youngster's real name was. It does appear that there is truth in the legend that an immigration official, when the boy arrived in London when he was 11 years old, could not figure from the boy's speech and documents what the spelling of his name was. So he put down Samuel Goldfish as the nearest he could come to it in English.

So Samuel Goldfish he remained during his four years in England. Then, in 1899, 15-year-old Sam came to America. Somehow he got into the glove business and eventually became a traveling salesman. We hear that he was pretty good at it. Also he was pretty good in other pursuits, which may have helped start the many stories about traveling salesmen and farmers' daughters that were popular off–color stories of their day.

In any event, Goldfish finally married Blanche Lasky. Lasky was the beloved sister of Jesse L. Lasky. The Laskys were children of a Californian whose shoe business had fallen on bad days. Jesse, who was quite handy with a cornet, and Blanche worked up a vaudeville act. Later Jesse went to Alaska in the 1898 gold rush, and then to Hawaii where he was for a time the only white musician in the Royal Hawaiian Band.

Lasky then went back to vaudeville, after a tour as manager for the magician Herrmann the Great. (This was Leon Herrmann, nephew of the real Herrmann the Great who died in 1899). Lasky was an amazingly good judge of talent and eventually became a booking agent. He made quite a lot of money, which he lost in a restaurant-cabaret, the first such opened in New York.

Lasky then hired a young playwright, Cecil B. DeMille, to help him work out a tabloid musical suitable for vaudeville presentation. Lasky had wanted the noted playwright William C. deMille, but Bill's mother talked Lasky into taking her younger son instead.

Now all these scattered threads from Poland, the

37

show business in California, and the New York theater came together in a knot. Goldfish, the glove salesman, began the entanglement.

Lasky was of the opinion that Blanche could have done much better than this highly opinionated glove salesman. But out of regard for Blanche, Goldfish was invited to the Lasky's for Sunday dinner. Also, it had been Jesse's wife Bessie who introduced Blanche to Goldfish. Sam had once cut cloth in the glove factory of Bessie's uncle.

Goldfish had seen his first movie in 1911. It was, according to Lasky's recollection, *Broncho Billy's Adventures*. "Broncho Billy" Anderson never made a film by that title, but he made a lot of other titles. Goldfish was immediately caught by the magic of filmmaking. He even spent some time around the General Film Company getting an idea of how it was all done.

Lasky was looking for a new enterprise to replace his cabaret failure. Goldfish suggested moviemaking. Lasky was outraged at the idea. Goldfish persisted, and Lasky grew more adamant.

But then Lasky and his friend DeMille went to see *Queen Elizabeth*. After that experience the idea of making movies did not seem as bad as it once had.

Goldfish continued his arguments. It appears now that there was more to his movie enthusiasm than just a love for films. Congress was considering a lower tariff on gloves. Goldfish wanted something to fall back on if the glove business fell to foreign competition.

Finally Lasky proposed the idea to his friend DeMille. He said he was only interested in features. These longer films were proving their worth, first with Zukor's importation of *Queen Elizabeth* and then with George Kleine's import *Quo Vadis?*, an Italian spectacle. In addition, Hobart Bosworth had secured feature film rights to all of Jack London's famous novels. Universal was cleaning up on *Traffic in Souls*, the first sex film shown outside of stag parties. It was in five reels and was being shown in the Shubert theaters.

Both Lasky and DeMille had been impressed by *Queen Elizabeth*. After careful thought Lasky decided that he could afford to risk his theatrical reputation on movie features.

According to DeMille, he and Lasky sketched out the formation of the company by scribbling on the back of a menu in Claridge's grill. Lasky was to be president and have his name on the company. This was because he was the only one with any money. Cecil B. DeMille was to be director-general and make the pictures. Samuel Goldfish (who later became Samuel Goldwyn) would sell the pictures to exhibitors. Arthur Friend, a lawyer, would handle the legal details.

Thus, very casually, the Jesse L. Lasky Feature Play Company was formed. The company very quickly established an excellent critical reputation. In time it would merge with Zukor's Famous Players, becoming the backbone of Hodkinson's Paramount Pictures distribution system.

Following Zukor's lead, Lasky wanted a star for his first film. Dustin Farnum, brother of the more famous William Farnum who had such a hit in *The Virginian*, agreed to star in the first Lasky feature, provided that Lasky could get *The Squaw Man* for him. This play by Edwin Milton Royal starred William Faversham on the stage. Royal agreed to sell his play for $5000. Farnum, refusing a quarter interest in the company for his role, also took $5000. Lasky only had $15,000 and sold the stock earmarked for Farnum to relatives to raise another $5000. After paying for the play and star, they had $10,000 left to produce the film.

DeMille, who had to make the film, had never seen a movie shot. He had no concept of the difference between the screen and the stage. Goldfish, who had some contacts in the industry, took DeMille out to see a movie lot in action.

Hobart Bosworth arranged for film rights to all Jack London's stories. This scene is from *John Barleycorn*. *Copyright 1914 by Bosworth Productions.*

It was a very thoughtful DeMille who returned. He told Lasky, "If that is the way movies are made, anybody can do it."

But he was smart enough to realize that he did not know enough to make the picture as they had planned. He had stopped in to see a film after he left the studio. This was to compare what he had heard and seen with a finished product.

His head was filled with strange terms such as "long shot," "close-up," "medium shot," "fade," and "dissolve." All these things comprised the "grammar" of film which D. W. Griffith had perfected, although he did not invent them as has been claimed so often.

As he analyzed the film he saw, DeMille recognized the value of this editing technique. He could see how it added variety and a dimension that was impossible on the static stage.

Oscar Apfel directs a scene on the open air set at Selma and Vine streets in Hollywood. Alfred Gondolfi is the cameraman—and owner of the camera. Dick LeStrange is behind the cameraman.

DeMille again talked to Goldfish, who found Oscar Apfel to help them get started in movie making. Apfel had been a stage director and then had become a movie director for a small company. In his later years Apfel became known as a character actor.

The next problem was a camera. DeMille found to his surprise that none was for sale. They were manufactured and controlled by the Edison trust. The independent producers—"outlaws" in the opinion of the trust—either were infringing Edison's patents by building their own or were getting Pathé cameras from France.

Again Goldfish's contacts came to the rescue. He found a cameraman named Alfred Gondolfi who owned a Pathé camera. Gondolfi, who had been working for Eclair and Rex companies, did not need a job. However, the offer of a salary for him plus money for the camera and the opportunity to travel west convinced him to take the position with Lasky.

It was Lasky's idea to film the picture in Flagstaff, Arizona. In his autobiography, Lasky said the decision was made because DeMille was restless, and Lasky wanted to give his friend a change of scenery. Oscar Apfal once said it was because some of Edison's detectives raided a production unit in New Jersey (where Lasky first intended to make the film) and seized an "outlaw" camera.

In any event, DeMille, Gondolfi, Dustin Farnum, and Farnum's valet entrained for Flagstaff. They got off and got back on again before the train pulled out. There were no accommodations in the frontier town. No one had thought to investigate the place before it was selected.

Apfel, talking swiftly while the train took on water, pointed out to DeMille that a number of companies were working in Los Angeles. They could find the extra cast members they needed, get their film developed so they could review each day's progress, and have better access to props.

The cast of *The Squaw Man* included seasoned players. Most of
them had previous motion picture experience. *Copyright 1914 by
Jesse L. Lasky Feature Play Company.*

Two days later Lasky in New York received a telegram asking permission for DeMille to spend $75 to rent a barn in Hollywood, California.

"Where's that?" a startled Goldfish asked.

"I have absolutely no idea," Lasky replied.

The barn was at the corner of Selma and Vine Streets in an orange grove ten miles from downtown Los Angeles. A man named Cristie had a studio there where he made two-reel comedies for Universal release, but *The Squaw Man* was to be the first feature filmed in Hollywood, the village that grew up to be the name that meant movies to the world.

Purchase of this truck caused Sam Goldfish to complain that DeMille would bankrupt the company. Oscar Apfel is seated at right. DeMille is standing on the opposite side of the engine. Dustin Farnum, Dick LaReno, Joseph E. Singleton and Red wing are in the center, surrounded by Indian extras. Picture was taken Jan. 5, 1914. *Copyright 1914 by Jesse L. Lasky Feature Play Company.*

Under Apfel's instruction, DeMille had broken *The Squaw Man* playscript down into a scenario which roughly sketched out each scene. Word had gotten around that a new movie company was in town and that it was loaded with money. So while Apfel supervised the erection of an outdoor stage, DeMille started casting. An actress named Jane Darwell came out, but her $60-a-week asking price was too much. In true Hollywood fashion, this too-expensive actress would one day play the queen of paupers, Ma Joad, in John Ford's *Grapes of Wrath*.

But DeMille got an excellent cast of true professionals: Monroe Salibury, Joseph E. Singleton, Billy Elmer, Winifred Kingston, and Red Wing, plus a girl named Carmen DeRue to play the little boy role. They billed Carmen as "Baby" DeRue to hide her sex. Carmen—about six—was already a veteran of Universal comedies.

In his autobiography DeMille said he picked Red Wing because he wanted a real Indian in the role of *The Squaw Man's* bride and not a professional actress. Red Wing must have done a con job on Cecil. She and her husband, also a full-blooded Indian, had been in vaudeville for years. Then she had made a number of pictures for Ince and others. She was probably the most experienced motion picture actress on the lot.

Apfel today is only a footnote to Hollywood's history. In the records Cecil B. DeMille is listed as the director of *The Squaw man*, usually with the notation in parentheses (with Oscar Apfel). But the truth is that *The Squaw Man* owes more to Apfel than to DeMille. DeMille acknowledged this in his autobiography when he said; "After working with Oscar Apfel for some months I felt able to direct a picture all on my own." The photograph of *The Squaw Man* set, taken by J. A. Ramsey, shows Apfel directing the scene.

Edwin H. Porter, Zukor's director, had considerable trouble at first in getting a natural performance from Hackett in *The Prisoner of Zenda*, but the actor settled down after seeing the first rushes of his exaggerated stage style. Apfel circumvented this with Farnum by taking him to a movie and disturbing the patrons by explaining things as the film unrolled.

Farnum came from a theatrical family. His father was a tragedian, and his mother was a singer. While the family was on the road, he and his two brothers grew up in Bucksport, Maine. William Farnum, the youngest brother, was the first to go on the stage. Dustin and Marshall followed him shortly after. Dustin's first job was with the Ethel Tucker Repertoire Company.

He told an interviewer: "I played 27 parts! I ranted and strutted and shouted—principally shouted—through them all."

He did it well enough to land on Broadway eventually. He made *The Ranger* and *Cameo Kirby* and was with his brother William and a little girl name Juliet Shelby in *The Littlest Rebel*, a Civil War story that Shirley Temple would someday film. Juliet Shelby a few years later became a Paramount star under the name of Mary Miles Minter. Dustin also was in the second company of Owen Wister's *The Virginian.*

Farnum was an outdoor type who thoroughly enjoyed himself during the making of *The Squaw Man.* He was on horseback ranging over the California hills every chance he got.

Under Apfel's direction, carpenters built a flat stage about two feet off the ground. Two-by-four braces were put up at each end to hold wires stretched across the top. Then muslin sheets were sewed together and rigged up with eyes to slip along the wires. Small cotton ropes were attached to pulleys so the cloth could be pulled over the stage. This softened and controlled the sunlight to give an even light on the set. The sets were no more than two flats pulled together to form the corner of a room. Proper furniture was then put in to make either an English drawing room or a Western saloon, as needed.

Horse stalls were remodeled into dressing rooms, and an office was partitioned off for DeMille. DeMille brought a truck to haul them on location for some of the shots. A sign reading "Lasky Feature Play Company" was tacked on the side. Dustin Farnum, DeMille, Apfel, and such members of the cast as were around climbed on the truck for a picture to send back to New York. DeMille was hopeful that the picture would impress his partners.

Shooting on *The Squaw Man* began on December 29, 1913, and was completed in 18 days. The story tells of James Wynnegate who takes the blame for embezzlement of charity funds committed by his cousin, the Earl of Kerhill (Monroe Salisbury). Wynnegate (Dustin Farnum) does this out of love for Kerhill's wife, Lady Diana (Winifred Kingston).

Lord of all he surveys, Jesse L. Lasky looks over the outdoor stage where the first Lasky films were produced. The famous Paramount barn is in the background. *Copyright 1914 by Jesse L. Lasky Feature Play Company.*

Wynnegate goes to the United States and then to Wyoming, where he saves an Indian girl, Nat-U-Rich (Red Wing), who has been attacked by a vicious rustler named Cash Hawkins (Billy Elmer). Apparently Wynnegate takes the same advantage of Red Wing that he prevented Cash Hawkins from taking. She becomes pregnant, and Wynnegate marries her, thus becoming the "squaw man" of the title. This was a frontier term attached to white men who married Indian women.

Then Lady Diana arrives in Wyoming to inform him that her husband is dead. Before his death Kerhill had confessed to the embezzlement that drove Wynnegate from England.

In the meantime, Cash Hawkins attempts to shoot Wynnegate in the back. Red Wing shoots Hawkins to save her husband. Nat-U-Rich then kills herself, in fear that she will be arrested for Hawkins' murder. She dies in Wynnegate's arms, clearing the way for the squaw man to return to England with Lady Diana and his son by Nat-U-Rich, Little Hal (Baby DeRue).

The shooting went smoothly with interiors at the barn stage and exteriors in the hills back of the studio. Once DeMille was shot at, and on another occasion some film was sabotaged in the processing laboratory. DeMille suspected that this might have been caused by scouts from the motion picture trust trying to put them out of business.

The story is often told of how DeMille tried to show *The Squaw Man* to Lasky and the film danced all over the screen. Frantic at the failure, the two partners rushed the print to Sigismund Lubin in Philadelphia. Lubin, who started in the business by illegally duplicating films of others and selling them as his own, took pity on the harassed beginners. In exchange for the print order, Lubin told DeMille that the trouble was due to a difference between the sprocket holes in the negative and those of the positive stock. These are the holes along the edge of the film. The projector gears engage the holes to pull the film along.

A corrected print was made and rushed to New York, where Sam Goldfish had arranged a trade showing. The audience was states' rights buyers, some of whom had already put a down payment on a territory. Others were waiting to see what Goldfish had to offer besides promises before buying prints.

Goldfish had lined up the states' rights buyers while the film was being made. This was the payoff. If they bought, the Lasky Feature Play Company was in business. If they turned the picture down, it meant bankruptcy. Therefore, it was three very nervous partners who opened the trade showing. Goldfish told Lasky that there was at least 60,000 "good" dollars among the exhibitors, "if the damned picture is any good." He glared almost accusingly at DeMille.

He had never shared Lasky's high opinion of their "director-general." Since Lasky invested only $20,000 in the film, $60,000 would represent a 200 percent profit on money that had been tied up for only five months at the very most.

"A man could get *rich* at this sort of thing!" Lasky gasped.

The trade showing was made in the Longacre Theater in New York. Cecil invited his mother and his brother, William C. deMille, to the screening. Mrs. deMille (all the family except Cecil spelled their name with a small "d") was a well-known play broker and agent. William had a number of stage hits to his name. Cecil wanted their opinion of the film.

Cecil and Jesse took seats at the back of the theater to watch the buyers' reaction during the screening. Cecil had run the picture at Lubin's, but Lasky was so nervous he refused to view it before the trade showing. Sam Goldfish had been too busy lining up the buyers. Cecil, then, was the only one who had seen *The Squaw Man* in its entirety. He told his two partners that he thought it was pretty good. This did not ease their nervousness. He had said the same thing about two plays he had written which had flopped miserably.

The audience sat quietly through the screening. There was no inattention. They were gripped by the drama on the screen. When the picture ended and the house lights went up, they crowded around a beaming Sam Goldfish to congratulate him.

DeMille said he was interested only in William's opinion. He looked inquiringly at his brother, who nodded slowly. "I knew we had won," DeMille wrote in his autobiography.

Dick LaReno, right, joshes the "English Dude" played by Dustin
Farnum in this scene from *The Squaw Man*. The seated man
behind LaReno is Cecil B. DeMille, taking an extra role to save
fi5. *Copyright 1914 by Jesse L. Lasky Feature Play Company.*

"LET HIM BEWARE WHO HARMS THESE HELPLESS ONES!"

William Farnum made *The Sign of the Cross* in 1914 for Zukor's Famous Players Film Company. Rosina Henley is the girl. *Copyright 1914 by Famous Players Film Company.*

Then Goldfish called him and Lasky to the stage to introduce them to the buyers. Jesse thanked them for their interest and told them that this was just the beginning. "You can expect bigger and better features from the Jesse L. Lasky Feature Play Company," he said.

This was the first Goldfish and DeMille knew that they were supposed to make more pictures. No plans had been made beyond *The Squaw Man*. The picture was released to the first states' rights distributors on February 15, 1914. Each buyer released the film in his own territory according to local schedules, so there was no nationwide release day for the film. Only East Coast distributors received the film at this time. But when word of the film's quality got around, Goldfish had every state in the union sold within three weeks.

According to DeMille, the film cost about $20,000 and grossed over $244,000. It was an outstanding success, both financially and critically. Critics spoke of its "clear photography" and sustained suspense.

A number of things aided the film's success. DeMille had a good dramatic story. Oscar Apfel, while certainly no D. W. Griffith, understood the technique of making pictures and the difference between a filmed story and a filmed stage play. DeMille understood dramatic composition and saw that the script developed it. Alfred Gondolfi was a very good cameraman. DeMille, as a result of his work with David Belasco, used good sets. And—one of the most important points of all—DeMille picked experienced actors. All except Farnum, the star, had previous film experience, and he caught on fast.

The Squaw Man had more natural acting than the exaggerated scene chewing of James O'Neill in Zukor's first film. Zukor was greatly impressed by the film and sent Lasky a telegram of congratulations. Then he immediately approached Dustin Farnum's brother William with a contract. William, after seeing Dusty's performance, signed to do Wilson Barrett's famous play, *The Sign of the Cross,* for Zukor. Rosina Henley, a noted actress of the day, took the feminine lead.

The story tells of the Roman patrician Marcus Superbus who rejects the advances of the wicked empress Poppaea for the love of a Christian girl, Mercia. Played against a background of the burning of Rome by Nero, Marcus renounces his pagan religion to follow Mercia to Nero's lions in the arena.

Zukor followed up his telegram of congratulations to Lasky with an invitation to lunch. Lasky was flattered. He later told Goldfish that Zukor was a brilliant man with some remarkable ideas about the future of the motion picture industry. He suggested that Goldfish also cultivate Zukor.

Zukor, however, kept his basic idea to himself. This was to create a company that would dominate the film industry as Rockefeller's Standard Oil Trust once controlled the oil industry. The other independent motion picture producers railed against the Edison trust and tried to break it up. Zukor simply wanted to take over in its place.

Congressional action, prodded by President Theodore Roosevelt, had outlawed many of the practices Rockefeller had used to control the rising oil industry. Zukor believed he could destroy his competition by cornering the most popular stars and by merging with his most formidable competition.

The Jesse L. Lasky Feature Play Company was just starting, but Zukor sized up its management as formidable future competition. It was aiming at exactly the same class of films that Zukor was making. Lasky himself had a high reputation in the theatrical world. The name of DeMille also was formidable through the plays of H. C. deMille, the late father of Cecil and William, through Mrs. deMille's play brokerage and through William's own

Edward Abeles repeated his *Brewster's Millions* role in Lasky's second film, directed by Oscar Apfel. Paramount later remade the story with Fatty Arbuckle and again with Bebe Daniels as *Miss Brewster's Millions. Copyright 1914 by Jesse L. Lasky Feature Play Company.*

plays. Cecil, of course, had not made his mark, but the dramatic quality of *The Squaw Man* definitely showed that he had film potential.

Then the way that Samuel Goldfish sold the entire national states' rights for the film in three weeks showed that the new film company was backing its creative talent with solid business talent as well. Zukor wanted these people working for him. His telegram and luncheon invitation to Lasky were the first shots in a campaign to bring this about. And it also proved to be the beginning of the drive that would someday make Paramount Pictures *paramount* indeed in the film industry.

The Squaw Man was a critical as well as a popular success. The New York *Dramatic Mirror* said, "And best of all, there is a real story told in photographed action, not in lengthy subtitles illustrated by fragmentary scenes."

The inexplicable hatred and contempt so many reviewers have had for Cecil B. DeMille over the years have obscured the extraordinary achievement of *The Squaw Man.* No one has made a study of this film, analyzing the film construction of this pioneer feature. It was not the first American filmed feature, but it was the first good one, although admittedly it fell short of the grandeur of the Italian-filmed *Cabiria* and *Quo Vadis?*

D. W. Griffith, for all his genius, was never taken seriously by critics until he began making features after Zukor and Lasky. He refined movie making and developed the first true film technique, but the short films he made—forced on him, it is true—did not provide sufficient dramatic scope to challenge the stage.

Zukor's American features that preceded *The Squaw Man* were mediocre films that were little more than filmed stage plays. The *Moving Picture World's* critic said, "This new method of thought transmission has a grander scope than the boxed-in stage presentation."

As for the three partners, they were elated and immediately began plans for more films. Lasky was able to get a new property. Edward Abeles had just closed in *Brewster's Millions,* based on the comedy by George Barr McCutcheon (famous for the Graustark novels). It was the story of a young man who would inherit a million dollars provided he could invest it wisely and make a profit by the end of the first year.

Abeles objected to signing for the movie role. DeMille then got Dustin Farnum to give him a pep talk. Dusty spoke glowingly of his film adventures, and Abeles signed. DeMille worked on the script but left Oscar Apfel alone to direct the film.

Lasky was now committed to do one film a month. He bought the Thomas Ross play, *The Only Son,* which Apfel also directed. The finances of the Lasky company had improved by this time to the point that DeMille—who did the casting—could pay Jane Darwell the $60 a week she asked, and she supported Ross in the film.

Lasky made an error in his next purchase, which was *The Master Mind* with Edmund Breese and Mabel Van Buren. He had admired the play on the stage, but Breese was no longer a juvenile. The harsh lighting and sharp lenses of the day made him look even older. Lasky had not yet learned what Griffith already knew: the best-looking motion picture actresses were teenage girls, and the best-looking male leads were men in their twenties.

Edmund Breese and Mabel Van Buren in *The Mastermind,* one of the films that Lasky said Oscar Apfel "ground out like sausages." *Copyright 1914 by Jesse L. Lasky Feature Play Company.*

Oscar Apfel directed *The Only Son* with Thomas Ross. *Copyright 1914 by Jesse L. Lasky Feature Play Company.*

Apfel continued to grind out pictures. The first eight after *The Squaw Man* were directed by him. DeMille worked on the scripts and helped Apfel, but he was aware that he did not know enough to direct a film by himself.

Then, by August 1914, they acquired another cameraman to supplement Gondolfi. DeMille took this new man, Alvin Wyckoff, and wrote a script based upon Stewart Edward White's novel *Conjuror's House*. He retitled it *The Call of the North*.

The story is laid in the Canadian northwoods. Robert Edeson in the leading role learns his father was unjustly accused of adultery and killed by the villain Theodore Roberts. Edeson narrowly escapes death himself through the aid of Winifred Kingston. He clears his father's name and finds happiness with Kingston. The picture got surprisingly good reviews, considering the trite story.

The New York *Dramatic Mirror* hailed it as "The latest and the best of the Lasky photoplays produced under the direction of Cecil B. DeMille and Oscar C. Apfel."

DeMille's next film was *The Virginian,* a classic Western. Dustin Farnum had the title role, and Winifred Kingston was Molly, the pretty school-teacher. The Virginian of the title was a happy-go-lucky cowboy whose friend Steve (played by J. W. Johnston) turned cattle rustler. Despite his own anguish, the Virginian tracks down and helps hang his old friend. He then kills Trampas, the man who led Steve wrong.

In one of the most famous scenes in the play and the four film versions, Trampas says to the Virginian, "You son of a---"

A quick draw and a gun pointed at his belly causes Trampas to stop his words right there (fortunately for the early film censors), and the Virginian says coldly, "When you call me that, *smile!*" The words became a catch phrase. Fifteen years later, when Paramount remade *The Virginian* with Gary Cooper, some of the posters only said, "When you call me that, *smile!*" and added the name of the theater. Everybody knew then that *The Virginian* was back.

The Virginian was the first Lasky film released under the Paramount banner. The previous films were all states' rights releases. When negotiations were completed to bring Lasky into the Paramount group, *The Call of the North* was ready for release. Goldfish wanted to hold it up and make *The Virginian* their first contribution to the new releasing company's schedule. He thought *The Virginian* was the stronger film. He was already jealous of the other producers in the Paramount group and wanted the first Lasky Paramount release to show up the rest, particularly Zukor's.

He got his wish. Zukor's first Paramount release was *The Lost Paradise* with Harry B. Warner, who was later billed as H. B. Warner to avoid confusing the public with the Harry of the Warner Brothers.

Goldfish was gleeful when *The Virginian* out-grossed the Zukor film. Zukor said nothing. It was characteristic of him to keep quiet and wait for an opportunity to strike back at his enemies.

And he was sure that Samuel Goldfish was his enemy.

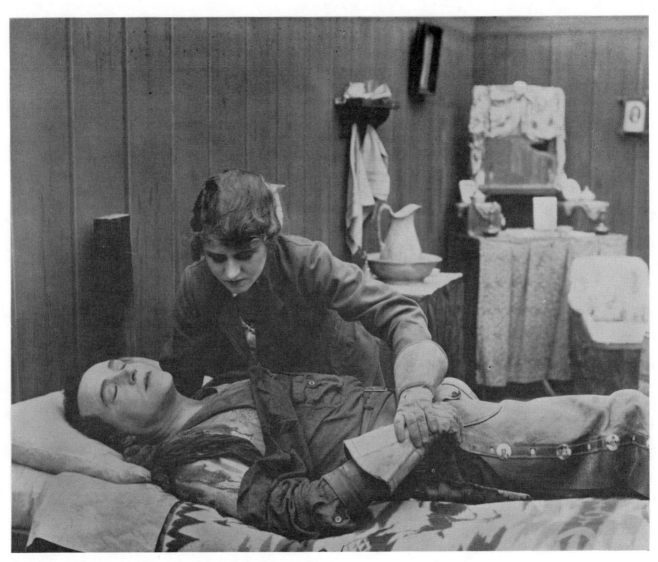

Cecil B. DeMille's *The Virginian* was the first Lasky picture to be released by the new Paramount Pictures distribution company. Dustin Farnum had the title role and Winifred Kingston was the schoolteacher. *Copyright 1914 by Paramount Pictures Inc.*

4

Little Mary and Others

Meanwhile, back at Famous Players, Zukor stumbled on the best break of his early movie career. This was the acquisition of Mary Pickford. Her importance to Famous Players cannot be overestimated. Zukor's idea of "famous players in famous plays" sounded wonderful, but was doomed to failure from the beginning. Others tried the same thing. Klaw and Erlanger, the Broadway producers, teamed with Biograph to present their own "famous plays in pictures." They lasted about a year. Lasky also tried to present stage stars in well-known plays. Only a very few were successful.

The trouble was that many of the famous players were unphotogenic and aging. James K. Hackett had done well in Zukor's *Prisoner of Zenda*. Dustin Farnum was very good in Lasky's *The Squaw Man* and the *Virginian*. But few of the rest impressed the movie public. The lenses and lighting of the day were not flattering to an aging actor. (Hackett was an exception. He was delighted when Edwin S. Porter's camera made him look younger than he was.)

When Zukor hired Lily Langtry (the "Jersey Lily"), Porter said she would photograph as an overweight old woman. Zukor insisted that people would flock to see such a famous woman. They did not, although enough came to keep the film from being a financial failure.

What Zukor failed to understand was that Broadway was not typical of America. A Broadway success will not necessarily appeal to the hinterlands. The people who filled the Broadway houses were not at that time moviegoer's. In fact, they often despised films. It was necessary for films to create their own stars, with faces and personalities that appealed to movie audiences.

D. W. Griffith understood this. His heroines, with very few exceptions such as Florence Lawrence and Linda Arvidson, were adolescent girls. The Griffith Girl was what moviegoers had come to expect. It was what they wanted.

To Zukor's good fortune, he had in Mary Pickford a genuine Griffith Girl. She came to him in late 1913 as part of a package Daniel Frohman arranged with David Belasco for the film rights to *A Good Little Devil*. The entire stage cast, which included Pickford, was part of the bargain.

Belasco insisted upon the play's being presented exactly as it had been staged. The result was not

Caprice was Mary Pickford's second film for Famous Players. Here she is with Howard Missimer. *Copyright 1914 Famous Players Film Company.*

54

good. Porter, mindful that Zukor had signed Mary Pickford at a salary of $500 a week, suggested that they withhold release of the picture until they could present their high-priced star in something better.

Zukor agreed, and the first Pickford release under the Famous Players banner was *In the Bishop's Carriage,* which Porter directed. House Peters, another Broadway star, played with Pickford. The film was released in September 1913. It did not set the world on fire. Her next film, *Caprice,* directed by J. Searle Dawley (an old friend of Porter's), also made money but was not an overwhelming success. This was followed by *Hearts Adrift,* based upon a magazine story discovered by Pickford. It was about a woman and a man (played by Harold Lockwood) who were cast away on a deserted island. They marry themselves and have a child. Then it seems that Lockwood's wife had not been drowned in the shipwreck that cast him upon the island. She hunts and finds him. Poor Pickford throws herself and her child into the sea. Released in February 1914, it was not a bad picture. Unfortunately, audiences preferred to see their heroines live and love.

Zukor then released *A Good Little Devil.* It did poorly, but the next Pickford film made by Porter was a smash hit, finally vindicating Zukor's faith in her.

This was *Tess of the Storm Country,* filmed—like *Hearts Adrift*—at Malibu, California, to avoid the harsh New York winter. The company made its headquarters in California. Although DeMille knew Pickford since both had worked in Belasco's *The Warrens of Virginia,* neither company bothered to visit the other.

Tess of the Storm Country was based upon Grace Miller White's novel. A wealthy miser buys land occupied by squatters. He tries to run them off the land, and a man is killed when the squatters resist. Tess's father is unjustly convicted of the crime, but the miser's son (Harold Lockwood) sympathizes with Tess. He grows to love her, but this love turns to disgust when he finds her with a fatherless baby that he thinks is hers. Angered by his lack of faith in her, Tess refuses to tell him the truth. Later the real killer is unmasked. Tess's father is released. Lockwood learns that the baby really belongs to his own sister. So Pickford and Lockwood live happily ever after, which is exactly what 1914 audiences wanted to see.

This is the picture that established Mary Pickford as the top star of the day. Her next film was *The Eagle's Mate,* in which she plays a young woman kidnapped by mountaineers and protected by James Kirkwood, who also directed the film. Zukor, trying to expand production from 30 to 52 pictures a year, hired several new directors, including Kirkwood, Sidney Olcott, and stage director Hugh Ford, who directed the next Pickford film, *Such a Little Queen.* Two other Pickford films were released in 1914, *Behind the Scenes* and *Cinderella* (both directed by Kirkwood).

Studios were business establishments, and for the most part the relationship between the principals was businesslike. That of Mary Pickford and Zuker

Harold Lockwood thinks the illegitimate baby is Mary's. She, angered by his lack of faith in her, will not tell him the truth in *Tess of the Storm Country,* directed by Edwin S. Porter. *Copyright 1914 by Famous Players Film Company.*

was an exception. Zukor was genuinely fond of his star and treated her like a daughter. She often was a guest at his home and accompanied Zukor and his wife to the theater. And Zukor, always on the lookout for new properties, took in every show opening in town.

Daniel Frohman, who was mainly responsible for finding stories, had a penthouse atop his Lyceum theater. Here he would host Zukor and Porter each week as they discussed possible future scripts. When a story was under consideration for her, Mary Pickford and her mother would attend the meetings.

Mary loved to come there because Frohman's retreat was actually a theatrical museum. Everything in it had a stage history, and the old man loved to explain to the young woman the story behind each item. His chair was the throne from *The Pride of Jennico* with James K. Hackett. The ivory letter opener on his desk had been used by Lily Langtry in another play. A framed caricature of Frohman was drawn—and remarkably well, too—by Enrico Caruso, the famous tenor. Framed autographed pictures of great stars crowded the walls, and every item in the room—including the rug—had once graced the set of one or another famous play.

The room was a living museum, and Frohman constantly added to it. He made a special production of adding each new item, as he did when he climbed up on the Hackett throne chair to drive a nail into the wall to hang Mary Pickford's picture with the other greats.

Scattered among the theatrical memorabilia were souvenirs of his friendship with people outside the theater. One was a framed drawing of a Kewpie doll by its creator Rose O'Neill. This doll was very famous in its day. O'Neill had an indirect association with films. She had married the son of Major Latham, inventor of the famous "Latham Loop" that figured so prominently in the early patents wars. Another drawing was by Grace Drayton, who invented the Campbell Soup kids of advertising fame. A later acquisition was a rag doll given to him by Bebe Daniels. The doll had been made by Phyllis Daniels, Bebe's mother, who sewed costumes for Kalem at one time. She left the face blank, and Bebe drew her own likeness on the doll. Frohman said it was a very good job. This, of course, came about long after Pickford had gone her way.

In his old age Zukor looked back upon this period as one of the happiest in his life. Movie making was fun then—a really family affair. It was not to last long. The ambitions of Zukor and Pickford and the growing dissatisfaction of Porter before many years would break up the friendly group.

Porter was not happy with Famous Players. All those who knew him agree that he had little interest in directing. He was much more interested in the camera and often shot his own pictures. Both Pickford and H. B. Warner have said that he gave little instruction to his actors. They knew what the story was, and he expected them to provide what action was called for without bothering him.

Although Zukor, Pickford, and others have disparaged Porter, he was one of the most inventive American filmmakers of his day. In 1901 he devised a revolving stand and took the first panoramic view for a motion picture. That same year he took the first known night motion pictures. This was at the Pan-American Exposition in Buffalo, New York. To show electrically lighted buildings at night, Porter used single frame exposures of 10 seconds each.

Porter has gone down in movie history as the first producer to tell a story with the camera. This honor is accorded to his 1903 film, *The Great Train Robbery.* However, early films restored by Kent Niver show that Porter filmed *Jack and the Beanstalk* in 1902, a year before *The Great Train Robbery,* the biggest hit of its time.

Porter's films were popular with the public. *A Good Little Devil* was not a success, but this was due

to Belasco's interference. *Hearts Adrift* was not successful either, although several historians and Mary
Pickford say otherwise. Zukor, on the other hand,
called it "a flop."

In any event, Porter thought he was not being
fairly treated and began to quarrel with Zukor over
stories and cast. Other directors were being brought
in, such as J. Searle Dawley and Hugh Ford, and
Zukor decided that Porter's days with Paramount
were numbered.

Hugh Ford was a stage director whom Daniel
Frohman brought into the company. His first picture
was *Such a Little Queen* with Mary Pickford and Carlyle
Blackwell, released in September 1914. Later Ford
would become director-general of Paramount's eastern
operations. Then, when all production was shifted to
the West Coast in the late 1920s, he would head Paramount's production in England. Except for Adolph
Zukor, Ford would have the longest continuous Paramount employment of any director, actor, or producer.

The formation of Paramount in late 1914 seemed the
answer to Zukor's and Lasky's distribution problems.
Now all they had to do was sit back and make films
on somebody else's money while Hodkinson worried
about selling them. However, it did not work out as
smoothly as everyone thought it would. Hodkinson
had very definite ideas about how the company should
be run. He thought that producers should concern
themselves solely with production and leave all the
rest to him. Zukor, on the other hand, was determined
to become the John D. Rockefeller of films. He quickly
decided that William Wadsworth Hodkinson was in
his way.

At the moment there was nothing he could do. But
he was a patient man. He waited for an opportunity.
In the meantime, Paramount had good pictures to sell
and an honest, able man to sell them. The company
prospered.

The original group included Bosworth Inc., Pallas,
Morosco, Lasky, and Famous Players. Bosworth held
the rights to all Jack London's books. The company had
adequate financial resources, and Hobart Bosworth was
an old-time actor who understood production values.
Tuberculosis forced him to leave the East. He was in
Los Angeles working in a local theater when Francis
Boggs, director for the Selig Polyscope Company, came
to town. He persuaded a reluctant Bosworth to join
him. Bosworth decided that he liked making pictures
and stayed with Selig for five years. Then, with backing

Hugh Ford was a long time Paramount director.

Phillips Smalley and Lois Weber were a husband and wife team.
Here they are in *The Traitors*, 1914, written and directed by Miss
Weber. *Copyright 1914 by Bosworth Inc.*

from Frank C. Garbutt, he founded Bosworth Inc.

He was soon joined by Lois Weber and Phillips Smalley, a husband and wife team. Weber had been a stock actress, and Smalley had been a lawyer. They were hired by Carl Laemmle, who was eccentric enough to permit Lois to direct her own pictures. Thus she became one of the first, if not the first, women to direct a motion picture. She also wrote her own scripts, which were well characterized, and boldly plunged into social aspects generally shunned at that time.

Some years earlier Kalem sent Sidney Olcott and a company to Europe to film in natural settings. The films were better than average, climaxing in the famous *From the Manger to the Cross*, which Olcott shot in Egypt and the Holy Land. Now Zukor tried the same thing. Porter and Hugh Ford were sent to Europe, going first to England and then to Rome, where they made Hall Caine's *The Eternal City*, released in 1915.

Although Zukor's Famous Players were not drawing, he still clung to the idea that their names alone would bring patrons into the theater. The evidence was clear that the public preferred fresh new movie faces to the wrinkled and sagging old stars. But he continued to present such films as *The Straight Road* with Gladys Hanson and *The Better Man* with William Courtleigh.

Fortunately, he finally got two genuine Broadway stars who were young and beautiful. One of these was Pauline Frederick. The other was Marguerite Clark. From the standpoint of the Paramount program, the two complemented each other perfectly. Frederick was an "emotional" actress, as they described intense actresses in those days. Clark specialized in cute, light comedy.

Since Clark's type of role was exactly what Mary Pickford was making, it would appear that she was not needed on the Paramount program .Some historians have hinted that Zukor hired her as a not-so-subtle hint to Pickford that she was not indispensable. Pickford and her mother were becoming increasingly difficult about salaries.

While Mary and Charlotte Pickford took a dim view of Clark, Zukor and the Pickfords were still on their professional honeymoon. Zukor has said that a still he saw of Marguerite in costume for *Prunella*, a Winthrop Ames stage production, was what decided him that he had to have Clark. *Prunella* was Clark's greatest stage triumph and years later would be her

most popular movie. The word "adorable" is the only one to use for her in those productions.

Marguerite Clark was the daughter of a well-to-do businessman, but when he died the family was destitute. The oldest sister, Cora, decided that Marguerite had stage possibilities. She then took the role in Marguerite's career that Minne Marx took in the Marx Brothers' and that Charlotte Pickford took in Mary's. Cora was 14 years older than her sister and a woman of great determination.

Marguerite Clark was a formidable rival to Mary Pickford in the early days of Famous Players. *Copyright 1916 by Paramount Pictures Inc.*

Marguerite got her first part at 12 and went on for a long and distinguished stage career. She was 27, but still looked like a child, when Zukor signed her to a three-year contract in 1914.

Her first picture for Zukor was *Wildflower*. Marguerite played an unspoiled child of the wood who was attracted to a wastrel who persuaded her to elope with him. Harold Lockwood rushes to stop the marriage, because he knows that his brother (James Cooley) is secretly married to an actress. He is too late to stop the wedding but forces Marguerite to go with him. The wedding is illegal because of Cooley's prior marriage. Marguerite then decides that she loves Lockwood after all.

The picture was a hit. Surprisingly, the advertising did not play up Marguerite's stage fame. Ben Schulberg—later to become a famous producer and discoverer of Clara Bow and father of novelist Bud Schulberg—was directing publicity for Zukor. Ben pointed out to Zukor that Broadway stars were not pulling like Pickford. He suggested they play down Marguerite's stage background and build her up as a motion picture star.

Zukor protested that Pickford had been a Broadway star, but Ben pointed out that she had been in only two Broadway shows. In one, *The Warrens of Virginia*, she played a minor child's role. In *A Good Little Devil* she did play the second lead, the blind girl, to Ernest Truex's lead. However, this play—and again this may inflame a lot of Pickford historians—was not a roaring success. The reason that Belasco agreed to let Zukor film it was because it had done poorly and Belasco had decided against sending it on tour with the original cast. He figured he might as well salvage as much out of it as possible by selling the film rights to Famous Players.

The stage had done little for Pickford, and she had done equally little for it. She was entirely a product of film, as far as her enormous popularity went.

After some soul searching, Zukor went along with Schulberg. Marguerite Clark's stage fame was not stressed. She was thrown cold upon an unsuspecting audience and triumphed through her own appeal, despite a trite and ridiculous story.

Also, considerable credit must be given to her director. He was Allan Dwan, making his debut with Famous Players. Dwan was no novice, however. He had already directed over 200 films at Essenay, American, and Universal. Dwan was trained as an electrical en-

gineer and supposedly helped develop the Cooper-Hewitt lights used in the early studios. He had gone to Essenay in 1909 to handle a lighting problem and fell in love with movie making. He worked for Essenay and American and then moved to Universal before jumping to Famous Players in 1914. Never a great director, Dwan nevertheless was an able one who handled some of the greatest stars of his time—and that time stretched from 1909 to the 1960s. In sheer active longevity he outlasted everybody, including Zukor, who was only a figurehead for the last 30 years of his association with Paramount.

Marguerite Clark figured in one of Zukor's sly schemes. He had already formulated his plan to absorb all his rivals. With this in mind, he had flattered Jesse Lasky. This began when Zukor sent Lasky a telegram of congratulations as *The Squaw Man* opened. He then invited Lasky to lunch, and the luncheons increased in number during 1914. Lasky was increasingly impressed by the acuteness of Zukor's ideas about the future of the motion picture industry.

Then suddenly the two new friends found themselves in direct competition. Lasky, Zukor, and two other companies were bidding for the screen rights to *The Goose Girl*. The story, by Harold McGrath, was about a lost princess who was raised by peasants and fell in love with a king in disguise.

Lasky outbid them all. He had gotten carried away in the bidding and paid more than he really wanted to. Also, he feared that his victory would alienate Zukor, whose friendship Lasky had come to prize.

So with this in mind, Lasky went to lunch at Claridge's with Zukor. He was determined to sell the film rights back to his rival. He would lose nothing actually but would regain Zukor's goodwill.

He approached the matter by suggesting that maybe Marguerite Clark would have been best for *The Goose Girl*. But before he could propose reselling the rights to Zukor, he was shocked by Zukor's saying, "You are absolutely right, Mr. Lasky. So I will be glad to loan you Miss Clark for this film."

Lasky was stunned. Loaning stars was unheard of. Later it became an accepted practice, but this was the first time it ever occurred. Lasky went away singing the praises of Zukor to DeMille and Goldfish. There seemed no reason for this unheard of generosity. Zukor asked nothing in return. He did not even charge extra, as producers later did, to make a profit on the deal.

Marguerite Clark defends her honor against S.N. Dunbar in *The Goose Girl*. Marguerite was the movies' first "loanout" star. *Copyright 1915 by Jesse L. Lasky Feature Play Company.*

Lasky merely paid Clark's salary and the expenses for her and Cora's trip to California.

Marguerite was not too happy over the deal. While she and Cora, her business manager, went along with it, she was rather temperamental and demanding during the shooting. She not only was irritated at having to leave New York but also was angry because Lasky would not use Harold Lockwood as leading man. Lockwood was her co-star in her first two films. Monroe Salisbury had already been signed for the king's role.

Fred Thompson, the director, did not have an easy time. However, this was the only time Marguerite caused trouble on the set, and it was all due to her irritation. On returning to New York she informed Zukor–through Cora–that she would never work for Lasky again. This was a sentiment heartily endorsed by Lasky's director-general, Cecil B. DeMille. Once, when Thompson was having trouble with Marguerite,

Marguerite made *Seven Sisters* in 1915. With her on the table are Madge Evans, Dorothea Comden, and Georgia Furnstman. In the background are Jean Steward, I. Feder, Lola Barclay, and Madame C. Dargurg. *Copyright 1915 by Famous Players Film Company.*

he called on the director-general for support. It was beneath Clark's dignity to argue, but Cora could and would draw swords with anyone. DeMille went down in defeat.

Marguerite's irritation with Lasky was so great that to the end of her career she would have no connection with the Lasky name. Even after the merger of Famous Players and Lasky into Famous Player-Lasky, Miss Clark's films were released under the Famous Players name alone.

It is common for the two reigning stars of a company to resent each other. Zukor claimed that Pickford and Clark were in this mold and that Pickford, while less open than her mother and Clark, did resent Marguerite. However, Marguerite–in Zukor's words–"could not have cared less."

Zukor kept her busy. Marguerite made seven films in 1915, all in New York with the exception of *The Goose Girl* for Lasky. All were moneymakers, and three were outstanding. These included *The Pretty Sister of José*, in which Marguerite took the role originated by Maude Adams on the stage. It is the story of a young woman who hates men because her mother had been wronged. A young bullfighter (Rupert Julian) loves her, but turns to Teddy Sampson when she spurns him. Only then does she realize that she loves him. He is fatally gored and dies with his head in her lap. Allan Dwan directed. The José of the title, whose pretty sister she was, was played by Jack Pickford, Mary's brother.

Another hit she made in 1915 was *The Seven Sisters*. She was the delightful Mici, a role created on the stage by Laurette Taylor, an actress still remembered for *Peg O' My Heart*. Mici was the third sister in a family of seven daughters. She wanted to get married, but under Hungarian custom she had to wait for her three older and plainer sisters to marry first. Mici, aided by Conway Tearle, cleverly arranges everything. Madge Evans played one of the younger sisters.

Where Mary Pickford more and more ran her own affairs, Zukor carefully plotted Marguerite's career– although a flinty-eyed Cora watched and approved every action. She was given outstanding stage plays with surefire roles created by the leading actresses of the day. Her directors were all experienced and highly capable. The director of *The Seven Sisters* was Sidney Olcott, a man who must be ranked second to Griffith at this time.

Olcott (real name Alcott) was born in Canada of Irish immigrant parents. He got into acting through amateur theatrics and was given his first professional job by John Ince, father of the famous Thomas H. Ince. He joined Biograph in 1904, working with Wallace (Old Man) McCutcheon as an actor and assistant director for two years. He then joined Kalem in 1907 as the new company's director. At this time he made friends with the Italian-American actor Robert G. Vignola and a former medicine show barker named George Melford.

Olcott's pet peeve was the ridiculously unauthentic backgrounds used in films of the day. After Kalem sent him to Florida to continue filming during the winter, Olcott made *A Florida Feud*, using genuine backgrounds. This film was so successful that he was able to persuade Frank Marion to let him take a company to Ireland. This was followed by a second and larger company the next year. Then, on a third trip, he expanded to Egypt and the Holy Land for *From the Manger to the Cross*, a reverent life of Christ filmed in the actual historical settings. It was one of the most acclaimed American motion pictures between *The Great Train Robbery* and *The Birth of a Nation*.

After a stint with Lubin in 1914, he came to Famous Players in 1915. Olcott's friend George Melford had joined Lasky the previous year. Melford was a workhorse who turned out assembly line pictures. He had the distinction of making what both Lasky and Zukor claimed to be candidates for the ten worst films of all time—but which made Paramount millions and gave the world a new synonym for great lover, *The Sheik*.

Olcott directed Mary Pickford in *Madame Butterfly* and *Poor Little Peppina*, but his heart was not in studio work. He wanted to go back to Ireland where the peasants loved him and flocked to help his films. And despite such lovable stars as Mary Pickford and Marguerite Clark, he preferred Valentine Grant. He met Grant one day and asked her if she would like to be a movie actress.

"But I know nothing about it," she replied.

"I'll teach you all you need to know," Olcott replied.

And so persuasive was his Irish charm that she agreed, and a little while later became his wife. Zukor gave in and agreed to finance another Irish expedition. Out of it came *The Innocent Lie*, a beautifully photo-graphed story of Irish fisherfolk. Then Zukor was astonished to hear that his Irish expedition was in Scotland. The result, *The Daughter of McGregor*, also with Valentine Grant, was good enough to justify the expense.

In the meantime Zukor was leaning more and more toward California, where filming could continue the year round. He bought the Fiction Pictures, Inc., plant at Melrose and Bronson streets as his California studio. Fiction Pictures was an ill-fated attempt by actor Wilfred Lucas to become a producer.

The search for new faces went on. Zukor got Pauline Frederick, who went to Rome to star in the Ford-Porter Film *The Eternal City*. The picture was a hit and established Pauline as a screen star. She was then 34, but she had a smooth beauty that withstood the harsh lenses and lights better than most actresses of the day. She gave Zukor a chance to present more

Valentine Grant in *The Innocent Lie,* a tale of Irish fisherfolk, was praised for its natural settings. *Copyright 1916 by Paramount Pictures, Inc.*

The Daughter of McGregor with Valentine Grant was filmed in Scotland by Sidney Olcott. *Copyright 1916 by Paramount Pictures.*

Thomas Meighan and Laura Hope Crews in *The Blackbirds,* the story of a woman smuggler who is reformed by the mysterious influence of an oriental rug. *Copyright 1915 by Jesse L. Lasky Feature Play Company.*

mature pictures that were beyond the range of Mary Pickford and Marguerite Clark—pictures of the type that had flopped with his middle-aged stars of the past.

Frederick's life reads like a plot from an early film. She was a society girl who sang so well at a church bazaar that a friend dared her to apply for a professional job. She did, and she got it: singing in vaudeville. This so enraged her father that she and her mother moved out. She worked in several shows and then landed a supporting role in *It Happened in Nordland*, the Victor Herbert musical starring Blanche Ring. Then, in true show business fashion, Blanche got mad and walked out during the national tour. Pauline stepped into the leading role, and a star was born.

After *The Eternal City*, released in April 1915, Pauline made *Sold*, directed by Edwin S. Porter, and then *Zaza*, again with Porter. *Zaza* is the famous story of a French chorus girl who is seduced by a married man. When she finds out that he is married, she goes

John Barrymore was a juvenile lead and light comedian for Zukor. Here he is as the imposter in *The Man From Mexico*. *Copyright 1914 by Famous Players Film Company.*

to tell his wife for revenge, but backs out when she sees her lover's little daughter. Gloria Swanson and Claudette Colbert both followed Frederick in this role.

Blanche Ring also made one Paramount picture, *The Yankee Girl*, for Zukor in 1915. However, her greatest contribution to Paramount was as a talent scout. It seems that her sister, Frances Ring, married a genial Irishman who had difficulty making a living. One day while sitting around discussing his future, the family decided that perhaps Tom had what it took to get into the movies. Blanche used her clout to get him in a couple of British pictures of little consequence. Then, when they returned to the United States, Blanche cornered Jesse Lasky. Blanche was the superpersuasive type (she was one of the first singers to get an audience to sing along with her). A reluctant Lasky said yes, and it was just as if Blanche had given him a check for $5 million, because Tom was the Thomas Meighan who became one of Paramount's big stars of the 1920s.

Tom had only one fault. He liked an occasional bender, but he was gentleman enough and sufficiently professional to do his drinking between pictures. The same could not be said for one of Zukor's best juveniles. This gentleman, who starred in popular brash young man comedies, was one John Barrymore. He was not too fond of acting anyway, having been forced into it after failing as an artist. He became a highly successful actor and was supposed to make films for Zukor in the daytime and, except on matinee days, perform on the stage at night.

Zukor put up with Barrymore's getting to the studio about noon, but one day, when he did not arrive at all, the angry producer sent director Marshal Neilan to pull him out of bed. This was like sending an arsonist to put out a fire. It was two days before Zukor saw either of them. Despite his drinking and sometimes disorderly conduct, Barrymore continued with Famous Players and its successors until 1920.

Lasky then pulled off a triple coup, gaining Blanche Sweet, Wallace Reid, and Geraldine Farrar. Farrar, an operatic sensation, was the most famous of the three, but Blanche Sweet and Wallace Reid made more money for the company.

Geraldine Farrar and Jeanie Macpherson. later DeMille's
scenario writer, battle it out in *Carmen,* 1915. *Copyright 1915 by
Paramount Pictures Corp.*

Pedro de Cordoba, left, Geraldine Farrar, and Wallace Reid were the stars of *Maria Rosa. Copyright 1916 by Paramount Pictures Corp.*

What Lasky and DeMille had in mind, putting an operatic prima donna into a silent film, was something that no one could figure out. In fact, DeMille was so sure she would be a poor actress that he suggested that they postpone filming *Carmen*, which was set as her first picture to cash in on the fame of her performances in the opera. He suggested *Maria Rosa* instead. It is the story of two Spanish peasants who love Maria. One (Pedro de Cordoba) kills a man with a knife belonging to the other (Wallace Reid). Wally goes to prison, but he is let out early for helping quell a riot. He returns just as Maria Rosa is to marry the real murderer. In a rage Maria stabs Ramon (de Cordoba), but before he dies he tells the police he fell on the knife.

The idea was to give Farrar practice in this film so that she would not be terribly bad in *Carmen*. She turned out to be a much better actress than anyone figured. *Carmen* was filmed after *Maria Rosa* and released first. Both films were hits, with critical praise heaped on both star and director.

The only mishap was that the story of Carmen deviated somewhat from the opera. This was because it was learned at the last minute that the opera was still copyrighted. William C. deMille, Cecil's playwright brother, then fashioned a scenario from Prosper Merimee's original story, which had inspired the opera.

Maria Rosa and *Carmen* were what set Wallace Reid's footsteps on the road to fame. The son of Hal Reid, the playwright and actor, Wally had been around for years, playing with different companies. Then DeMille and Lasky were impressed by a bit he played as a fighting blacksmith in Griffith's *The Birth of a Nation*, and invited him to join them.

Finally Lasky closed the year with a smash hit, topping a season that had produced one hit after another. This blockbuster—and a motion picture milestone—was *The Cheat*. It was an original play by Hector Turnbull, an ex-newspaper critic, whom William C. deMille persuaded to join Lasky.

The story was lurid and shocking. A society woman (Fannie Ward) gambles away charity funds in her custody. She covers the loss with a loan from a rich Japanese (Sessue Hayakawa) in exchange for the promise of what could only be hinted at in those days. But she manages to get the money from other sources and reneges on her promise to Hayakawa. Angered, he brands her naked shoulder as he brands all his property. She shoots him. Her husband takes the blame but is exonerated when she bares her shoulder in court.

Hayakawa got the critical acting raves. A master at underplaying in a time of scene-chewing actors, he went on to a remarkable career, the first Oriental to play romantic leads in the United States. Thomas H. Ince saw him in a stage play and persuaded him to make films. Later he changed to Lasky and played villains until *The Cheat* established him.

Blanche Sweet was the other big acquisition for Lasky in 1915. Jesse had seen her in *Judith of Bethulia* for Biograph and signed her as soon as she was free. She made such films as *The Warrens of Virginia, The Captive*, and *The Secret Sin*.

Fannie Ward reacts after injuring Sessue Hayakawa in *The Cheat*, a popular and critical success. *Copyright 1915 by Jesse L. Lasky Feature Play Company.*

Maud Allen, a famous dancer, and Forrest Stanley were in *The Rug Maker's Daughter*, a Bosworth release on the Paramount program. *Copyright 1915 by Bosworth Inc.*

The other Paramount releasing companies were doing well. Pallas and Morosco had combined, and Oliver Morosco had acquired the major interest in Bosworth when Hobart Bosworth, angered at financial restrictions on his artistic ambitions, withdrew and joined Universal. One of Bosworth's hits of this period was *The Rug Maker's Daughter* with dancer Maud Allan and Forrest Stanley.

Bosworth also got Paramount involved with the censors. Lois Weber's *Hypocrites*, released in late 1914, finally got to Boston in 1915. Mayor Curley objected to scenes of an allegorical "truth" portrayed by a nude woman. The picture was banned.

According to *The Movie Magazine* (June 1915), a Bosworth representative then hired an artist to paint a gown on Edwards (the nude) frame by frame.

By this time Lois Weber and Phillips Smalley had already gone back to Universal. Also, Oscar Apfel had moved from Lasky to Bosworth. So 1915 closed on a happy financial and artistic note for all the companies associated with Paramount. The producers were happy, too, with the single exception of Adolph Zukor.

For one thing, Zukor was having trouble with Mary and Charlotte Pickford, who demanded more and more money. But more irritating than this, he saw his dream of dominating the movie business threatened by a new company. This was Triangle, organized by a human dynamo named Harry E. Aitkin. It suddenly became very clear to Zukor that Aitkin had the same ambition

as Zukor: to dominate the film business. What was even more shocking to Zukor, it appeared that Aitkin had a very good chance of doing it, too. Zukor started planning for war.

Hypocrites, written and directed by Lois Weber, was praised for its pictorial beauty. Here nuns weeps for the murdered priest, played by Courtney Foote. *Copyright 1914 by Bosworth Inc.*

Blanche Sweet joined Lasky after her success in Griffith's *Judith of Bethulia.* Here she has a dual role of twin sisters in *The Secret Sin* with Thomas Meighan. *Copyright 1915 by Jesse L. Lasky Feature Play Company.*

5

The Shark of Films

Harry Aitkin had been the sparkplug in the Mutual group. Then he and his brother financed—at great sacrifice—D. W. Griffith's *The Birth of a Nation*. Griffith's extravagance and epic approach almost bankrupted the Aitkin brothers, but fate was with them. The film made cinematic history, and the brothers owned the gold mine. The financial arrangements provided subtantial cuts to Griffith and Thomas Dixon, who wrote the story, but Aitkin controlled the film.

This tremendous success—and tremendous is the only word to describe it—gave Aitkin delusions of grandeur. He decided to organize the greatest film factory of them all. He pulled out of Mutual and persuaded Adam Kessel and Charlie Bauman of the New York Motion Picture Company to join him. Kessel and Bauman brought with them Mack Sennett and Thomas H. Ince. Griffith also joined. The company was built around these three producers (Griffith, Sennett, and Ince) and was called Triangle.

With the success of *The Birth of a Nation* to support his quest for money, Aitkin had no trouble raising funds. He immediately went wild on Broadway, signing up 60 famous players ranging from Douglas Fairbanks to Beerbohm Tree. He flatly announced that Triangle would have the best directors, the greatest stars, and the finest pictures in the business. With names like Marie Doro, Texas Guinan, Tully Marshall, Willard Mack, Frank Keenan (grandfather of Keenan Wynn), Helen Ware, DeWolf Hopper, and others, it appeared that he might make good his threat.

Many of these stars had been approached by Zukor and Lasky but had refused to make films. The enormous success of *The Birth of a Nation* awoke them to the possibilities of films, and Aitkin's lavish checkbook brought them in.

There was a hasty meeting of Paramount executives. Lasky, who had a lot of experience in going bankrupt, claimed Triangle could not support its galaxy of high-priced stars. DeMille, who was having trouble finding enough good stories to keep his own plant going, doubted that Aitkin could get enough stories himself. Also, DeMille said that he could do anything Griffith could do or better if Hodkinson would stop being so cheap with money. Oliver Morosco had little to say, and Zukor said even less. Samuel Goldfish ventured the opinion that they

Jesse L. Lasky, left, and Adolph Zukor as they looked in 1916 when their companies combined to make Famous-Players Lasky. *Copyright 1916 by Famous Players-Lasky Corp.*

would run Aitkin out of business in 18 months.

Zukor, instead of talking, investigated. He found that a banking firm associated with the Rockefellers was financing Aitkin. He did not see how anyone could have a more solid financial base than that. When his own Allan Dwan quit to join Triangle, he began to have nightmares involving the possibility of Mary Pickford doing the same thing.

Yet at the moment there seemed little he could do to head off this new threat to his own grandiose plans. The next he heard was that Aitkin had taken over the Knickerbocker Theater as the New York showcase for Triangle and planned a three-picture premier on September 23, 1915, to launch Triangle to the trade. The opening program was to be Douglas Fairbanks and Seena Owen in *The Lamb* supervised by Griffith but directed by Christie Cabanné, Mack Sennett's *My Valet* with Raymond Hitchcock, and Thomas H. Ince's *The Iron Strain* (a sort of Alaskan *Taming of the Shrew*) with Dustin Farnum and Enid Markey. The admission price was set at $2.

Triangle was off to a roaring start. Zukor was finally prodded into action. His answer was a merger to build a production company stronger than Triangle. Lasky was agreeable. Shortly thereafter Famous Players-Lasky was formed, absorbing Zukor's Famous Players, Lasky's Jesse L. Lasky Feature Play Company, Morosco, Pallas, and Bosworth. The Bosworth name was soon dropped. Pallas-Morosco continued for a while and then disappeared.

In dividing up the authority, Zukor became president of the new company. Jesse L. Lasky was first vice–president in charge of production. Cecil B. DeMille was director-general. There was no real job for Samuel Goldfish, but since he owned 25 percent interest in Lasky, something had to be done for him. He was given the title of chairman of the board. This was supposed to be a figurehead position. Goldfish was as arrogant, egotistical, and Napoleonic as his partners. He had no intention of being less than the ruler. So the seeds were formed for a power struggle.

The merger got off to a bad start. As the new production head, Lasky selected *Less Than the Dust*, a story of India, for their top star Mary Pickford. Pickford called it the worst picture of her career. Lasky agreed.

Then Goldfish began interfering. Zukor, as part of his last salary negotiations with Mary Pickford, signed her brother Jack to a $500-a-week contract. Goldfish canceled it saying, "It's too much for the snotty little bastard." This description was concurred with by most people who knew him except the young man's doting sister and mother.

Goldfish also resented the enormous salary paid to Mary. Pickford in her autobiography claims she was told that Goldfish once looked out the window and saw her walking across the set. "For her salary she should run instead of walk!" he groused.

Relations between Goldfish and Zukor continued to deteriorate. It was only a matter of time before there would be a complete break. It would have come earlier except that Zukor always moved slowly and cautiously. There are several stories about what the final straw was, but it appears that Mary told tales that provided the catalyst.

According to Lasky, he was discussing a story with Mary Pickford when Goldfish burst in. "Jesse, don't let Zukor butt in on this picture. We've always made better pictures than Famous Players, so see that you keep the production reins in your hands."

Pickford reported the outburst to Zukor. The next day Zukor informed Lasky: "I am sorry to tell you this, but Famous Players-Lasky is not big enough to hold Mr. Goldfish and myself."

The stock had been split 50-50 for the merger. If the entire Lasky group held fast behind Sam, it would be a standoff. In that case Zukor said he was prepared to sell out to the others. Lasky consulted DeMille, and together they agreed to back Zukor over Goldfish. Goldfish resigned and received almost a million dollars for his stock. He joined Edgar Selwyn in Goldwyn Pictures, a name formed from a combination of their names. Sam liked the name so well that he adopted it for his, thereby becoming the famous Samuel Goldwyn. It was almost 40 years before he again spoke to Lasky, DeMille, and Zukor.

He only met with them then because the State of California declared the old Lasky barn an historical landmark. He was invited to the ceremony and hated to see the others get all the publicity.

The Goldwyn matter was only one of Zukor's troubles. His greatest problem was a running battle with W. W. Hodkinson. Under the contracts with Paramount, Hodkinson advanced $35,000 to the producers for each five-reel film. This was an advance against profits. Paramount had to recoup this advance before the producers shared in the returns. Then they got 65 percent of the gross.

Zukor resented the $35,000 lid on production expenses. It was adequate in the beginning, but Triangle's lavish production plans changed this. Zukor felt that he had to have more money to meet the Triangle challenge. *The Birth of a Nation* and his own *The Eternal City* (1915), which cost $100,000, proved that bigger pictures meant bigger profits.

Violet McMillan played Ojo in *The Patchwork Girl of Oz*, filmed by L. Frank Baum and released by Paramount in 1914. *Copyright 1914 by L. Frank Baum.*

Also, Zukor resented Hodkinson's taking in independent work on which the producers got none of the profit, since only Zukor had stock in Paramount itself and this was only 10 percent. One such independent deal was *The Patchwork Girl of Oz*, made by Author L. Frank Baum for his own Oz Film Manufacturing Company. Pierre Cowdere, the French acrobat, played the title role, and Violet McMillan, a well-known vaudeville star, was Ojo the Munchkin boy. The picture was a critical success and a total box office failure. No one knew why. The *Wizard of Oz* had been an enormous stage success with Montgomery and Stone.

This failure was in late 1914, but Hodkinson continued to gamble on independent productions which Zukor rightly felt competed inside the Paramount distribution system with his own films.

Up to this time Wall Street money had been afraid of the film industry. By 1915 there were 200 companies producing, and the bankruptcy rate was high. Then Benjamin B. Hampton, a vice-president of the American Tobacco Company, did a survey that showed that films were a $600 million annual business and growing. He argued that a well-run trust could dominate the industry. With the backing of Percival Hill, president of American Tobacco, Hampton tried to bring about a giant merger that included Paramount. He failed because Zukor would not join unless the producers got stock and could hold office in the distribution company. Hodkinson adamantly refused. He continued to insist that production, distribution, and exhibition were separate fields that required separate expertise.

While the merger failed, it was a tremendous aid to Zukor because he had many talks with Hampton and came away with a more thorough knowledge of how Wall Street worked. He then talked with financier Otto Kahn, laying the foundation for future financing. But first he had to get rid of

Hodkinson. The founder of Paramount had become a roadblock to Zukor's ambitions. He immediately began buying up Paramount stock from Hodkinson's partners, a group of exhibitors. Hampton warned Hodkinson, but the warning did not take effect.

"I don't think he can do it," Hodkinson said. "But if he does, then I will start over again. I've done it before."

Hodkinson's confidence was based on his belief that Zukor lacked the capital to buy enough stock to dominate Paramount. But somehow the determined little man from Famous Players-Lasky got the others behind him. It was whispered that Otto Kahn had a finger in it. And so it happened in the fall of 1916 that Hodkinson found himself surprised. He was voted out, and Hiram Abrams became president of Paramount. Hodkinson then organized a new distribution company to finance and distribute independent productions under his own name.

Hi Abrams refused to be the rubber stamp Zukor wanted at the helm of Paramount. Soon he was out, and Zukor took over the presidency himself. B. P. Schulberg, who started with Zukor in 1913 as publicity chief, resigned to go with his friend Abrams. Schulberg had an idea that would eventually cost Zukor dearly. This was that stars should take over production—an idea that led to the formation several years later of United Artists.

While this corporate manipulation was going on, production continued at the studios. Although it was all one company now, the production units were still split between the Lasky group in Los Angeles and the Zukor group in New York. Although the ads called Cecil B. DeMille "director-general," he was in fact only the director-general for West Coast production. After Edwin S. Porter left the company in 1916, Hugh Ford assumed production direction for the eastern studio. Lasky, of course, was over DeMille and Ford but rarely interfered in production matters. He functioned mainly as a talent scout for stars and stories and okayed budgets. Under the merger agreement, all films produced on the West Coast were "Presented by Jesse L. Lasky." Those produced on the East Coast were "Presented by Adolph Zukor." Daniel Frohman had served his purpose and was dropped from the company.

Porter left production completely. He settled his stock options for over $800,000 and joined a company manufacturing Simplex projectors. It was a good move. Theaters were expanding and creating new markets. Most important of all, within four years there would be a trend toward two projectors in each theater. At that time there was only one. The audience waited while the projectionist changed reels. It was 1922 before it became a general practice to have two machines to provide continuous showings.

This is done by printing two sets of cue marks on the end of a reel of film. When the film approaches the end of the reel, the projectionist watches for the first cue flash. At that moment the projectionist starts the second machine running. A douser or sliding trap in front of the lens prevents this second film from showing on the screen. Then, when the second cue mark flashes in the upper right corner of the screen, the operator drops the douser on the first machine and opens the douser on the second machine. To the audience it appears only as a normal change of scene.

Among the new stars who appeared for Paramount in 1916 were stage actress Marie Doro in the *Heart of Nora Flynn* for DeMille, Thomas Meighan in *Common Ground* for George Melford, and then the Zukor group for the third remake of *Oliver Twist*. It was the custom then for small women to play major boys' roles. In addition to Marie, this all-star Oliver cast had Tully Marshall as Fagin, Hobart Bosworth as Bill Sikes, and Raymond Hatton as the Artful Dodger. It was a very good picture in every respect but was eclipsed in movie history by the later fourth remake with Jackie Coogan and Lon Chaney, Sr., for First National.

Mary Pickford made *Poor Little Peppina* with Sidney Olcott directing; *The Founding, The Eternal Grind,* and *Hulda from Holland* megaphoned by John B. O'Brien; and the disastrous *Less Than the Dust,* which was directed by John Emerson, who came to Zukor from Triangle.

Over in the Pallas division, Dustin Farnum was back after a sojourn with Triangle where he starred in *The Iron Strain.* He made *The Son of Erin, The Call of the Cumberland,* and *David Garrick,* which was based upon the life of the famous English actor.

The best remembered of all the newcomers in 1916 was a Follies dancer named Koenig, who chose the stage name of Mae Murray. She had done a Follies skit called "Little Mary Pickum," which was a burlesque

of a famous lady. In time Mae would marry royalty, queen it over Hollywood, and become the very archetype of a star.

In 1916 Mae made *Sweet Kitty Bellairs, To Have and to Hold,* and *The Plow Girl. To Have and to Hold* was her first film, and it was her misfortune to draw "Whispering" George Melford as her director. They called Melford "Whispering" because he could be heard two miles away screaming at his actors and actresses, as Mae found out. She was a dancer, not an actor, and if it had not been for the kindness and help of her co-star Wallace Reid, Melford would have packed her back to Zukor who was the "idiot"— Melford's designation—who hired her. The story by historical writer Mary Johnston was about an indentured bride who came to the Virginia colony to marry a planter.

Marie Doro, Thomas Meighan, and child actor Billy Jacobs in *Common Ground,* a tear jerker about a fighting D.A. who got framed. *Copyright 1916 by Jesse L. Lasky Feature Play Company.*

David Garrick, based upon the life of the great English actor, starred Dustin Farnum and Winifred Kingston. *Copyright 1916 by Pallas Pictures.*

Marie Doro was filming *Oliver Twist* on the adjoining set. She said that Melford screamed so loudly that she sometimes got confused as to which director was yelling at her. Once she grabbed her Fagin (Tully Marshall) and gave him a resounding kiss in answer to a loud command from Melford to Murray.

Marguerite Clark made seven films this year, climaxing in *Snow White* (beating Disney to the punch by 23 years) for the Christmas trade. Pauline Frederick made eight films. When you worked for Paramount, you *worked*.

At the end of 1916 Mary Pickford seemed to be in trouble for the first time in her movie career. After the flop of *Less Than the Dust*, she demanded her own way on the next film. It was *Pride of the Clan*, directed by Maurice Tourneur, a very fine craftsman. It, too, was poorly received. Mary and Francis Marion, the scenario writers, then decided they knew more about filmmaking that Tourneur. So they began adding bits of business and ad-lib gags during the filming of her next picture, *The Poor Little Rich Girl*.

Tourneur was among the first great artists of the screen. He had been a painter in France before turning to acting and then to motion picture directing in 1912.

Mae Murray's first picture was *To Have and to Hold*, Wallace Reid co-starred. *Copyright 1916 by Jesse L. Lasky Feature Play Company.*

78

Marie Doro, Tully Marshall, Hobart Bosworth, Raymond Hatton, and an unidentified actor in *Oliver Twist. Copyright Famous Players-Lasky, 1916.*

He came to the United States in 1914. His pictures always had pictorial beauty, with each scene composed like an artist's canvas. He was strong on low-key and back-lighting effects. In fact, he often sacrificed movement and action for pictorial beauty. Despite his shortcomings, he was highly regarded and had a long career. He quit Hollywood in 1929 because of front office interference but continued work in France until he was 72.

Tourneur was a methodical director who liked to have everything planned in advance. Consequently, according to Mary Pickford in her autobiography, he was horrified by the ad-libs. He repeatedly asked Mary and Marion where they found that in the script.

A hidden mask reveals to Mary Pickford that her lover is a road agent in *A Romance of the Redwoods*—one of Cecil B. DeMille's lesser efforts. *Copyright 1917 by Famous Players-Lasky.*

The picture was previewed by the Paramount staff and produced nothing but gloom. What was supposed to be a comedy evoked no laughs. A highly deflated Mary permitted Zukor to send her to California to work under DeMille. Before she left, Mary wrote DeMille a letter in which she assured the director-general that she would not interfere in any way with the direction of the picture. The letter was sent on Zukor's orders.

The film was *A Romance of the Redwoods*. The story is laid in the gold rush period. Mary saves her road agent lover from the vigilantes by pretending to be a young mother. The baby she clutches as she desperately pleads for Elliot Dexter's life is only a doll.

As the fliming wound down on this trite story, word came from New York that the ugly duckling, *A Poor Little Rich Girl*, was turning out to be the biggest financial success of Mary's career to date. She was bewildered, because it was poorly received at the company showing in New York.

Lasky told her why. He had not been in New York when the brass reviewed the film, or things would have been different. "The same thing happened to me with *Brewster's Millions*," he told Pickford. "The trouble was that it was being viewed by a handful of worried people who had worked on it. They did not find it funny. We thought we had a flop, but when it opened in a full theater with a fresh audience who could spur each other to join in the laughter, we had a roaring success. Never show a comedy to a small group of people."

The Pickford pictures had always been Paramount's most popular items. This worked well, because Zukor invented the block booking system. He forced exhibitors to take some turkeys in order to get the Pickford films. This was great until Mary and her mother found out the Pickford pictures were carrying the rest. She demanded more money, finally raising herself to $10,000 a week plus half the profits of her films. This actually meant that Paramount was making less net profit on her films than on those of Marguerite Clark and Pauline Frederick. But her films brought in more profit in the long run because they forced the sale of films that could not have been sold on their own merits.

Pickford finally became so expensive that something had to be done. All Paramount films were sold at the same price. Zukor did not want to change this system. So he founded Artcraft, a company to exploit special films. It is not true, as is sometimes reported in various histories, that the company was designed only for Pickford and that she would not permit any other woman's films to be distributed through it. Artcraft was set up to get higher rentals for Paramount's more expensive premium films. Shortly thereafter, Realart was organized to distribute what later was called B films. Paramount continued as the distributor for the A film line. In this way Paramount could set rentals higher and lower than the Paramount standard price. Lasky looked on Realart as a training and developing ground for featured players who would move up to Paramount release as they became bigger drawing cards.

The year 1917 was scheduled for 104 features—two a week. This broke down into a weekly Paramount release, plus 18 Artcrafts and 34 from Realart.

Not one single exhibitor complaint was heard about the Realart subsidiary with its lower rentals, but the cries of anguish were resounding about the jacked-up prices of Artcraft. Each Artcraft was sold separately and for all the traffic would bear. Among the bitter denunciations was the claim that Zukor was a "shark who intends to devour us all!" The bitterness got worse when Pickford's Artcraft films tripled in price over what they brought under the Paramount program plan.

As proof that Pickford did not jealously try to keep other women stars out of Artcraft, Elsie Ferguson's first film, *Barbary Sheep*, was released as an Artcraft special. The film was directed by Maurice Tourneur with his usual sense of beauty that brought out Ferguson's loveliness to perfection. The story concerned a titled British man who neglected his wife while he went hunting the rare Barbary sheep in the mountains of Algiers. While he stalked his sheep, an Arab chief (Pedro de Cordoba) stalked Lady Wyverne (Elsie). The success of the picture was a triumph of star and director over story.

Ferguson, overcoming parental objections, had become a chorus girl in 1901 and attained stardom with *Such a Little Queen* (later filmed with Mary Pickford) in 1909. She remained a top Broadway star until Zukor overcame her reluctance with a $5000-a-week offer to make six pictures a year for the next three years. She was then 35 years old—old for a motion picture star—but she photographed like a girl 15 years younger.

She said later that the camera frightened her so much that she would go home at night during the filming of *Barbary Sheep* and cry. She claimed she would never have gotten through the film except for the gentleness of Tourneur. She found in him the audience she missed, playing to him as she would to a packed house.

Artcraft's biggest triumph, next to Mary Pickford, was the acquisition of Douglas Fairbanks. Triangle brought Fairbanks to Hollywood in Harry Aitken's big star grab. Fairbanks was doing well on Broadway in a series of all-American youth plays but accepted Aitken's offer because of his admiration for Griffith.

Barbary Sheep introduced Elsie Ferguson to the screen. Here she is with Pedro Cordoba. *Copyright 1917 by Famous Players-Lasky.*

Fairbanks' contract specified that he would be directed, or at least supervised, by Griffith personally. Griffith was contemptuous of Fairbanks' screen possibilities, advising the bouncing young man to try Mack Sennett.

The Lamb, Fairbanks' first film, was one of three chosen to open the first Triangle program in New York. It immediately showed that Fairbanks, if handled properly, could become a new star. Even so, Griffith was too immersed in his plans for *Intolerance* to give attention to anything else.

Fairbanks used this neglect to break his Triangle contract. He set up his own studio to release through Paramount's Artcraft. His first Artcraft release in 1917 was *In Again, Out Again*. It was followed by *Wild and Woolly, Down to Earth, Man From Painted Post, Reaching for the Moon*, and *A Modern Musketeer*. In the latter, his final release for 1917, he had a short flashback sequence of himself as D'Artagnan which foreshadowed his later triumph in *The Three Musketeers* and *The Iron Mask*.

Zukor tried still another company to raise film rentals. This was the Cardinal Film Co., organized for the sole purpose of exploiting Cecil B. DeMille's first spectacle, *Joan the Woman*, with Geraldine Farrar as Joan of Arc.

This was the last straw, and exhibitors declared war. That "shark" Zukor was out to swallow them all, and they intended to destroy him. It is significant that no fury was directed toward Jesse L. Lasky. It was all centered on Zukor, which showed that they knew where the real power in Paramount was centered.

Thomas L. Tally, as befitted an ex-cowboy, was first to draw a gun in this film range war. According to movie legend, Tally rode into Waco, Texas, after a season on the range. He was surprised to find someone was showing pictures that moved. He went in, was captivated, got into the business, and became the leading exhibitor in Los Angeles. Then he joined with J. D. Williams, another prominent exhibitor, to bring together a national group of showpersons.

After three days of wrangling, owners of theater chains in eight major states announced that they were forming the First National Exhibitors Circuit. The new company would furnish pictures to the theaters of its owners, who claimed $20 million in annual admission receipts.

In the beginning the company intended to operate as Paramount had under Hodkinson. That is, it would finance and distribute the films of independent producers. Later, when this did not work well, the circuit became First National Pictures and—for a time—a formidable rival of Paramount.

Triangle was on the verge of falling apart, and Zukor no longer feared its competition. This new company was something else, because it controlled a huge block of first-run theaters, which gave it a guaranteed outlet for its films. This was a very serious threat because it could cut Paramount, Artcraft, and Realart out of these theaters, lessening Zukor's market.

By concentrating on the biggest stars, he had been able to force exhibitors to meet his increasing rentals. They had to have Mary Pickford at any cost, or their competition would book her films. He had at first hoped that this would continue to be true. Then J. D. Williams, who was running the new First National, scored by grabbing off the only star who could hope to match Mary at the box office: Charlie Chaplin.

In the meantime production went on. Jack Pickford was beginning to be a minor draw in pictures like *Freckles* with Louise Huff, although he never achieved top billing. Julian Eltinge, the female impersonator, made several pictures, including the 1917 film *The Clever Mrs. Carfax*. Eltinge was a rather nondescript-looking man, but when he put on a wig, a dress, and powder, he was more beautiful than many women stars. William Desmond Taylor moved from Pallas to Famous Players to direct Lewis Sargent in *Huck Finn* and Jack Pickford in *Tom Sawyer*. Fannie Ward, Ann

"COME OUT FROM BEHIND THAT BUSH. WE KNOW YOU."

DOUGLAS FAIRBANKS
IN
"IN AGAIN - OUT AGAIN"

This is Douglas Fairbanks, Sr., under the fake beard in *In Again—Out Again. Copyright 1917 by Artcraft Pictures.*

Pennington, Billie Burke, George M. Cohan, and Kathlyn Williams also made films for Artcraft and Paramount. Cecil B. DeMille made another spectacle, *The Woman God Forgot*, with Geraldine Farrar and Wallace Reid. Mae Murray made *A Mormon Maid* with Hobart Bosworth, by then out of the producing business.

The novelty of the year was Paramount's only

Joan the Woman, with Geraldine Farrar, was DeMille's first spectacle. It was a good picture, but its huge costs kept it from being very profitable. *Copyright 1917 by Famous Players-Lasky Corp.*

venture in the then-popular serial field with *Who Is Number One?* Cullen Landis and Kathleen Clifford were the stars. And—sowing seeds for future trouble and tragedy—Fatty Arbuckle moved from Mack Sennett to Paramount, where he began making feature comedies.

The United States entered World War I in April 1917. At first this had little effect upon the studios. Only a few stars left to join the Army. Most found some way to get themselves draft deferred. Business boomed through 1917. Then a heavy government war tax hit theater admissions. This was followed by the cruel Spanish influenza epidemic of 1918. Theaters were closed. Many excellent pictures piled up losses because they could not get sufficient bookings.

Zukor, in the meantime, had become the secret partner of Lewis J. Selznick in Select Pictures, which had Clara Kimball Young and Norma and Constance Tal-

Jack Pickford and Louise Huff were in the sentimental *Freckles*. Jack was signed by Paramount, hoping the Pickford name would draw audiences. He was never a great success. *Copyright 1917, Paramount Pictures Corp.*

madge under contract. Paramount and Zukor's partners had no part in this deal. If it seemed unethical for Zukor to finance a Paramount competitor, he excused himself with the claim he did it just to control Selznick. This venture did not last long. It soon broke up because Selznick–like his sons Myron (who became a famous agent) and David O., who made *Gone With the Wind*–was a Napoleonic character himself. He would take dictation from nobody.

Despite all the trouble and the business losses that required substantial cutbacks, there was a big break for Paramount in the collapse of Triangle. Bad management, poor pictures, and extravagance brought the company to the point of bankruptcy. The big three of Triangle–Thomas H. Ince, D. W. Griffith, and Mack Sennett–pulled out. Zukor offered them independent production deals like the one that brought Fairbanks into the Paramount fold the previous year.

This was going against Zukor's plan to have complete control of Paramount's pictures. Under his agreements with these producers, Paramount provided financing. After the financing costs were recouped, profits were split. It was similar to the arrangement Famous Players and Lasky had with Hodkinson. This cut Paramount's profits, but it kept these great producers from going with a rival.

Hobart Bosworth, Edythe Chapman, and Mae Murray were in *A Mormon Maid*. Frank Borzage, later a famous director, played the hero in this picture. *Copyright 1917 by Famous Players-Lasky Corp.*

When Julian Eltinge, female impersonator, put on paint and powder, he was more beautiful than many real leading ladies. Here he is shown in *The Clever Mr. Carfax. Copyright 1917 by Paramount Pictures Corp.*

It also brought in some of the greatest stars of the day. Ince brought Dorothy Dalton, William S. Hart, and Charles Ray. Griffith brought Lillian and Dorothy Gish, Bobbie Harron, and others. Mack Sennett brought himself and his zany crew of comedians, gagsters, and—no small asset—the Bathing Beauties.

Who Is Number One? was Paramount's only serial. It starred Kathleen Clifford and Cullen Landis. *Copyright 1917 by Paramount Pictures Corp.*

Griffith first made *Hearts of the World.* Although financed by Zukor personally, this was not a Paramount picture. Griffith's first film for Artcraft was *The Great Love* with Robert Harron, Lillian Gish, and Henry B. Walthall. It was about a young American who enlisted in the British army. While in London he saves a young girl from a fortune hunter.

This potboiler was followed by *The Greatest Thing in Life* in 1918 and by *A Romance of Happy Valley, The Girl Who Stayed at Home, True Heart Susie,* and *Scarlet Days* in 1919. In addition, he made a series of Dorothy Gish pictures at his Mamaroneck studio in New York. Richard Barthelmess played in several of these. One made in 1919, *Out of Luck* (also known as *Nobody Home*), had Rudolph Valentino in an early role.

Richard Barthelmess had earlier supported Marguerite Clark in several pictures and then played the lead in Griffith's final Artcraft picture, *Scarlet Days,* in 1919, a story of the California Robin Hood-like character Joaquim Murietta. It was not an overwhelming success, and Barthelmess did not have his first great hit until *Broken Blossoms.* Zukor advanced the money for *Broken Blossoms,* but, in the settlement of Griffith's break with Paramount, this milestone film was Griffith's first United Artists release.

Robert Harron was in D.W. Griffith's *The Great Love,* released by Paramount. *Copyright 1918 by Artcraft Pictures.*

MACK SENNETT COMEDIES

Mack Sennet's Bathing Beauties did not demand that a man be
handsome. Even cockeyed Ben Turpin had a chance with them.
Copyright 1919 by Mack Sennett.

After years of threatening to do so, Mary Pickford finally broke with Zukor in 1918, accepting an offer from First National. Both Pickford and Zukor have claimed the break was amiable. He was just unable to pay her increasing demands. Famous Players-Lasky stock dropped from 85 to 22½ on the day her departure was announced.

Out of Luck (also called *Nobody Home*) was produced by D.W. Griffith. Dorothy Gish and Ralph Graves were the stars. Rudolph Valentino, left, had a supporting role. *Copyright 1919 by Artcraft Pictures.*

According to Pickford, Zukor told her he was abandoning the star system and would henceforth concentrate on story appeal. He did not do so. Instead he secured Mary Miles Minter, a Pickford type but without her talent, and groomed her to take Pickford's place. Minter had been on the stage since childhood, playing *The Littlest Rebel* (later a Shirley Temple movie) on stage with Dustin and William Farnum. She made a series of pictures for American before Zukor signed her.

Despite Zukor's statement to Pickford that he was abandoning dependence on stars, the Paramount star system continued with only one exception: Cecil B. DeMille. DeMille had a long talk with Zukor and Lasky. At this point he had ceased to be director-general in all except title. He was operating under an independent production contract that gave him control over everything in his pictures except finances.

What DeMille said in effect, although he put it more modestly, was that he was the star of his pictures and he needed no other. It was wasteful to pay enormous salaries to people like Pickford, Fairbanks, and their kind. He intended to use only featured players and build them into stars. He sited Wallace Reid as a prime example of how this could be done. Once they were stars, he had no more use for them. They could then move on to other Paramount productions.

Lasky was skeptical, but DeMille's thinking was right along the line of Zukor's wistful hopings. He was sick of stars demanding more money, although he knew that no company could continue without them. He was willing to back DeMille financially. The director-general quickly proved his point with films like *Male and Female, For Better For Worse,* and *Don't Change Your Husband.* All featured a fugitive from Mack Sennett's gag factory named Gloria Swanson.

Scarlet Days was Griffith's last picture for Paramount's Artcraft. Richard Barthelmess, shown here with Eugenie Besserer and Carol Dempster, plays a romantic bandit. *Copyright 1919 by Artcraft Pictures.*

In a short time Swanson would become queen of the Paramount lot, the most popular woman star of them all. The daughter of an army officer, she began at Essanay as a teenager, married Wallace Beery, and then went to Keystone. DeMille saw something in her that others missed and made her a star. When she finally left DeMille, it was at his insistence, not hers. She had become too much of a star for the course he had planned for himself. In this period of his career, DeMille was literally a star maker.

Mary Miles Minter was signed by Paramount's Realart subsidiary as a replacement for Mary Pickford. *Copyright 1917 by American*.

Those who remember DeMille only by his garish and often tasteless later work will be surprised to know that he was considered to be in the top five of all producers before 1920. Some considered him second only to Griffith. He was inventive in those days and often struggled to get significance into his work. After the failure of *The Whispering Chorus* and the near failure of *Joan the Woman*, DeMille, in his own words, decided "to make pictures for the public and not the critics." Certainly his record shows that few in Hollywood ever understood the public's desires better.

DeMille, likable or not, was a star. Paramount recognized this. In a 1922 ad listing pictures of all the company's stars, everybody pictured was an actor or actress except one. It was DeMille right where he deserved to be—among the stars. For the rest of his time with Paramount he remained a star, outshining any member of his cast.

As the decade closed, Griffith and Fairbanks left to join Mary Pickford and Chaplin (both of whom quit First National) to form United Artists with Hiram Abrams. Geraldine Farrar had already gone to Goldwyn. Ince and Sennett, disliking Zukor's domination, were still in Paramount but already making plans to leave.

William S. Hart was the king of the cowboys. Jack Holt, a fine actor and a genuine gentleman, was heading for stardom. Ethel Clayton, who had been with Paramount since the Lasky days, was still a drawing card.

Bebe Daniels, a newcomer to Paramount, was being groomed for bigger things. After several years as Harold Lloyd's foil, she accepted a DeMille offer and played a small role in *Male and Female*. She was cute and had the qualities to be another Mabel Normand, DeMille thought.

Gloria Swanson was just starting her climb to stardom when she made *Don't Change Your Husband* for Cecil B. DeMille. *Copyright 1919 by Artcraft Pictures.*

The smash hit of 1919, however, came not from the regular Paramount stable but from one of its independents. This was from Mayflower Productions, which had been organized to exploit the talents of George Loane Tucker. Tucker had been around a long time. In fact, he was with the IMP company that took Mary Pickford to Cuba in 1911. After IMP became Universal, Tucker in 1913 directed the famous *Traffic in Souls*, based upon the Rockefeller Commission's exposure of prostitution in New York. Tucker then went to England, where he directed for several years before returning to join Mayflower.

The film he made was *The Miracle Man*, based upon a play by George M. Cohan, which in turn was based upon Frank L. Packard's novel. It was the story of a band of crooks who tried to take advantage of an old faith healer in order to pull their confidence game on the public. Their leader was Thomas Meighan. The girl was Betty Compson. Lon Chaney, Sr., played the fake cripple whose "cure" was supposed to set off the con game. But the old man's goodness reformed them all.

The story itself was not what made *The Miracle Man* the extraordinary hit that it was. It was a good story for the time, but its real appeal lay in perfect casting, from Meighan at the top on down to the child Frankie Lee (brother of Davey Lee who would someday be Al Jolson's "Sonny Boy"). The cast seemed to live the parts, and this was directly due to Tucker's direction. Lon Chaney—one of the greatest actors of all times—said in a later interview that Tucker crouched under the camera and guided them through the more touching parts of the play, whispering constant instructions while tears rolled down his cheeks. He was as much into the characters as the actors themselves.

Bound in Morocco was one of Douglas Fairbanks' last films for Paramount before he left to help form United Artists. Here Doug uses a lance to pole–vault to a convenient horse to escape Arabs who have stopped his car. *Copyright 1919 by Artcraft Pictures.*

Lon Chaney and Joseph Dowling were in the star-making hit *The Miracle Man,* an independent production released by Artcraft. *Copyright 1919 by Mayflower Productions.*

Wanda Hawley, Clara Horton, Violet Heming (the star), and, standing, Margaret Loomis and Mildred Reardon were in George Melford's production of *Everywoman,* a morality play. *Copyright 1919 by Paramount Pictures Corp.*

The picture was remade in 1931 with Chester Morris, Sylvia Sidney, and Boris Karloff. It was just a shadow of the original.

The year 1919 was a productive one. Some other hits were DeMille's *Male and Female* with Gloria Swanson and Thomas Meighan, *The Grim Game* with Houdini the great magician, *The Sporting Chance* with Jack Holt and Ethel Clayton, *The Invisible Bond* with dancer Irene Castle. An unusual entry was *Everywoman*. Violet Heming was Everywoman, and her companions were actresses portraying the virtues of an innocent young woman. In the course of the film, each of these leaves her one by one.

In the seven years since Zukor imported *Queen Elizabeth* he had become president of the largest and most profitable film factory on earth. This became threatened by First National and United Artists. So as the new decade of the 1920s opened, Zukor had to change his objectives.

The big threat was the way First National was cutting Paramount out of many first-run theaters. Zukor realized he could not build a film empire on stars alone, as he had tried to do. He had to have his own theaters or gradually wither on the competitive vine.

So Zukor began the new decade determined to fight First National on its own grounds: Paramount would acquire its own theater chain.

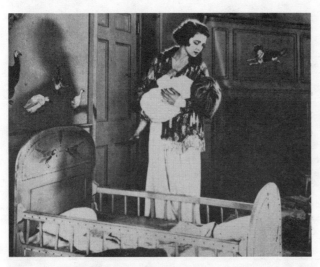

Irene Castle, the famous dancer, was in the Paramount's *The Invisible Bond. Copyright 1919 by Artcraft Pictures.*

Gloria Swanson is threatened by a lion in the flashback scene from DeMille's *Male and Female. Copyright 1919 by Paramount-Artcraft.*

Jack Holt is not really a chauffeur. It is all a disguise in *The Sporting Chance* with Ethel Clayton. *Copyright 1919 by Paramount-Artcraft.*

6

The Turbulent Twenties

The end of World War I in November 1918 left all the studios with a heavy inventory of war pictures that suddenly no one wanted to see. They were tired of war. They wanted fantasized escape, and no one was better suited to give it to them than Cecil B. DeMille. In 1922, at a time when the entire motion picture industry was reeling under the impact of a recession and the worst scandals in Hollywood history, Zukor told *Motion Picture Classic* magazine that the DeMille "society dramas" were the type of picture the public preferred.

It is true that DeMille's pictures were good grossers, but Zukor overlooked the fact that this period produced—for other companies—Mary Pickford's *Pollyanna,* Lubitsch's *Passion,* (which established Pola Negri), Griffith's *Way Down East,* and Von Stroheim's *The Devil's Pass Key.* All were 1920 releases and were sensational hits, and none resembled DeMille's "society dramas."

Paramount also did not do too badly in non–sex-oriented films this year. John S. Robertson made *Dr. Jekyll and Mr. Hyde.* John Barrymore, breaking out of his brash young man comedy role, gave a splendid performance in this picture. Frank Borzage

Frank Borzage's *Humoresque* with Gaston Glass and Alma Rubens was produced by Hearst's Cosmopolitan Productions for Paramount release. *Copyright 1920 by Cosmopolitan Productions.*

Jim Hawkins is played by Shirley Mason in Maurice Tourneur's *Treasure Island*. William Ogle, right, is Long John Silver. Lon Chaney, Sr., is Merry. Chaney also took the role of the blindman Pew. *Copyright 1920 by Paramount-Artcraft.*

proved himself a director of the finest caliber with *Humoresque*. This was Fannie Hurst's story of a boy whose mother's sacrifices made him a great violinist. Gaston Glass, Alma Rubens, and especially Vera Gordon as the mother drew raves for their performances. Maurice Tourneur made a beautiful film in *Treasure Island*, although it was spoiled by the inclusion of a modern romance at Lasky's insistence. Shirley Mason played Jim Hawkins, Charles Ogle was Long John Silver, and Lon Chaney was good in the double roles of Pew the blind man and pirate Merry.

Some other films were Wallace Reid and Bebe Daniels in *The Dancin' Fool* and *Sick-a-Bed*; Jack Holt, Lewis Stone, and Agnes Ayres in *Held by the Enemy*; Dorothy Gish and James Rennie in *Remodeling Her Husband* (directed by Lillian Gish); Douglas McLean and Doris May in the amusing *Mary's Ankle*; Fatty Arbuckle in *The Round Up*; the great escape artist Houdini in *Terror Island* (directed by James Cruze); Gloria Swanson, Bebe Daniels, and Thomas Meighan in DeMille's *Why Change Your Wife*; and Mary Miles Minter made *Judy of Rogue's Harbor*. Unfortunately for her, Minter fell in love with the distinguished but aging director of this film, William Desmond Taylor, whose personal tragedy is discussed later in this chapter.

There were some very good pictures in this list, but *Why Change Your Wife* topped them all at the box office. DeMille spent $130,000 on it and the gross was $1 million.

Pictures are no good without theaters to show them in. Hundreds of new movie companies had sprung up over the years and then died quickly for lack of a market. First National was expanding its chains and franchises and building a huge new studio to start making its own films. William Fox was buying all the theaters he could get to insure a market for his films. Marcus Loew, the vaudeville theater owner, bought into Metro.

Zukor first tried to bring a group of theater owners into a booking scheme by which he would supply them

with pictures, somewhat on the order of the First National circuit. When this failed, he turned to theater buying and building on a grand scale. He backed Pop and Sid Grauman in building the Million Dollar Theater in Los Angeles. Sid later pulled out of the deal and built the Egyptian and Grauman's Chinese theaters in Hollywood.

George Melford staged this desperate battle between Fatty Arbuckle and Wallace Beery for *The Round Up.* *Copyright 1920 by Famous Players-Lasky Corp.*

Harry Houdini made *Terror Island* in 1920. It was directed by James Cruze who later made *The Covered Wagon*. Copyright 1920 by *Paramount-Artcraft*.

Some of Zukor's other theater deals were not as clean as his deal with Grauman's, and he came in for some unpleasant publicity. He made a deal with Stephen E. Lynch, a North Carolina exhibitor, who had been one of the original backers of Hodkinson's Paramount Pictures. Lynch was a businessman of the old school who believed in destroying your competition. He came to Zukor with a plan to bring all the southern part of the United States into the Paramount theatrical fold.

Zukor agreed. He had plenty of money. Wall Street bankers had just floated an additional $10 million in Paramount stock to finance theater buying. He had already bought heavily into the Stanley Company with its string of theaters on the East Coast. Wrapping up the South exactly fitted his plans.

Among theater owners Lynch and his men became known as the "wrecking crew." Heavy pressure was put on circuit owners either to sell or franchise with Paramount for sole showing of Paramount features. Those who did not were hit with new theaters as competitors. They were cut off from all Paramount products and undercut in admission prices.

One of those Lynch ruined in this manner was E. H. Hulsey, who had a circuit affiliated with First National in Oklahoma and Texas. Hulsey had reinvested his money in expanding his chain and was on shakey financial ground. He could not withstand the Lynch blitz and was forced to sell to Paramount to avoid bankruptcy after Lynch frightened Hulsey's financial backers.

Hulsey had a representative on the First National board of directors. Part of the deal was that the sell-out to Paramount would not be immediately revealed. This permitted Hulsey's man to remain on the First National board as a Zukor spy.

While a lot of pictures—104 features—were ground out under Lasky, George Melford (Old Whispering George, who was said to have never made a good picture in his life) produced the Paramount hit of the year. Both Zukor and Lasky are on record as saying that it was the worst picture they had ever seen. Even silent picture enthusiasts would be hard put to remember another picture from 1921, but they remember this one. It starred Agnes Ayres, supported by Adolphe Menjou and a newcomer to Paramount named Rudolph Valentino. It was called *The Sheik*.

Valentino had been around for several years, playing minor roles before scoring a sensational hit in Metro's *The Four Horsemen of the Apocalypse*. For some odd reason, neither Metro's production head Richard Rowland nor the *Horsemen's* director Rex Ingram showed any further interest in Valentino. The actor went to see Lasky, who did not think he had a suitable story for the future "Latin Lover" until a secretary pointed out that *The Sheik* was an ideal story. Lasky had bought the story earlier but had shelved it for lack of a suitable lead.

Why Change Your Wife was a $1 million grosser in 1921. The cast includes Thomas Meighan, Gloria Swanson, and dancer Theodore Kosloff. *Copyright 1921 by Famous Players-Lasky Corp.*

Paramount officials considered *The Sheik* a disaster, but it proved to be an enormous hit. Here is Rudolph Valentino with Agnes Ayres. *Copyright 1921 by Famous Players-Lasky Corp.*

After the amazing success of *The Sheik,* Paramount gave the director, George Melford, tremendous billing on *The Great Impersonation,* his next film. Kathlyn Williams is shown with James Kirkwood. *Copyright 1921 by Famous Players-Lasky Corp.*

The novel, by woman writer E. M. Hull, had been a big hit. It is the story of a willful, dynamic woman, Diana, who arouses the interest of an Arab sheik while visiting in North Africa. He attacks her caravan and drags her off to his desert oasis. She escapes, but her horse breaks a leg. She is found in the desert by the villainous bandit Omir (Walter Long). The Sheik comes riding to the rescue and recaptures her. A French writer (Menjou) is a friend of the Sheik's and tries to get him to release the woman, but before anything can be done, the bandit chief grabs Diana again. One of his other wives advises Diana to kill herself rather than submit to Omir's cruelty. Omir chases Diana around the harem. Walter Long had a lot of practice at this sort of thing. He had done something similar in Griffith's *The Birth of a Nation*. But before poor Diana suffered a fate then regarded as worse than death, the Sheik comes charging to the rescue and kills Omir in a hand-to-hand fight.

Now this was a novel published in England by a British woman. In those days it was unthinkable for a British woman to marry a low foreigner. So the Sheik is almost killed in the fight. While he hovers near death, Menjou reveals to Diana that the Sheik is not an Arab at all. He is the son of a British father and a Spanish mother. An old sheik found him in the desert after his parents were killed and raised the boy as his own son. This made a happy ending possible.

While a postwar depression had set in that was hurting box office receipts, everyone thought this was only temporary. Paramount was in the best position of its career. The huge theater-buying program was paying off, both as a guaranteed market for Paramount films and as an investment. With the company producing, distributing, and exhibiting, there was no wholesaler anywhere to dilute profits. The bankers on the Paramount board of directors, who had come in to oversee the expenditure of their loans, thought Zukor a genius.

Then in true movie script fashion the sky fell in. Three calamities in a row left the company reeling. The entire motion picture industry was threatened. There was a nationwide demand by some church groups for a constitutional amendment banning motion pictures. While films had always had their critics, this time the situation was desperate.

The trouble exploded on September 21, 1921, when a young actress named Virginia Rappe died in a San Francisco hospital. Paramount comedian Roscoe "Fatty" Arbuckle was charged with her murder. The woman died of complications following a ruptured bladder. Police charged that the rupture occurred from the weight of Arbuckle's body during a rape of Rappe. This supposedly happened during a wild party the 320-pound actor threw in the hotel suite.

A death that occurs during commission of a felony— as rape is—is chargeable as first degree murder. However, at the preliminary hearing the charge was reduced to manslaughter.

Paramount had three Arbuckle films in release. Their appearances on the screen caused such a violent public reaction that all were withdrawn from circulation. *Freight Prepaid* was never released, and *Gasoline Gus* only got a few showings. A scheduled film, *One Glorious Day*, was canceled and made the next year (1922) with Will Rogers in the Arbuckle role.

Trouble for Arbuckle and Paramount was compounded because of an earlier scandal. Shortly before the death of Rappe, an official in Massachusetts was indicted for the alleged cover-up of a 1917 incident involving Arbuckle and Paramount. This involved a sale convention in Boston. Arbuckle had been present to plug his films. After the sales pitch for Paramount's seasonal schedule, the group adjourned to a local house of prostitution that catered only to the elite.

Someone talked. Zukor was informed that it would take $100,000 to hush the scandal. Somebody—it was never revealed who—paid the money. Then, for political reasons, the scandal was dredged up four years later. The official said to be instrumental in the cover-up was indicted.

The combination of these two scandals put Paramount in an embarrassing position. Actually, Arbuckle was under contract to Joseph M. Schenck, but Paramount financed and released the Arbuckle films. One-half million dollars was tied up in the negative costs. In addition, the lost profits would have been up to another million dollars.

The general public, like the cast shown here in *Freight Prepaid*, wanted to hang Fatty Arbuckle in 1922. This picture was never released. *Copyright 1922 by Paramount-Artcraft.*

The trial resulted in a hung jury. If the case had been restricted to Arbuckle alone, it might have passed over quickly. But sordid details of Hollywood life came out that smeared the entire industry. Arbuckle went back on trial, reviving all the old stories. Then in the middle of this second trial, William Desmond Taylor, the Paramount director, was murdered in his apartment.

Mary Miles Minter, Paramount's virginal-looking replacement for Mary Pickford, rushed to the dead man's apartment as soon as the news broke. She was weeping and screaming about her great love for Taylor. Mabel Normand, the comedienne, also hurried over to try to retrieve letters she had written Taylor.

Taylor had been a man of spotless reputation. Whenever intellectuals visited Hollywood, they were taken to see Taylor and William C. deMille (Cecil's brother) to impress them with the high caliber of the movie colony.

Will Rogers, shown here with Lila Lee, replaced Fatty Arbuckle in *One Glorious Day.* It was the story of a spirit named Ek who took over the body of a timid man (Rogers) and made him into a hero. *Copyright 1922 by Famous Players-Lasky.*

The facade crumbled with his death. He turned out to be a genuine B movie mystery man. Nothing in his past, as told in his official biography, could be proven. No record was found of him in the place in which he claimed to have been born. His stage experience with Sir Charles Hawtry's company in England was denied, as were other claims, including his attendance at Bristol College. It was shown that he deserted a wife and daughter in New York, adventured in the gold fields of Alaska and Colorado, and was an actor in Hawaii.

Through the aid of a well-placed woman, he got into the movies, working at Balboa as an actor and director and then with Vitagraph as an actor. He directed Dustin Farnum at Pallas. Jack Pickford liked him so well that he recommended Taylor to Mary Pickford. Taylor directed her in *How Could You, Jean?, Johanna Enlists,* and *Captain Kidd, Jr.,* before leaving Hollywood to join the British Army in 1918. Upon his return he made important films with Ethel Clayton, May McAvoy, and, released after his death, *The Green Temptation* with Betty Compson and Mahlon Hamilton.

Mystery piled on mystery. Scandal after scandal was uncovered. Tales of frightful dope parties and sex orgies came out. Hearst claimed to have sold more papers because of the Taylor case headlines than he did during the war. The case had mysterious aspects: a monogrammed lady's nightgown in a bachelor's apartment, torrid love letters that disappeared and then reappeared, gangsters, and beautiful women stars.

Evidence came out that Taylor had incurred the enmity of a drug ring because he tried to stop it from servicing Mabel Normand. There is good reason to believe that Taylor was killed by a paid hit man on orders of a drug ring chief. This came out in evidence that was hastily suppressed. Illicit drugs had such a hold on Hollywood at the time that all the studios feared what might come out if this line of investigation was pursued. Heavy pressure was put on the police and city authorities, and Taylor's mysterious missing valet was made the scapegoat. At one time this man, Edward Sands, offered through letters to the press to return and testify. Nothing came of it because nobody wanted Sands' testimony, which could have revealed who was. at a sex and drug party at which Taylor broke down in tears because he could not get Mabel Normand to leave. A number of studios' stars were involved in that affair.

While every studio in town was scared, Paramount took the worst lumps. It had Mary Miles Minter, Fatty Arbuckle, Taylor, and William S. Hart in trouble. Hart was forced off the screen for two years because of a woman's claim that he was the father of her illegitimate daughter. Hart was later cleared, but at first no one knew how the case would go. Lasky feared another substantial loss like the one suffered on Arbuckle.

Hart was beginning to drop in popularity due to the competition of the flashier Tom Mix and Buck Jones, both at Fox, but he was still a powerful draw for Paramount.

The public cry for movie censorship and a cleanup of Hollywood became so strong that in March 1922, one month after Taylor's death, the newly formed Motion Picture Producers Association announced that Will Hays, the postmaster general in President Harding's cabinet, had resigned to become its president. Hays' job, the producers fervently declared, was to provide a code that would eliminate all the objectional features that the public was opposed to. They spoke of Hays as a "czar" who would make Hollywood behave. Actually he was a public relations man hired to make sure that politicians in Washington did not do anything to hurt the film industry.

Some of the narcotics aspects of the Taylor case investigation created great concern. So in the summer of 1922 there was a secret meeting of film moguls to consider the danger of the situation. It appeared by this time that the Los Angeles police investigation of the Taylor drug angle had been successfully diverted. However, there was a strong possibility of other scandals involving some very profitable stars. A list was drawn up of those stars who might create new scandals. The conferees recommended that they be dropped as quickly as possible. Unfortunately, they were too big and there were too many of them. The financial jolt this would have caused was more than the studios dared to risk. It could have bankrupted three of them.

One of the names on the list was Paramount's highly popular Wallace Reid. Zukor was greatly disturbed, and called Lasky from New York. Lasky, who believed the best of everyone, asked Reid if he was hooked.

Reid solemnly assured Lasky that the rumor was untrue.

Arbuckle was tried a second time, and again the jury failed to agree. A third trial was set for the fall. In the meantime Gloria Swanson, Thomas Meighan, Bebe Daniels, and the new European import Pola Negri continued to bring in crowds despite a poor year generally. The tempestuous Pola had been a hit in Germany, but her first American triumph was in Ernst Lubitsch's *Passion*. The American rights to *Passion* were offered to Zukor, but he passed, letting his old rival First National introduce Pola to the West.

Zukor's lack of foresight was based primarily on his genuine belief that the public did not want period pieces. *Passion* dealt with the French revolutionary period. Also, there was still a lot of hatred of all things German left over from World War I. But once *Passion* made such a hit, he rushed to sign the new star.

William Desmond Taylor's last film was *The Green Temptation* with Mahlon Hamilton and Betty Compson. *Copyright 1922 by Famous Players-Lasky.*

Lewis Sargent played the disturbed boy in William Desmond
Taylor's *The Soul of Youth*. Taylor was a highly regarded director
until his mysterious murder. *Copyright 1922 by Realart Pictures.*

DeMille had a well-liked picture in *Manslaughter* with Leatrice Joy as a spoiled "brat." Her lover, Thomas Meighan, has to prosecute her for reckless driving which resulted in the death of a motorcycle policeman. Rudolph Valentino forged ahead with *Blood and Sand* with Nita Naldi as the femme fatale who stole the young matador from his gentle sweetheart, Lila Lee. *The Young Rajah* with Valentino and Wanda Hawley was generally conceded to be miserable, but Valentino was still coasting on the fame of *The Sheik,* and the film made money.

But as it appeared that Paramount would weather the Arbuckle and Taylor scandals, the Wally Reid mess began to boil again. Reid was going to pieces. It could no longer be kept under cover. He looked so haggard and beat in *Clarence,* the William C. deMille film made in late 1922, that an agitated Lasky forced him to tell the truth: Reid was hooked on cocaine.

This was a greater calamity than the Arbuckle incident. Reid was the all-American boy and one of the top male box office draws of his time. Where Paramount lost $.5 million in unreleased Arbuckle films, it stood to lose $2 million in Reid pictures, plus his expected earning in the future. Public reaction to another scandal, coming on the heels of the other two, could very well destroy Paramount completely.

Lasky, goaded by an outraged Zukor, had Wally put under a doctor's care. He was isolated in a padded room, where he underwent the agony of withdrawal. He later seemed to be getting better, but his apparent improvement was the result of a return to the narcotic. Despite the Paramount guards and precautions, Reid kept getting drugs. It was done very cleverly. The narcotics were sent to him by mail from New York in specially marked fan letters.

Rudolph Valentino and Wanda were wasted in *The Young Rajah*. *Copyright 1922 by Famous Players-Lasky.*

Cecil B. DeMille had another hit in *Manslaughter* with Thomas Meighan and Leatrice Joy. It is the story of a man who has to prosecute his sweetheart after she kills a motorcycle policeman while speeding. *Copyright 1922 by Famous Players-Lasky.*

Nita Naldi in the vamp and Lila Lee is the sweetheart of Rudolph Valentino in *Blood and Sand. Copyright 1922 by Paramount Pictures.*

Reid collapsed on the set in November 1922, and the scandal could not be contained any longer. Lasky took the brunt of Zukor's fury. Zukor had warned Lasky about Reid, and nothing had been done. Lasky was told very definitely that his neck was on the block.

The bankers who financed Paramount's great theater expansion were frightened for their money. Heavy pressure was put on Zukor to dump Lasky. The vice-president for production was saved by two things. One was a brilliant publicity campaign to turn Reid into a hero.

The actor's addiction was acknowledged. The claim was made that he innocently was hooked when given too much morphine after injuring his neck in an accident while filming *Forever*, the film adaptation of the famous play *Peter Ibbetson*, in which he starred in 1921 with Elsie Ferguson. This beautifully made film was the high point of Reid's acting career.

The continual flood of stories gave a blow-by-blow description of Reid's heroism in fighting his addiction.

Police officials were quoted to the effect: "Breaking the dope habit is a terrific fight. If a man wins, he should be praised."

And the stories went on to claim that Wally was winning his agonizing fight. The public was with him. Most people idolize a gallant hero, and that is what Paramount publicity made Wallace Reid. His pictures played to overflow crowds. Then on the afternoon of January 18, 1923, Wallace Reid died—and was hailed as a hero.

Elsie Ferguson and Wallace Reid are the ill-fated lovers in *Forever,* based upon the famous play by *Peter Ibbetson.* Paul McAllister is with them here. *Copyright 1921 by Paramount-Artcraft.*

The ravages of his dope addiction were apparent when Wallace Reid played *Clarence. Copyright 1922 by Famous Players-Lasky.*

The publicity blitz took some of the banker pressure off Lasky, but what really turned Paramount back into a corporate giant came in March 1923 when *The Covered Wagon* opened at the Criterion Theater in New York. The story was a mediocre *Saturday Evening Post* serial, but Lasky's enthusiasm turned it into a genuine epic and one of the big money makers of the 1920s.

The story revolved around the conflict between Alan Hale and J. Warren Kerrigan for the hand of pretty Lois Wilson during a wagon train trek to Oregon. Lasky alone saw the film in epic terms. He removed George Melford and Mary Miles Minter, who had been set as director and star. He picked James Cruze to make the film solely because he heard that Cruze had some Indian blood.

There were no big names in the cast. Kerrigan, the male lead, had been a star for Universal but had long since declined. Wilson, the feminine lead, was an ex-schoolteacher, who had played undistinguished

The Covered Wagon was an epic film directed by James Cruze. The success of this film helped Paramount recover from the Arbuckle-Taylor-Reid scandals. *Copyright 1923 by Paramount Pictures, Inc.*

parts for Universal before coming to Paramount. Hale, the villain, was a very good actor but never a major star. The character parts were all excellently cast with people like Ernest Torrence, Tully Marshall, Ethel Wales (a former Lasky secretary in the Vine Street barn days), and Charles Ogle.

The trite story line added nothing to the film. The true villains of *The Covered Wagon* were the natural hazards: flooding rivers, prairie fires, Indian fights, and the everyday troubles of life and death. The true heros and heroines were the massed people in their wagons.

The picture ran 59 weeks at the Criterion before going into national release. According to Lasky, the film—which cost slightly over $750,000—made back its negative cost in showing at the Criterion in New York and Grauman's Egyptian in Hollywood alone. It is one of the all-time greats of the silent screen.

In other activity in 1923, Pola Negri made *Bella Donna*, a remake of the wicked woman story which Pauline Frederick filmed for Zukor in 1914, and *The Spanish Dancer*. The latter was based upon the same story as Mary Pickford's *Rosita*, also released that year. *Rosita* was Ernest Lubitsch's first American film. Critics had a field day comparing the two. The general opinion seems to be that the Pickford film was more polished, but the Negri film was more entertaining.

William S. Hart made *Singer Jim McKee* and *Wild Bill Hickok* after his return to the screen. Bill, once the greatest of the cowboy stars, was getting old and (even worse) old-fashioned. Tom Mix and Buck Jones were the new heroes. Hart was told that he could no longer have production control of his films. He quit, going to United Artists to make one film, *Tumbleweeds,* before closing his career.

With the DeMille unit, Milton Sills did such a good job in *Adam's Rib* that he was picked up by First National and went on to top stardom in such pictures as *The Sea Hawk, Burning Daylight,* and *The Barker.*

DeMille, with his egomania, could not be expected to keep turning out society dramas in the face of the adulation being given to James Cruze after *The Covered Wagon.* He had to top this film. And he did it—after a bitter fight with everybody in Paramount. He won the battle but, as the expression goes, he lost the war. The ax was out for his neck, and in about one year he was told that Paramount no longer needed his egotistical, expensive presence in the company he helped found and did so much to make successful.

The screens' first singing cowboy—in a silent movie!—was
William S. Hart, shown here with William Russell, in *Singer Jim
McKee. Copyright 1923 by Paramount Pictures, Inc.*

7

Paramount Indeed

DeMille's bid for glory was *The Ten Commandments,* the most lavish picture made to that time. *Motion Picture News* reported:

Thirty-three thousand yards of cloth were required for the costumes which numbered more than 3,000, and $18,000 worth of special harness, of ancient design, had to be made.

Transportation over the heavy sand, where motors and horse wagons were out of the question, was accomplished by means of sand sleds. Three Cadillac cars provided fast film transportation to and from the studio in Los Angeles. A car would leave Camp DeMille at 7 o'clock at night with the film shot that day, and would start back to Guadelupe [site of the filming] with the developed film at 2 p.m. the next day, arriving in time to show Mr. DeMille and his assistants after dinner.

The big set representing the ancient walled city of Ramseses was 750 feet wide and 109 feet high. It was the largest ever constructed for a motion picture [yes, it was larger than Griffith's *Intolerance* set], and was approached by an avenue of 24 sphinxes. This avenue was designed and built under the direction of Paul Iribe, Mr. DeMille's art director. To make the huge set required 55,000 feet of lumber (enough to build 50 ordinary five-room bungalows), 300 tons of plaster, 25,000 pounds of nails and 75 miles of cable and wire for bracing.

Both Zukor and S. R. Kent, Paramount's vice-president for sales, had approved the budget of *The Ten Commandments.* But as the cost mounted, they became uneasy and then frightened as banker pressure increased. Lasky warned DeMille, but the director flew into a rage. He asked sarcastically, "Do they want me to quit now and release it as *The Five Commandments?*"

Pressure became so great that DeMille arranged financing through the Bank of America to buy the film for $1 million. Frank Garbutt of the Paramount management staff cautioned Zukor, "Don't sell what you haven't seen."

Production continued, with a final cost of almost $1.5 million. The gross was almost $4.2 million. This should have made DeMille the fair-haired boy again. But the financial backers of Paramount did not look at the profits in quite that way.

According to Benjamin B. Hampton, the gross on each film had to be reduced by about 25 percent to arrive at net profits. This would mean, by the system in use in 1923, that *The Ten Commandments* made about 100 percent profit. This compared with other DeMille films in this way:

Theodore Roberts was Moses in *The Ten Commandments,* De-Mille's answer to Griffith and Cruze. *Copyright 1923 by Paramount Pictures,Inc.*

Don't Change Your Husband—Cost: $74,000; earned: $300,000.

Why Change Your Wife—Cost: $130,000; earned: $1,000,000.

Manslaughter—Cost: $385,000; earned: $1,200,000.

Adam's Rib—Cost: $400,000; earned: $880,000.

In other words, every one of DeMille's recent pictures earned as much as or *more than the money invested* as did *The Ten Commandments.* He could have turned out three pictures of the ordinary variety in the time he made *The Ten Commandments,* and a failure would not have been as catastrophic as the failure of an epic would have been.

The difficulty was that DeMille's contract gave him complete artistic control of his films from casting to cutting. The only control Paramount had over him was financial. As Lasky pointed out when the New York office was screaming about the extravagance of *The Ten Commandments:* "The Director-General is a law unto himself."

In other 1923 activity, *The Cheat* was remade with Pola Negri in the Fannie Ward role and Charles de Roche in the Sessue Hayakawa role. Cosmopolitan, the Hearst film unit releasing through Paramount, made a profitable film in *Enemies of Women* with Alma Rubens and Lionel Barrymore.

While Hearst is usually sneered at by movie historians, the pictures his company made were not all that bad. The worst were those featuring his close friend Marion Davies, and this was only because of Hearst's personal intervention demanding that she be played up to the detriment of the story line. Even so, she sometimes broke through with a winner like *When Knighthood Was in Flower,* a story of the days of Queen Elizabeth I, released in 1922. Robert Vignola, an old friend of Sidney Olcott and George Melford, was the director.

Cosmopolitan pictures that did not feature Marion were often quite good. What a lot of film writers don't seem to acknowledge is that the famous *Broadway Melody,* the first MGM musical and a talkie milestone, was a Cosmopolitan picture produced by the Hearst unit. It was released by MGM, and Thalberg, despite what one sometimes reads had nothing to do with producing it.

Adam's Rib with Milton Sills. Pauline Garon, and Anna Q.
Nilsson was the kind of picture Paramount's bankers like to see.
It earned 100 percent profit. *Copyright 1923 mount Pictures, Inc.*

Even when good Marion Davies' pictures (as a number of them were) were money losers because of too much partying on the set and too little work, Paramount, and later MGM, were willing to absorb the loss for favorable publicity in the Hearst newspapers.

In another profitable move, suggested by Sidney Kent, head of sales, Paramount got back in the short subject business. No new films were made. The old Mack Sennett–Paramount two-reelers were dusted off and given new subtitles, which sometimes greatly altered the story line. Sennett, who had gone to Pathé and did not share in these rereleases, thought it most unkind of Zukor to go into competition with him using Sennett's own films.

In the meantime, Paramount had government trouble. While it was Will Hays' job to use his political skills to keep government agencies from digging into Hollywood deals, the cries of exhibitors who felt themselves wronged by Paramount became too loud to sweep under the political carpet.

The Federal Trade Commission held a series of hearings in major cities in the summer of 1923 to hear exhibitors' complaints. In Philadelphia the Commission learned how Zukor gained control of the large Stanley circuit and cut out all independent producers from selling films to the circuit. Zukor loaned the Stanley Company $1,250,000, taking stock for collateral.

The government investigator asked, "At the time the loan was arranged, wasn't it understood that you were to take 100 percent of the Famous Players output, as you have since done?"

The witness said this was not the understanding. His questioner then said, "Then you believe that Famous Players is in the loan business."

"No," the witness replied. "We just looked upon it as a friendly turn" (reported by *Motion Picture News,* July 7, 1923).

In the New York hearings a small theater owner told how he had been forced to book an entire season's Paramount program of two pictures a week for $85 a picture. At first he refused. Then the manager of the Paramount exchange in Buffalo, New York, "clocked" his house while he was showing a Goldwyn picture and told Goldwyn that the owner was getting enough trade to warrant paying more. Goldwyn immediately raised his fees. He then signed with Paramount. "I figured everybody was going to raise the price on me," the witness said. "Paramount Pictures are easier to put over than those of any other company."

In later testimony a witness was asked which distributor had the best consistent average of pictures for the past two years. (This would have been for 1921 and 1922.) The witness said, "Famous Players." Then he added that others were moving ahead in some respects. "The main thing today is pictures like *Robin Hood* [the Fairbanks film] and *Safety Last* [Harold Lloyd's thrill special]. Nobody can compare, for example, *Bella Donna* with them."

In other words, Pola Negri could not compete with Fairbanks and Lloyd. This was true everywhere. Paramount was still the best overall, but selected stars were cutting deeply into this superiority.

The remake of *The Cheat,* the hit of 1915, with Pola Negri and Charles de Roche in the Fannie Ward and Sessue Hayakawa roles, fell woefully short of the original. *Copyright 1923 by Famous Players-Lasky.*

The Mack Sennett release *The Little Widow* was one of the short subjects recut and retitled for rerelease in 1923. *Copyright 1919 by Famous Players-Lasky Corp.*

Salome vs Shenandoah was another Bennett two-reeler retitled by Ralph Spence for Paramount re-release. *Copyright 1919 by Famous Players-Lasky Corp.*

The government investigation fizzled out without accomplishing anything. Paramount moved ahead, developing new stars to take the place of Charles Ray, Dorothy Dalton, Ethel Clayton, Elsie Ferguson, Pauline Frederick, and others of the old-timers who moved on to other pastures.

The new stars were Lois Wilson, Richard Dix, Jack Holt, Thomas Meighan, and Bebe Daniels, who moved up from Realart to Paramount release. Gloria Swanson, with a string of hits like *Zaza, The Impossible Mrs. Bellew, Bluebeard's Eighth Wife,* and *Prodigal Daughters,* held her place as queen of the lot. Pola Negri got lots of publicity, but Hollywood dampened her style. Most of her American pictures were inferior to those she made in Germany.

Another who failed to sustain his initial promise was James Cruze. After *The Covered Wagon,* Cruze was Paramount's hope for the future. He was born Jans Cruz Bosen in Ogden, Utah, in 1884. After knocking about in carnivals and traveling shows, Cruze became a movie actor in 1912. His most famous role was as the newspaper reporter hero in the sensationally successful serial *The Million Dollar Mystery.*

Cruze turned to directing and joined Paramount in 1919. He made a number of Wallace Reid pictures, several with Fatty Arbuckle, and *Terror Island* with Houdini. All these were good workmanlike jobs. Outside of the classic *The Covered Wagon,* his best films were *Hollywood* (1923), *Merton of the Movies* (1924), and *Beggar on Horseback* with Edward Everett Horton (1925).

Hollywood was a grand satire. A movie-struck young woman comes to the movie capital. Her entire family and boyfriend follow her. They all end up in the movies, except the poor girl herself. But she marries the boyfriend, who is now a big star, and lives happily ever after.

Cruze used unknowns for the family but threw in every real star he could persuade to do a bit part, including a scene with William C. deMille going through the motions of directing a picture. The film gave the impression of seeing an inside view of the real Hollywood.

The stars making cameo appearances include Thomas Meighan, Lila Lee, Hope Hampton, Agnes Ayres, Will Rogers, Charlie Chaplin, Fritzi Ridgeway, William deMille, Cecil DeMille, Owen Moore, Lois Wilson, J. Warren Kerrigan, Walter Hiers, Jack Holt, May McAvoy, Ben Turpin, Douglas Fairbanks, Mary

Pickford, Leatrice Joy, T. Roy Barnes, Nita Naldi, Bull Montana, George Fawcett, Betty Compson, Lloyd Hamilton, Pola Negri, William S. Hart, Viola Dana, and a glimpse of the banned Fatty Arbuckle.

Cruze married Betty Compson and directed several of her Paramount pictures. While many of his films were entertaining, he never again reached the heights of *The Covered Wagon.*

In 1924 DeMille turned out three of the kind of pictures the company liked. *Triumph* had Leatrice Joy and Rod La Rocque. *Feet of Clay* featured Vera Reynolds, La Rocque, Julia Faye, and Ricardo Cortez *The Golden Bed* (not released until 1925) had Lillian Rich, Warner Baxter, and Rod La Rocque.

Stardom was beckoning to Lois Wilson *To the Last Man. Copyright 1923 by Paramount Pictures, Inc.*

Glenn Hunter is *Merton of the Movies* in James Cruze's version of the famous stage play. *Copyright 1924 by Paramount Pictures Corp.*

DeMille's *Feet of Clay* had Rod LaRoque, Vera Reynolds, Julia Faye, Richardo Cortez, and (in back) Robert Edeson in major roles. *Copyright 1924 by Paramount Pictures Corp.*

Adolphe Memjou and Ricardo Cortez in a very tame orgy from D.W. Griffith's *The Sorrows of Satan. Copyright 1925 by Paramount Pictures Corp.*

Plans were made for DeMille to make *Sorrows of Satan*, from the Marie Corelli novel, but at the end of 1924 DeMille's contract expired. Negotiations for a new one were hot and bitter. DeMille got the same ultimatum that drove William S. Hart out of Paramount: he had to give up artistic and production control. This meant he would have to make whatever story was handed him and with the cast stipulated by the production head. The studio also demanded that he give up the production staff he kept on the Paramount payroll between pictures.

The final decision was made in a meeting between Zukor, Lasky, Sidney R. Kent, and DeMille. DeMille wrote in his autobiography: "My long life has had few bitterer moments than when one of those gentlemen said to me, and the other two heard it in unprotesting silence: 'Cecil, you have never been one of us.'"

DeMille did not identify the speaker, but he is not hard to deduce. Zukor was always "Mr. Zukor" and always addressed Lasky and DeMille as "Mister." The use of the name Cecil in the quote rules him out. A letter Lasky wrote DeMille indicates a continued friendliness that does not tie in with the statement. That leaves Kent.

So DeMille went into independent production, which was doomed to failure because William Fox, First National, Paramount, and the newly emerging Metro-Goldwyn-Mayer were sewing up all the major first-run theaters.

Zukor sought D. W. Griffith to fill the prestige void left by DeMille. Griffith's first effort with Paramount money had to be released through United Artists because of prior contractual commitments. This was *Sally of the Sawdust*, which introduced W. C. Fields to feature films. Years before, Fields was in some minor shorts. Then for Paramount release Griffith made *That Royal Girl*, with Fields and Carol Dempster, and *Sorrows of Satan* (which had been slated for DeMille), with Adolphe Menjou and Ricardo Cortez. Neither set the screen on fire, and Griffith—now definitely a has-been—faded into oblivion with a few more undistinguished films for United Artists. Like so many others, he failed because he could not keep up with changing audience attitudes. The public no longer wanted the sweet Lillian Gish image that Griffith tried to force Carol Dempster to portray. Clara Bow mirrored the new trend in heroines.

Tragic Clara came to Paramount as part of the deal to bring back Ben P. Schulberg. Schulberg started with Zukor in 1914 in the scenario department and then switched to publicity and finally production. He left with Hiram Abrams and was the genius who originated the idea of United Artists. When Abrams deftly cut Schulberg out of the UA profit picture, Ben went into independent production. His Preferred Pictures made some good films, but, like all independents, he was hampered for lack of exhibition houses. Money on films was and still is made by rentals in first-run houses in key cities. Rentals for small 250- to 500-seat small-time theaters might be as low as $5 a day. While the additional income was welcome, this was only a drop in the total bucket.

The jewel in Schulberg's talent crown was Clara Bow. A star-struck Brooklyn kid, Clara won a talent contest sponsored by Eugene V. Brewster, publisher of *Motion Picture Magazine*. Out of the hundreds who won these magazine promotion contests by Brewster, only Clara, Mary Astor, and Allene Ray got anywhere.

The prize was supposed to be a real part in a picture. Brewster had to bribe W. Christie Cabanné to give Clara a bit part in *Beyond the Rainbow*. Tradition and Clara's various histories claim that her bit was cut out, breaking her heart, but that the bit was restored in later releases after she became famous. Like so many legends, this one is suspect, because an ad for the film that appeared in an Indianapolis newspaper in 1922 lists Clara in the cast. This was before she made *Down to the Sea in Ships* and proves that she did get on the screen in her first effort.

She came under personal contract to Schulberg. So when Ben joined Paramount in 1925, Lasky agreed to assume the contract. Clara made *Dancing Mothers* and *The Runaway* for William C. DeMille and then scored a hit in the picture that made her reputation, *Mantrap*, directed by Victor Fleming, who also had a short romance with Clara. Fleming got his start as an Artcraft cameraman with the Fairbanks' pictures and eventually won film fame as the director of *Gone With the Wind*.

After Schulberg came, the lineup at Paramount had Schulberg in charge of the West Coast studio, Walter Wanger heading the East Coast studio, and both reporting to Lasky. Sidney R. Kent as sales manager was moving closer to Zukor and was actually more powerful than Lasky in the company. Kent's days were numbered, however, because a man named Katz was coming up strong to cut Kent down.

Walter Wanger, one of the most famous names connected with film production, was a young college graduate in 1919 when Lasky was looking for someone to manage Charles Frohman, Inc., which Zukor had bought with Paramount money. Wanger was recommended as just the man, but after talking to him, Lasky was so impressed with Wanger that he hired him as his assistant instead. When Hugh Ford, who headed the East Coast studio, went to England to manage Paramount interests there, Wanger was put in his place. Wanger went on to great notoriety, including serving a jail sentence for shooting an agent he suspected of seeing too much of Joan Bennett (Wanger's wife at the time) and producing the colossal *Cleopatra*, which practically ruined 20th-Century-Fox.

There was intense rivalry between the two studios, and the West Coast production seemed to have the better of the deal. The star of the East was Herbert Brenon, whose *Peter Pan* (photographed by James Wong Howe) was the hit of 1924.

Peter Pan was a triumph for all concerned with it. Newcomer Betty Bronson was perfect as Peter, and Mary Brian was good as Wendy. Unfortunately, both had such sweet, little-girl faces that they could not buck the trend to the Clara Bow–Colleen Moore flapper ideal of the time. After a great beginning in *Peter Pan*, both excellent talents languished in sweet girl roles that added nothing to their careers. A typical example was Bronson's second film, *Are Parents People?* It was a cute picture. Adolphe Menjou and Florence Vidor were separating in the roles they played. So Miss Fixit, their daughter (Betty Bronson),

Mantrap in 1926 was the picture that made Clara Bow at Paramount. She plays the tramp wife of Ernest Torrence, right, who tries to vamp Percy Marmount, left. Victor Fleming directed. *Copyright 1925 by Paramount Pictures, Inc.*

Lasky agreed to take over Clara Bow's contract as a condition for B.P. Schulberg to join Paramount. This is Clara in *Rough House Rosie. Copyright 1927 by Paramount Pictures, Inc.*

rigs up a deal to make them think she is getting involved in a scandal. In their concern for her, they come back together. It got good reviews, but any ingenue could have played the role.

In the last half of the 1920s, new stars began to take over. After *A Sainted Devil* and *Monsieur Beaucaire* (both 1924), Rudolph Valentino left. Gloria Swanson decided she had the qualifications of a producer and left in 1927. Pola Negri faded. Thomas Meighan held on, but his fame was decreasing. Richard Dix, in a series of dramas such as *The Vanishing American* (1926), became a top star. Bebe Daniels left Realart behind and became Paramount's best comedienne in such films as *Senorita* (1927), in which she masqueraded as a dashing Spanish swordfighter because her father had been conned into believing he had a son instead of a daughter. In another delightful comedy she was a desert charmer who switched the situation in *The Sheik* and kidnapped an Englishman (Richard Arlen) for herself. It was called, appropriately enough, *She's a Sheik*.

While Paramount got a spate of new handsome male faces such as Charles "Buddy" Rogers, James Hall, and Reed Howes, an oddity was the rise of genuinely homely leading men in this period. Paramount put out a list of the ten biggest drawing films in 1926, and the leader was *Behind the Front*, a World War I spoof with Wallace Beery and Raymond Hatton.

It was made before the Laurel and Hardy era, but it had Stan and Ollie's lunacy. In one memorable scene the boys see an American soldier in No Man's Land. They crawl through a deadly night barrage to rescue the poor fellow. But when they get him back to the trenches, they discover it is their hated lieutenant.

"Let's take him back!" Wally said in a subtitle.

Hatton agreed, and they hoisted him over the trench and started back to the shell hole where they found him, oblivious to the artillery and machine gun fire. That is pure Laurel-Hardy logic.

A hastily shot sequel, *We're in the Navy Now*, was rushed out and grabbed the number two spot in box office receipts after *Behind the Front*. Edward Sutherland, a Mack Sennett alumni and later the husband of lovely Louise Brooks, directed both. The others among the top ten for 1926 were:

The Grand Duchess and the Waiter—Adolphe Menjou and Florence Vidor
Let's Get Married—Richard Dix
The Vanishing American—Richard Dix
Mantrap—Clara Bow, Percy Marmont, and Ernest Torrence
The Quarterback—Richard Dix
The Campus Flirt—Bebe Daniels
Padlocked—Lois Moran
The Blind Goddess—Jack Holt and Esther Ralston

Aloma of the South Seas with shimmy dancer Gilda Gray, *Kid Boots* with Eddie Cantor and Clara Bow, and *So's Your Old Man* with W. C. Fields were also hits. All but two Dix films were made by the West Coast studio. Shortly afterward the East Coast operations were shut down, and all production was sent to the West Coast.

Paramount's big hit in 1924 was *Peter Pan*. It was directed by Herbert Brenon, shown here with Ernest Torrence who played Captain Hook in the film. *Copyright 1924 by Paramount Pictures, Inc.*

Betty Bronson, fresh from her triump in *Peter Pan*, unites her parents, Adolphe Menjou and Florence Vidor, in *Are Parents People?* Copyright 1925 by Paramount Pictures, Inc.

Jack Holt was doing well in a series of Zane Grey westerns, but the big films of 1927 were *Beau Geste* with Ronald Colman and *Wings*, an aviation epic with Clara Bow, Buddy Rogers, and Richard Arlen. This was truely a vintage year. In addition to these classics, Clara Bow made Elinor Glyn's *It* and forever after was known as the "It Girl." After his enormous success in a bit part in *Wings*, Gary Cooper had the lead in *Nevada*, a Zane Grey western intended for Jack Holt. Victor Fleming's *The Rough Riders*, a saga of the Spanish-American War, was very good and very popular. While *Metropolis*, the Fritz Lang UFA import, became a science-fiction classic, it did not do well at the box office. The story was ridiculous, and the film was redeemed only by extraordinary visual effects of the world of tomorrow. Since it depicted the struggle between capital and labor, it was popular in leftist circles.

The *Metropolis* story line concerned an industrial dictator who had his chief scientist build a robot model of the woman who was leading the worker revolt. This was done in order to discredit her by the robot's actions. She is aided by the industrialist's son, and everyone makes friends in the last feet of the final reel.

The big new star to burst forth was another homely man, George Bancroft. Bancroft was rented into show business, or so he claimed. When a stock company needed a baby for an act in 1882, almost one-year-old George got started in show business. He played child parts until he was 14. Then, being large for his age, he joined the U.S. Navy for a five-year hitch. After that he was a blackface comedian and played Uncle Tom in 1901. He eventually landed on Broadway. In 1925, when times got bad for him, he got extra work at Fox. Then his big break came when James Cruze cast him as Jack Slade, the killer in *The Pony Express* (1925). He drew raves from the public and the critics. This was an extraordinary feat, considering that he was

Bebe Daniels, masquerading behind a moustache, bests William Powell in a duel. The picture is *Senorita. Copyright 1927 by Paramount Pictures Corp.*

Foppish roles like *Monsieur Beaucaire* almost ruined Rudolph Valentino's career. *Copyright 1924 by Paramount Pictures, Inc.*

Antonio Moreno discovers that Clara Bow has "it" in the film called *It*. William Austin, left, is the third player. After this hit, Clara was known as the "It Girl." *Copyright 1927 by Paramount Pictures Corp.*

George Bancroft, right, caught public attention as the killer Slade in James Cruze's *The Pony Express* in 1925. Here he is with Ernest Torrence, left, and Ricardo Cortez. *Copyright 1925 by Paramount Pictures Corp.*

competing against such scene stealers as Wallace Beery, Ernest Torrence, Betty Compson, Ricardo Cortez, and exceptionally cute little Donzelle Darr.

Ricardo Cortez was the star, the rider who carried the dispatches on Lincoln's election to California to save that state for the Union. Cortez had a good career with Paramount for several years. According to legend, someone told Lasky there was a "nice Jewish lad" named Jacob Krantz that he should help out. Lasky pointed out that there was no demand for nice Jewish lads that season, but agreed to see Krantz just to be polite.

As it happened, the demand was for Latin lovers, due to the Valentino craze. It appeared to Lasky that Krantz had a Latin look about him and only needed a Latin name. So he took Ricardo from a cigar box.

Then going through the alphabet, he clicked off Spanish sounding names until he got to the the C's and found Cortez.

Following the success of Bancroft in *The Pony Express,* Paramount did not know quite what to do with him. He made some lightweight pictures like *Tell it to Sweeney* with Chester Conklin and in 1927—two years after the Slade role—he was tagged by an odd person whom Paramount had picked up for no reason that anyone could fathom.

He called himself Josef von Sternberg. Some of those who disliked his airs claimed he was plain Joe Stern, an ex-pants presser who should have stayed in that trade. Legend seems to indicate that Sternberg considered himself a genius, and the evidence indicates he may have been right.

Von Sternberg's *Underworld* made George Bancroft a top star. The film also featured Evelyn Brent and Clive Brook. *Copyright 1927 by Paramount Pictures Corp.*

Gary Cooper was not ready to play the role he was given in *Children of Divorce,* but Clara Bow insisted on having him. *Copyright 1927 by Paramount Pictures Corp.*

132

He began in the processing department of a studio and then became an assistant to Emile Chautard, an early director. His first directorial achievement was *The Salvation Hunters* (1925), a beautifully artistic but practically motionless bit of realism that was panned so badly it was withdrawn. He floated around for a couple of years and then earned Lasky's gratitude by hastily shooting some new scenes for Frank Lloyd's *Children of Divorce* with Clara Bow, Gary Cooper, and Esther Ralston. Lasky then trusted him with a Ben Hecht script called *Underworld.* This hard-hitting picture was a sensation, ushering in the gangster cycle that led directly to Edward G. Robinson, James Cagney, George Raft, and their imitators.

Bancroft became a star in the role of "Bull" Weed, a gangster chief who is condemned to hang for killing a man who tried to cut in on his woman (Evelyn Brent). His henchman Rolls Royce (Clive Brook) is supposed to arrange a jail break, but the plan fails. Bull thinks this is so that Royce can have Feathers (Brent) for himself. He breaks jail to kill Brook. Brook is fatally wounded in aiding Bull. Realizing he was wrong, Bull surrenders to accept his own fate.

By 1928 Paramount was being reluctantly forced into the sound era. But before silent pictures died, there were to be two genuine triumphs: Von Sternberg's *The Last Command* and Von Stroheim's *The Wedding March.*

Pat Powers, one of the pioneer producers, remembered Von Stroheim's success *Foolish Wives* from the day when both worked for Universal. So when Von Stroheim outlined his idea for *The Wedding March,* Powers agreed to back it. As usual the director-actor was so lavish in his extravagance that Powers ran out of money and begged Lasky to bail him out. Lasky was aware of the troubles everyone had had trying to work with Von Stroheim during the years. However, he went ahead.

The story dealt with a wastrel young aristocrat in old Vienna who abandons his true love (Fay Wray) to marry the homely daughter of a corn plaster king. It was an acknowledged masterpiece. Even Lasky and

Powers, shocked at the expense, admitted that. However, it was shut down before it was completed. According to Lasky, "So again Von Stroheim was absent by request at the final 'butchering' of one of his more artistic triumphs." Lasky finally cut it directly in half, releasing the picture as two films: *The Wedding March* and *The Honeymoon.*

Von Stroheim the actor plays Von Stroheim the director's idea of a balcony love scene. Fay Wray is the girl in *The Wedding March. Copyright 1928 by Paramount Pictures Corp.*

133

The other director was more fortunate. His *The Last Command* was one of the glories of the silent screen. The original idea came from Ernst Lubitsch and was about a Russian general who was ruined by the revolution. He ended as an extra in Hollywood, playing a Russian general for a director who had been one of the people the general had persecuted in Russia. Emil Jannings, the great German actor, gave a superb performance as the general. William Powell never did better than in the part of the director. Evelyn Brent was also marvelous.

This film was Emil Jannings' last hurrah on the American side. He was one of the truly great screen actors but was seen in the United States only in imported films until he came here in 1926. Paramount had earlier used him in *Deception,* in which he gave a splendid portrayal of Henry VIII. He gave an even better performance as the acrobat who killed his faithless wife in *Variety.* In his brief American career before sound sent him home, he made *Sins of the Fathers, The Way of All Flesh, The Patriot* (directed by Ernest Lubitsch in his first Paramount appearance), and *The Betrayal* with Gary Cooper and Esther Ralston. Paramount also had a chance at *The Last Laugh* in which F. W. Murnau directed Jannings in an acting tour-de-force. Universal took the film when Paramount and MGM declined it. It was a critical success and a box office failure. As Zukor predicted, it was too grim for the American public.

While the production side was making some of the best pictures in Hollywood history, the power struggle went on back in corporate headquarters.

In 1926 Paramount bought into the Balaban and Katz theater chain in Chicago. Abie Balaban and Sam Katz had once been piano players in the early nickel theaters. They saved their own nickels and became theater magnates. The merger resulted in all Paramount and Balaban and Katz theaters uniting into a theater division under Sam Katz.

Katz believed that studios existed only to feed exhibitors what they wanted. He immediately ran afoul of sales manager Sidney Kent, who thought theaters existed only to take the block bookings the sales department forced on them. The theater unit was known as the Publix Theaters Division of Paramount.

To bolster Katz's ego and increase the importance of the theater division, Lasky suggested to Zukor that the corporate name be changed from Famous Players–Lasky to Paramount–Publix Corporation. So from that time on the names of the founding companies were no longer carried under the Paramount Pictures name.

This did not settle the trouble. Katz and Kent continued to fight. It was a bitter struggle in which Katz, Kent, and Lasky lost, leaving quiet but iron-hard Adolph Zukor in shaky possession of the corporate battlefield.

But first they all had to go through the agony of the conversion to sound pictures.

Evelyn Brent and William Powell supported Emil Jannings in
The Last Command, a superb von Sternberg film. *Copyright 1928
by Paramount Pictures Corp.*

8

The Awful Noise

Paramount was not ready for sound. It should have been. Daniel Frohman was one of the first to hear of Edison's pioneer mating of phonograph and projector. Griffith experimented with sound for *The White Rose* in 1921. In 1923 Eddie Cantor sang "Oh, Gee, Georgie!" for a short made by Lee DeForest. Also, Al Jolson made a talking short in which he sang "Rockaby Your Baby to a Dixie Melody" before he made *The Jazz Singer.* The signs were all there.

While Fox was rushing in after Warner Brothers' pioneering effort and First National was selling out to Warners, Paramount continued to stick with silent films. They were good movies, but they did not make money. *Old Ironsides,* which the company expected to be another *Covered Wagon,* flopped miserably and brought James Cruze's Paramount career to an end. *Tillie's Punctured Romance* with W. C. Fields and Louise Fazenda was a good comedy. The only relation between this film and the famous Marie Dressler–Charlie Chaplin Sennett film was the title. This one concerned a circus lost behind the German lines in World War I and the struggles of Fields, Chester Conklin, and Fazenda to get home.

When it became apparent that sound was a seri-

ous threat, attempts were made to add sound effects to silents not yet in release. *Wings* was the first one so scored. Roy J. Pomeroy, the technical genius who parted the Red Sea for DeMille, added the roar of engines and the crack of machine guns.

Sound backgrounds also were added to William Wellman's *Beggars of Life* (1928), which had splendid performances by Wallace Beery, Louise Brooks, and Richard Arlen. This was known as "goat glanding" in the trade.

After Warners released *The Lights of New York,* the first all-talking picture, Zukor realized at last that silent films were doomed. Pomeroy was sent to RCA and Western Electric to learn about recording sound. When Roy returned, Lasky scheduled *Interference* with Clive Brook, Evelyn Brent, and William Powell as Paramount's first all-talkie.

Immediately Lasky ran into interference from Pomeroy. The technician felt that his work for Paramount had never been sufficiently rewarded. He demanded the directional assignment for *Interference.* Since he was the sound authority, Lasky grudgingly gave in.

Some historians list the picture as jointly directed by Pomeroy and Lothar Mendes. It appears that Mendes

Wallace Beery gave a rollicking performance in James Cruze's *Old Ironsides*. The film was supposed to be an epic, but something went wrong and it failed. *Copyright 1928 by Paramount Pictures Corp.*

W.C. Fields, Louise Fazenda, and Chester Conklin masquerade as
German soldiers in *Tillie's Punctured Romance. Copyright 1928 by
Paramount Pictures Corp.*

directed the foreign version. William C. deMille served as Pomeroy's assistant, according to both deMille and Lasky. The elder deMille wanted to learn about sound, and Lasky wanted someone with a director's training to back up the inexperienced Pomeroy.

Wallace Beery and Louise Brooks were in *Beggars of Life*, based upon Jim Tully's story of hobo life. William Wellman directed. *Copyright 1928 by Paramount Pictures Corp.*

In the story William Powell was reported to have been killed in the war. His wife (Doris Kenyon) marries a famous doctor (Clive Brook). Powell is content to be an Enoch Arden, but Powell's ex-girlfriend (Evelyn Brent) uses the information that Powell is alive to blackmail the doctor's wife. Powell, to save his ex-wife, kills Brent. He turns himself in to the police but does not identify himself. He knows he will never come to trial, because the doctor, not knowing his identity, told him that he has only a short time to live, due to heart trouble.

Lasky did not like Pomeroy. He wrote: "Pomeroy sat in his little domain with earphones on, lord of all he surveyed. Terrified silent picture stars were ushered into the Presence for voice tests."

"The little domain" that Lasky contemptuously referred to was a small, one-set stage that had been rigged up for sound tests. It had to be small because it was padded to keep outside noises from reaching the microphone.

Lasky said that since Pomeroy had parted the Red Sea, written the Ten Commandments in letters of fire, and raised a wall of fire to protect the Hebrews, perhaps the technical wizard could be excused for placing himself on the same level as the original author of these deeds.

In *Interference*, Paramount's first all-taking film, the actors had to turn to face the microphone to deliver their lines. Here Clive Brook, as the doctor, tells William Powell he has only a short time to live. *Copyright 1928 by Paramount Pictures Corp.*

140

It would appear that Lasky was being spiteful. DeMille said, "Roy was most gracious in accepting me as an assistant and devoted considerable time to my instruction."

As to the film itself, Mordaunt Hall wrote in *The New York Times*: "The film is so remarkable that it may change the opinions of countless sceptics concerning talking photoplays. The vocal reproductions are extraordinarily fine, and the incidental sounds have been registered with consummate intelligence." This was a very fine tribute to Pomeroy.

In an interview with the *Times* after the picture was released, Clive Brook also spoke of Pomeroy's helpfulness. Brook was in the British army in World War I and was invalided out of the service in 1918. Because of a shortage of leading men, he became an actor. After the war he made several British films and was brought to the United States by Thomas H. Ince.

He had a good voice and stage training. He had nothing to fear from the microphone, but he had not wanted to make *Interference*. He felt that he had been losing ground since his last good part in *Underworld*. He wanted a stronger part.

Brook also gave an account of how the early voice tests went. He was horrified at the way his voice sounded, but Pomeroy told him that few people recognized their own voices when they heard them recorded for the first time. He asked Brook to try again but to avoid stage declamation. "Speak as you would in a small room," he told the actor. "Don't think of the gallery. I am the gallery now."

Brook tried again. The results were better. "I had learned my first lesson in sound recording," the actor said.

On the other hand, William Powell relished his part. For years he had been a stock Paramount villain in such roles as a thief in *Beau Geste*, a gambler-gunman in *Nevada*, and a gangster in *The Drag Net*. While *Interference* cast him as a murderer, he was a "nice" killer for once.

Latter-day critics condemn the picture as "too talky" and stilted. They are judging by contemporary standards. For its day, it was an impressive technical achievement.

The greatest enemy of directors and actors was the lack of mobility. The actors had to turn and face the camera as they spoke their lines. They could not move beyond the microphone range. Cameramen also were cramped. The need to keep the camera crew in a box restricted the fluid camera movement that is the mark of a good picture.

Actors commented on how unnerving the total silence was. Worse, the need for silence kept the directors from giving instructions during filming. Many actresses and actors performed well only when a director could coach them during the actual filming. This need, as much as poor voices, ruined some big stars.

As far as a poor voice was concerned, this was no excuse for throwing out a popular star. Voice dubbing was already being used. This was revealed

William Powell was a stock villain at Paramount for many years. Here he is with Gary Cooper and Thelma Todd in *Nevada*. *Copyright 1927 by Paramount-Famous-Lasky.*

E.H. Calvert, William Powell, and Eugene Pallette are the detective trio in *The Canary Murder Case. Copyright 1929 by Paramount-Famous-Lasky.*

in an enlightening story by Mark Larkin in the July 1929 issue of *Photoplay* magazine. Larkin said that a man named Lawford Davidson dubbed the voice of Paul Lukas.

In another case, Margaret Livingston—who later married Paul Whiteman—dubbed the voice of Louise Brooks in the initial S. S. Van Dine murder mystery *The Canary Murder Case.*

According to the *Photoplay* article: "They called Miss Livingston to the studio one day and said, 'Miss Livingston, we are up against it, and we think you can help us out. We want to turn *The Canary Murder Case* into a talkie, and Miss Brooks is not available. We think you can double for her. Will you do it?' "

The film was based upon a very popular book written by Willard Huntington Wright under the pseudonym of S. S. Van Dine. Wright was an art critic who had done numerous highbrow type articles on the screen as an art form. His character Philo Vance was a supercilious dilettante, but for some odd reason he struck public fancy. He popularized the theme of the amateur detective who outwits the stupid police. The rage for his type continued until Dashiell Hammett came along and, with Raymond Chandler, ushered in the private eye era.

The story, like all of Van Dine's earlier books, was based upon fictional solutions to famous crimes. *The Canary Murder Case* was a fictionized version of the unsolved murder of the Broadway star Dot King.

Louise Brooks was dressed in a feathered costume as the Canary and swung out over the stage audience on a trapeze-type swing. Her feathered cap looked startlingly like the hat worn by Evelyn Brent in *The Drag Net.* William Powell had the role of Philo Vance. Eugene Pallette was Sergeant Heath, and E. H. Calvert was District Attorney Markham who brought Vance into the case.

All four were well cast, and for once the book was faithfully followed. Powell's role was played with more strength than the original character written by Van Dine.

The story dealt with the Canary's heartless treatment of several men, anyone of whom had reason to kill her. She is finally killed in a locked room. Men outside her door heard the voice of the murderer, but when they broke the door down, there was no one inside except the murdered girl. The windows overlooked a

sheer drop to the street, and the killer could not have gotten out that way.

The book is still available on library mystery shelves, so it will not be revealed here how the murderer in his ingenious way could commit his crime in an apparently locked room and then escape himself. Vance had a theory that men revealed their true character in the way they play poker. So he got the suspects into a poker game. One man, seemingly the quiet, methodical type, was revealed as the most daring of the group. Thus pinpointed, Vance, in the person of William Powell, worked out the solution.

B. P. Schulberg, the head of West Coast production for Paramount, wanted to remake the film as a talkie, scrapping the old version. Zukor disapproved wasting so much money, and the film was reshot in portions. Livingston doubled for Louise Brooks in some reshot scenes where the actress' face did not need to show, and she dubbed her voice in others. Many of the shots did not have to be remade at all, because

William C. deMille and H.B. Warner discuss the script of *The Doctor's Secret,* Paramount's second all-talking picture. *Copyright 1929 by Paramount-Famous-Lasky.*

they had no dialogue in them. Since this was basically a silent film, it did not have as much dialogue as a script intended for a talkie. Some early sound film screenwriters seemed to think that every moment had to be filled with words.

According to *Photoplay:* "Miss Livingston took up a position before the 'mike' and watched the picture being run on the screen. If Miss Brooks came in a door and said, 'Hello, everybody, how are you this evening?' Miss Livingston watched her lips and spoke Miss Brooks' words into the microphone. Thus a sound track was made and inserted in the film. This operation is called 'dubbing'" ("The Truth About Voice Dubbing," July 1929).

Although it was shot in 1928, *The Canary Murder Case* was not released until 1929. Some Louise Brooks fans hotly denied that her voice had been dubbed in this film when the *Photoplay* article was published.

Brooks did not return to Hollywood after this film. She went to Germany, where she showed how talented she was in *Pandora's Box.*

Paramount's second talkie was *The Doctor's Secret* with H. B. Warner and was directed by William C. deMille. According to Lasky, deMille learned enough about sound to handle a picture himself. Whereupon Lasky joyously sent Roy Pomeroy back to his special effects department, but he quit and went to *RKO*.

There was no complaint with the way *Interference* was directed. Pomeroy might well have developed into a very good director. Unfortunately, his high-handed methods had irritated B. P. Schulberg and Jesse L. Lasky. Lasky's anger still showed 28 years later when he wrote his autobiography, *I Blow My Own Horn:* "Not even Sam Jaffe, the studio manager, or I could invade the chief's sanctum sanctorum without asking permission," Lasky wrote. "Pomeroy overplayed his hand by demanding $3500 a week after his first talkative movie. By then William C. deMille . . . had surreptitiously picked up enough knowledge to direct the next picture himself. [DeMille said himself that Pomeroy was very gracious in teaching him.] And we had organized a 'radio squad' of telephone-trained sound engineers who were happy to carry on at salaries not exorbitant for technical experts in their field. By the time *Interference* opened at the Criterion [in New York] on November 16, 1928, Pomeroy was dethroned, a fallen despot."

When the authors asked for background on Pomeroy at the Academy of Motion Pictures Arts and Sciences library, we were told there was no file on him. The man who made Paramount's first all-talking picture and who "parted" the Red Sea for the first time since Moses deserves a better fate than being forgotten.

The second all-talkie, *The Doctor's Secret,* was based upon Sir James M. Barrie's play *Half an Hour.* DeMille said that the title was changed because *The Doctor's Secret* promised something possibly scandalous while *Half an Hour* sounded dull. The film had Ruth Chatterton (whose stage career had fallen on evil days), H. B. Warner, and Robert Edeson. Edeson was a veteran of the old Lasky barn, while Warner got his movie start with Zukor in the Famous Player days.

The success of *Interference* decided Zukor. He gave orders to drop all production of silent films except those close to completion. Unfortunately, the late start meant a wait of six months before the studio could turn out a full talkie schedule. In the meantime, the studio had to continue releasing the silents it had on hand in order to fill contractual obligations.

The reason for the delay was lack of equipment. Zukor had decided to go with the sound-on-film method instead of the Vitaphone sound-on-disc system. Lack of channels—that is, complicated wiring for the recording systems—was a bottleneck. The demand was so high that manufacturers could not meet schedules.

Sam Jaffe, then West Coast studio manager, got the idea of shooting around the clock. The limited sound stages could be utilized twice as much, and some of the open stages could be used because noise was less in the small hours of the morning.

This had little effect on the employment of screen directors. At first there was a rush to import stage directors. But with the exception of a few like George Cukor and Reuben Mamoulian, they faded quickly or were downgraded to dialogue coaches. They did not understand the difference between stage and screen techniques. Lasky told Zukor that it was easier to teach the old gang to handle dialogue than to teach the newcomers screen technique.

William C. deMille wrote: "It is something of a tribute to the 'old guard' that, in 1938, out of 244 recognized, active picture directors, only 21 were brought from the theater to the screen after the advent of sound, while 136 were recognized picture directors before 1928."

The other 87 in deMille's total were mainly men who climbed from the ranks of assistant directors.

Mitchell Leisen, who had been art director for Cecil B. DeMille, and Henry Hathaway were two notable examples. Others were foreign imports.

The remaining silent films rushed out to clear the decks fared badly in towns where sound had already arrived but did well in the provinces. But it was the large cities that produced the big grosses, so many

Clara Bow was still Paramount's top woman star when she made *Ladies of the Mob* in 1928. *Copyright 1928 by Paramount-Famous-Lasky.*

This picture looks like an exotic Eastern drama, but *His Tiger Lady* with Adolphe Menjou and Evelyn Brent is a backstage story. *Copyright 1928 by Paramount-Famous-Lasky.*

of these pictures lost money. They would have been hits but for the coming of sound.

Among the better silent movies was Clara Bow's *The Fleet's In,* with James Hall. She also was in *Ladies of the Mob,* written from a prison cell by a convict and said to be very realistic.

In *The Fleet's In,* Clara was Peaches Deane, a dance-hall girl. When James Hall found she was a pushover, he fell in love with her, and they were married. Then there was a fight, and he was jailed. But you can bet that true-blue Clara and her buddy Searchlight Doyle (Jack Oakie) got the judge to release Hall in time to sail with his ship. He sailed with the promise that she would be his girl in every port forever after.

Adolphe Menjou and Evelyn Brent made a backstage story called *His Tiger Lady.* It was supposed to be very good, but like all the "clearance silents," it was lost in the noise.

Another good picture was *Doomsday,* based on the popular novel by Warwick Deeping, author of *Sorrell and Son.* It was directed by Rowland V. Lee and had Gary Cooper and Florence Vidor.

Florence, as Mary Viner, had to choose between Arnold, a farmer, and Percival, a rich landowner. Having known poverty all her life, she chose wealth in the form of actor Lawrence Grant. The poor farmer was left to his dirt and cows. Those who remember Gary Cooper as the aging lawman of *High Noon* do not know what an uncommonly handsome young man he was. The audience knew, and thereby much of the suspense was lost. The women anticipated that Florence would return in the end to farmer Gary. She did. And they were happy with the movie, which was what movies were for in those fantasy days before social significance became a factor.

So 1928 faded into history, and Paramount closed in on what it hoped would be a happier 1929. The future looked good—as rosy as the ending of one of the company's romantic pictures. Unfortunately, the worst years in Paramount's history lay before it.

Florence Vidor and Gary Cooper made a lovely couple in *Doomsday. Copyright 1928 by Paramount-Famous-Lasky.*

9

Days of Despair

Americans celebrated New Year's Day 1929 with the feeling that this was surely the greatest of all times. Never before in its history had the country been so prosperous. The stock market had proven to be a gold mine for anyone who could get enough to pay 10 percent down on some stock. One never expected to pay any more, because the stock kept rising. On paper many people were wealthy.

Hollywood, after its first cold fear of the new talking pictures, was breathing somewhat easier for the most part. There were still some stars who had not yet made the transition to sound, but it now looked as if more would survive than originally thought. Some even hit higher popularity than they ever had in the old silent films.

At Paramount, silent pictures were just about through. Films for 1929 were all-talking ones except for the silent *Betrayal*, the part-talking *The Carnation Kid*, and *Redskin*, which had sound effects only.

Betrayal was Emil Jannings' last Hollywood film. At the end of 1928 he had been given the first Oscar for his acting in *The Last Command*. Unfortunately, Jannings could not speak English and had no desire to learn. Even before *Betrayal* was released, Jannings had

Gary Cooper was the seducer who returned to find Esther Ralston married in *Betrayal. Copyright 1929 by Paramount-Famous-Lasky.*

149

Love blooms over ice cream sodas in The Shopworn Angel *with Gary Cooper and Nancy Carroll. This was a very popular picture. Copyright 1929 by Paramount-Famous-Lasky.*

settled with Paramount and departed for Germany. Both Lasky and Zukor acknowledged his great gift as an actor, but they knew he was hopeless in American talking pictures. Esther Ralston and Gary Cooper were in the picture also, but being a silent in a talkie landslide, the film got little attention.

The story was depressing as well. Emil Jannings was an aging burgomaster in a small alpine town. Esther Ralston was his young wife who permitted herself to be seduced by Gary Cooper. While Jannings played many types of parts in his long, illustrious career, the theme of the wronged husband ran through a surprising number of them. Some, like *Variety* and *The Blue Angel*, became classics. *Betrayal* is not one of them.

Gary Cooper was much better served by *The Shopworn Angel*, directed by Richard Wallace and released with the final reel in dialogue as "Part Talking!" The exclamation mark was intended to arouse public interest in the ads. It was a very good picture and gave star Nancy Carroll one of her best roles. Paul Lukas' voice had to be dubbed because of his thick accent, but Cooper, in his first speaking role, showed that Paramount could breathe easier about his future. He was far better in the role of the shy soldier in love with a tough snow–world tramp than his friend James Stewart was in the 1938 remake with Margaret Sullivan in the Carroll role.

The shopworn angel of the title was played by Nancy Carroll and is a chorus girl who is being kept by the financial backer of the show in which she dances. As the favorite of the backer, Paul Lukas, she is hard to handle. She upsets rehearsals by being late, and the harassed stage manager can do nothing but tear his hair.

Then the chorine meets a lonesome, shy, Army private from Texas. The soldier, Gary Cooper, is on leave before being shipped to France to fight in World War I. He buys her an ice cream soda instead of the usual cocktails she is used to and takes her walking in the park instead of to a bachelor apartment. They fall in love, and he asks her to marry him before he leaves for the battlefield.

She tells Lukas, who wishes her a cynical good-bye. The couple are married just before Cooper sails. Carroll, without her rich protector, is now just another chorine,

and the sarcastic dance director takes out on her his long pent-up spite.

In the final scene of the film the chorus line is rehearsing to the theme song "A Precious Little Thing Called Love." Suddenly, in the middle of the song, Carroll has a vision of Cooper in France. The audience sees it as a double exposure superimposed over her. The troops are crossing no-man's-land. We see the bullets flying, and Cooper stumbles and falls.

Nancy breaks her step and cries out in anguish as the vision fades. The angry dance director yells at her. She picks up the step again. Tears stream down her face as she begins to sing about how, when her heart misses a beat at footsteps in the street, it is "a precious little thing called love." The film fades on that.

It is possible that a different ending was substituted later. This sometimes happened when audiences disapproved of an ending. A film like this would be dis-

It was during the filming of *The Wolf Song* that Gary Cooper met Lupe Velez. *Copyright 1929 by Paramount-Famous-Lasky.*

151

missed as sentimental today, but when it came out the audience sat trully "spellbound." This film had ony one reel of talking.

Cooper's *The Wolf Song* with Lupe Velez was a goat–gland silent with a sound track grafted on to bring it up to date. The background sound included a few words and some songs. It was a story about fur trappers and made little impact. That is, it made little impact on audiences, but it made a decided impact upon Cooper's personal life. Gary's hectic affair with Clara Bow, which began during the filming of *Wings,* had run its natural course. Clara thought he was "pretty," but he wasn't lively enough for her. So Cooper turned his affections to his co-star Lupe Velez, who in many ways was like Clara: she could never be still, cussed a blue streak, and didn't give a damn for anybody's opinion.

Both women were far removed from what one would expect a man of Gary Cooper's public image to take up with. But he was quite serious about both for a while. When Harry T. Brundage interviewed Cooper during the making of *The Wolf Song,* he asked the actor what the most exciting thing was that had happened to him in Hollywood. True to his screen image, Cooper replied in a monosyllable: "Lupe!"

And Velez was an exciting person. Unfortunately, she was also a tragic one. Guadalupe Velez de Villalobos was born in Mexico about 1908. All her life she had wanted to be an actress. She told John Barrymore how she dressed in her brother's pants and strutted and aped him and members of her family. Her mother said that this was impolite. Lupe replied, "Who wants to be polite when she can be an actress?" At 13 she was dancing in a Mexico City show. At 16 she was in Hollywood, and at 19 she made her first hit with Douglas Fairbanks in *The Gaucho,* released in 1927.

She had a continual string of romances, but the one with Cooper was the most serious. It lasted three years—a long time for a woman like Lupe. Harrison Carroll, the Hearst columnist, wrote after her death, "I am certain she was never able to give her other romances the same adoration she bestowed on Gary Cooper in the days when both were young and trying to carve out their places in Hollywood."

After the romance ended, Lupe married and divorced Johnny Weissmuller, the screen Tarzan. She later killed herself rather than give birth to an illegitimate baby alleged to have been that of Harald Raymond, a continental actor who was ostracized by Hollywood after Lupe's tragic death in 1944.

The best thing that happened to Cooper in 1929 was *The Virginian.* Apparently this is a story that could not fail. The Cooper version was its third filming, and it was a success every time, unlike most remakes that never approach the greatness of the original. DeMille made it with Dustin Farnum and Winifred Kingston. Preferred Pictures remade the film in 1923 with Kenneth Harlan and Florence Vidor. William S. Hart played the role for two seasons on the stage.

The book, by Owen Wister, was a realistic account of cowboy life and justly a huge success. The play and movies reduced the book to two major events: the romance of the Virginian and the hanging of his friend Steve. Mary Brian was the sweet schoolteacher in the 1929 version, and Richard Arlen was Steve. Walter Huston, father of director and occasional actor John Huston, was the villain Trampas.

The Virginian is a ranch foreman. Steve, his best friend, is the top hand. The two are inseparable and often up to highjinks together. In one scene, at a dance, the men slip into a room where the married women have put their babies to sleep while they square dance and mix up the babies. (This incident in the film is based upon an actual event. Paramount's publicity for the film included a picture of the house where this had occurred.) The mothers are in hysterics while they try to figure out which baby is theirs.

The Virginian has a run-in with Trampas, suspected of being a cattle rustler. Cooper explains to Huston that he has his eye on him.

Trampas says, "You son of a --" He gets no farther because the Virginian has his gun out and rams it into Trampas' middle. "When you call me that—smile!" he says.

The Virginian with Gary Cooper and Richard Arlen was a hit.
Although Arlen and Cooper are drinking buddies here, soon
Cooper would help hang Arlen for cattle rustling. *Copyright 1929
by Paramount-Famous-Lasky.*

Those became very famous words due to the various *Virginian* versions of stage and screen. So some of the posters for the 1929 films had only these words on them and the name of the theater. Nothing else was needed. Everybody knew *The Virginian* was back.

Steve turns out to be weak. He begins stealing calves and then throws in with Trampas in cattle rustling. The rustlers are holed up in the mountains, and the Virginian is the only person who knows the trail. The posse asks him to lead them. He is torn between friendship and duty. Duty wins. After the battle, he has to help hang his friend.

Hal Skelly played the burlesque comedian in *The Dance of Life,* repeating his Broadway role. *Copyright 1929 by Paramount-Famous-Lasky.*

William S. Hart always maintained that the story was false. No true cowboy would ever turn against a friend. Hart was not so lucky himself, because his close friends turned against him.

The Virginian cinched Cooper's position, and he went on to become one of Paramount's top male stars of the 1930s.

The feminine honors for 1929 went to Nancy Carroll. She made *Close Harmony* with Charles "Buddy" Rogers and Jack Oakie; *The Shopworn Angel* with Cooper; *Illusion* again with Rogers; *The Wolf of Wall Street* with George Bancroft, Paul Lukas, and Olga Baclanova; *Sweetie* with Helen Kane and Jack Oakie; and *The Dance of Life* with Broadway star Hal Skelly repeating the role of the burlesque comedian he played on the stage. Nancy Carroll had the biggest hit of her career to that time as the self-sacrificing partner that Skelly abandoned on his way to Broadway glory. But when the crash came, naturally it was little Bonnie who picked up his pieces and put him together again.

Just rereading the plot outline, one finds it hard today to see what the shouting for this film was all about, but it was regarded as a gripping drama in spite of some atrocious jokes. In one song-and-dance patter, Skelly says he likes the dangeroos best of the zoo animals. "Dangeroos?" Nancy repeats between her tap dancing so the word will sink in to the audience.

"Yeah, dangeroos—d-a-n-g-e-r-o-u-s!" Skelly replied. And then they go into their dance.

Anyway, it was a hit. However, it did not do much for Skelly himself. He made *Behind the Makeup* with William Powell and then faded after a failure in D. W. Griffith's *The Struggle.*

Powell continued to improve in popularity with every film. One was *Pointed Heels,* about a fashion designer. The biggest success, however, was Ruth Chatterton. An important stage star in the early twenties, she had fallen on barren days. Paramount snapped her up solely because she could talk, and Ruth quickly became the first lady of the talking screen.

Although they were late getting into musicals and the vogue was dying out, Paramount kept trying. After the success of Skelly in *The Dance of Life,* the studio signed Eddie Dowling to make his stage success, *The Rainbow Man.* It bombed, and Dowling went back to Broadway. Zukor was having to learn a second time that the film public preferred to make its own stars rather than to have Broadway's choices shoved on it.

The Hollywood actors in most cases were doing better than the imported ones. Former supporting actors suddenly were the new stars. One of these was Jack Oakie. Oakie first came to serious notice with his amusing portrayal of Searchlight Doyle in Clara Bow's *The Fleet's In*. He also got excellent notices in *Sweetie*, the Nancy Carroll musical about a girl who inherits a boys' college. Oakie, a supporting player in this film, later would play Nancy Carroll's role in a remake called *Collegiate*, where the plot was changed to a man inheriting a girls' school.

Oakie was to go on to a long and fruitful career, living until 1978. He made a few pictures as the lead, but mainly is remembered for his supporting roles. He never failed to brighten any film he was in. But he did have a snotty attitude toward his fans. He once told a young autograph hunter: "Get away, you little bastard. Don't bother me."

When Bing Crosby insulted an autograph hunter in a nightclub in the 1940s, there was a hue and cry. But apparently Oakie was in the same class as W. C. Fields. People thought it funny when he insulted youngsters. One sort of expected it of him.

Oakie's real name was Offield. He was born in Missouri in 1903. His first job was as a clerk for a brokerage house, but he decided he would rather be a chorus boy in a musical comedy. He was pretty good at it and was in a long string of successes—but only in the male choruses. Then, during the run of *Peggy-Ann* by Rogers and Hart, Oakie broke up the show by standing behind the lead and mimicking him in a love scene.

He was thrown out of the play and blackballed on Broadway. Undaunted, he headed for Hollywood. There, in 1928, he managed to get a couple of bit parts. Then Paramount picked him up for the Clara Bow film, and Oakie found a home for the next eight years. He was so popular in 1929 that he made six pictures for his home studio and an additional two on loan.

Another supporting actor who found himself in great demand was Eugene Pallette, a real veteran. He was born in 1889 in Kansas. He attended military school and then became a touring actor like his parents. He joined the movies after being stranded and once said his first part was as an extra playing a Union soldier in *The Birth of a Nation*. He was soon playing leads for Triangle. After time out to serve in World War I, he went back to Hollywood. He was considered a very handsome man in those days, and Douglas Fairbanks, who got acquainted with him in their joint Triangle days, chose Pallette to play Aramis, the handsomest of the soldiers, in *The Three Musketeers*.

Alas, with the passing years, his face and belly grew fat. So when Fairbanks tried to reassemble his original musketeer cast for the 1929 production of *The Iron Mask*, Pallette drew the role of Porthos (originally played by George Sleigman), the fat musketeer. Fairbanks jovially referred to Eugene as "our baby elephant."

He was a solid hit as Sergeant Heath in *The Canary Murder Case* and repeated the role, also in 1929, in *The Greene Murder Case* and the next year in *The*

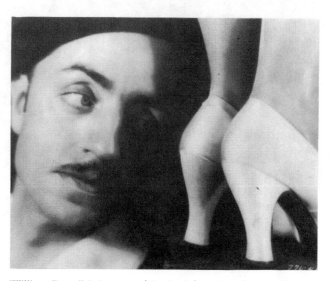

William Powell is interested in the lady's shoes because he is a fashion designer in *Pointed Heels. Copyright 1929 by Paramount-Famous-Lasky.*

Paramount hired famous minstrel man Eddie Dowling to make *The Rainbow Man* with Frankie Darro and Marion Nixon. *Copyright 1929 by Paramount-Famous-Lasky.*

Benson Murder Case. Also in 1930 he had an amusing part as the buddy of Jack Oakie in *Sea Legs*.

While many of the Broadway imports fell by the wayside, Jeanne Eagles–the girl who created the stage role of Sadie Thompson in *Rain*–was a hit in *The Letter*, based upon a Somerset Maugham short story. Bette Davis later starred in a remake for Warner Brothers.

The highly dramatic story involved the wife of a rubber planter in Malaya, played by Herbert Marshall. In a jealous rage the wife shot her lover because of his growing away from her. She claimed he had attacked her and thus escaped prosecution. However, the man's Eurasian mistress had a letter the wife had written to the dead man. This proved that she had passionately insisted that he visit her the night he was killed. To keep her from facing a murder charge, her husband (Herbert Marshall) beggared himself to buy the letter from the vengeful Eurasian. He destroyed the letter and told his wife she was safe. He forgave her and added that her ordeal was her punishment. In a highly charged ending, she screamed, "My punishment is that I still love the man I killed!"

Eagles died not long after this and never fulfilled the promise of her first talking film.

Two of the biggest successes of the year were foreign stars, Maurice Chevalier and Marlene Dietrich. The stories are a bit blurred about how Chevalier came to Paramount. Zukor said that he had known Maurice for years and always dropped in to see him when in Paris. Lasky claimed that it was all his idea. He saw Chevalier in a revue while in Paris. He was struck by how the Frenchman went over with American tourists and talked to Maurice about signing a contract.

"Would I see 'Doog' and 'Maree' if I come to America?" Maurice asked.

"I'll personally introduce you," Lasky said, and they shook hands on the deal.

Lasky claims that both S. R. Kent and Zukor were aghast. They insisted that Chevalier's accent would doom any picture he was in. Hadn't they just shipped the great Emil Jannings back home for that very reason? Lasky accepted this rebuke cynically. He knew, even if the others had forgotten, that they turned down Jannings only partly because of his poor English.

Jannings was difficult to handle. His pictures, while great prestige items, were not great money makers, with the exception of *The Last Command*. They were glad to be rid of him.

As for accents, they were paying Americans right then to assume accents for roles as foreigners. Why ask Adolphe Menjou, for example, to speak with a French accent when one could get the genuine article? The only reason Paul Lukas' accented voice was dubbed was because he was playing an American.

When Lasky signed Chevalier, he had in mind a book they had bought the previous year. It was called *Innocents of Paris*. It was about a French junk dealer who attracted crowds to his flea market sales by singing. He was heard by an impresario and raised to revue status but went back to the girl he knew in the flea market.

George Wallace directed from a script by Ethel Doheny, based on the book by Clarence E. Andrews. Filming was done in Astoria, New York, which had been reopened so Paramount could get stage stars to work in films without interrupting their broadway runs to go to the West Coast. The hit song from *Innocents of Paris* was "Louise," a tune that would by identified with Chevalier for the rest of his life.

The picture premiered on May 25, 1929. The reception convinced Kent and Zukor that accents–at least Chevalier's kind—were here to stay. Zukor was especially pleased because Ziegfeld had borrowed Chevalier for six weeks while the script was being prepared for shooting at the Astoria studios. This was a break for Paramount. The personal appearances were great publicity, making Chevalier known in a city where the reception was always highly touted in Paramount's promotions in the rest of the country. In addition, Paramount was paying Chevalier $1500 a week and getting $5000 for his services from Ziegfeld.

S. R. Kent told Lasky, "Why not stop making pictures and just rent out stars?"

Lasky, who had once been a booking agent, replied sadly that there was only one Chevalier. Besides, his major problem was not in booking stars but in

Jeanne Eagles, the famous "Rain" girl, was in *The Letter*. The film was remade later with Bette Davis in the Eagles role. *Copyright 1929 by Paramount-Famous-Lasky.*

keeping the police from booking them. One he had in mind was Clara Bow, whose publicity was turning sour.

Everyone was happy with Chevalier's first film. The happy-go-lucky Gallic charm came through nicely. The success of *Innocents of Paris* caused Lasky to rush his charming Frenchman into *The Love Parade*, with Ernst Lubitsch as director. Chevalier's co-star was a soprano Lasky heard in a Shubert musical, 26-year-old Jeanette MacDonald. Lasky liked her. Lubitsch thought she was great. So did the public. Chevalier did not. However, he went on to make two more Paramount pictures with the often temperamental MacDonald. Later, when he shifted his contract to Metro-Goldwyn-Mayer, Chevalier was disgusted to have MacDonald shoved on him again for *The Merry Widow*.

Von Sternberg had an offer to direct Emil Jannings in the German star's first talkie at UFA in Germany. Since Paramount still owned considerable UFA stock, Zukor agreed to release the director. But before he left, Von Sternberg made *Thunderbolt* with George Bancroft and Richard Arlen.

It was a poor copy of the underworld silents Von Sternberg had made with Bancroft. Thunderbolt (George Bancroft) is hiding from the police who want him on a murder charge. His girl Ritzy (Fay Wray) has fallen for Bob Moran (Richard Arlen), a young bank clerk. Thunderbolt goes to kill his rival but is interrupted by a dog, and this leads to his capture.

From his death cell, Thunderbolt arranges to frame Bob on a murder rap. Bob is placed in death row where Thunderbolt intends to kill him. He is not content to let the state get his revenge for him. He must kill Bob himself. Then, to his surprise, Ritzy gets permission to marry Bob before he goes to the electric chair. The wedding is held in the cells. Thunderbolt, who is to die the next day, confesses he framed Bob. He does this solely to get the chance to shake hands with Bob. At that moment he intends to kill the boy with his fist.

Before he can carry out his plan, he learns that Bob never stole Ritzy from him at all. He stole her from Bob. The boy and girl had been childhood sweethearts. Hearing this, Thunderbolt gives up his plan to kill Bob and goes to the electric chair roaring with laughter.

The story was inconsistent and filled with coincidences and improbable action. It was no credit to anyone concerned. When Von Sternberg left for Berlin, Lasky told S. R. Kent, "I hope he stays."

In Berlin Von Sternberg met Marlene Dietrich—Marlene being a contraction of her real name Maria Magdalena.

Dietrich has never shown a fondness for the past, especially her own. So there is some vagueness about it. But it seems that she was the daughter of a police officer. After his death her mother married a man who was killed in World War I.

Innocents of Paris with Sylvia Beecher (handing out programs) was Maurice Chevalier's introduction to American film audiences. *Copyright 1929 by Paramount-Famous-Lasky.*

Marlene's first ambition was to be a concert violinist, but this changed to an interest in the stage. After a number of turndowns, she got her first break as a chorus girl in 1921. The following year she had a part in a UFA production called *The Little Napoleon*. After that she alternated between stage and screen for the next seven years.

Thunderbolt was a continuation of the gangland pictures George Bancroft had been playing for Josef von Sternberg. Richard Arlen is the object of Bancroft's rage in this scene. *Copyright 1929 by Paramount-Famous-Lasky.*

Despite all her publicity as a creation of Von Sternberg, Dietrich was a well-known personality in Berlin before Sternberg. She played stage roles for Max Reinhardt and was in 17 German films.

The Jannings film was to be Heinrich Mann's *Professor Unrath*, the story of an aging professor who falls in love with a faithless woman. Von Sternberg reworked the story and renamed it *The Blue Angel*, after the night club where Lola sang.

Marlene got the Lola role. Von Sternberg, who was not always accurate in his autobiography, claimed he forced her on Jannings. This is part of the legend. Jannings had worked with Dietrich before. She had a small part in his 1924 film *Tragedy of Love*, which also dealt with an aging man's infatuation for a fickle woman. He liked her—then. He changed his mind later.

Dietrich is on record as saying she was nothing before Von Sternberg. This slights some pretty fair directors. She worked for Joe May, William Dieterle, and Alexander Korda before "Jo" came along.

In any event, Von Sternberg was smitten by Dietrich. He sent word to Lasky asking Paramount to sign her. S. R. Kent was going to Europe to check on Paramount's foreign sales staff. Lasky asked him to scout this "sensation" Von Sternberg was raving about. Kent went, looked, and wired back, "She *is* sensational! Sign her!"

Marlene Dietrich's role in *The Blue Angel* earned her a Paramount contract. *Copyright 1931 by Paramount-Publix Corp.*

After he mailed the contracts, Lasky had a sudden panicky thought. He wired Von Sternberg: "Does she have an accent?"

Other successes of 1929 included Clara Bow who passed her talkie examinations well enough. She made *The Wild Party* with Dorothy Arzner directing; *Dangerous Curves*, a circus picture, for Lothar Mendes; and *The Saturday Night Kid* with Jean Harlow and Jean Arthur under Eddie Sutherland's direction.

Harold Lloyd made his talkie debut in *Welcome Danger*, doing well enough, but the comedy sensation was *The Coconuts*, introducing the Marx Brothers to the screen.

Based on the Kaufman-Berlin musical, *The Coconuts* had Groucho Marx as owner of the Hotel de Coconut. It had 600 rooms all filled, but only one paying guest. She was rich Margaret Dumont, who gained eternal fame as Groucho's foil in a series of pictures. The story involved a plot to steal Dumont's necklace, which was foiled by Harpo. Whereupon hotel clerk Oscar Shaw got to marry Dumont's daughter, played by Mary Eaton from the New York stage. Chico and Zeppo, the other Marx brothers, had little to do except wander in and aid with the gags.

Groucho was the only one of the brothers who had real talent, but their zany style was a novelty that pulled crowds. They were put into a series of pictures that got successively worse. The others were *Animal Crackers*, 1930; *Monkey Business*, 1931; *Horse Feathers*, 1932; and *Duck Soup*, 1933.

If the titles seem odd at this time, it is because slang dates quickly. All were popular phrases of the day. For example, horses do not have feathers. So if you retorted "Horse feathers!" when informed of some questionable "fact," it meant that you doubted the veracity of the speaker. Likewise, in some manner the idea got around that "duck soup" was easy to make, so something easy became duck soup. "Monkey business" seems to have survived and gone into permanent language.

In explaining the failure of the later Laurel and Hardy films, Stan Laurel once said, "The producers thought we needed no plot. They just strung a bunch of gags together." This also explains the quick decline of the Marx Brothers at Paramount. There was no strong plot to keep the picture going between gags, and there are not enough gags and their twists to keep a feature star or stars going picture after picture without a strong element of suspense to support them. Harold Lloyd knew this, and suspense was the foundation upon which he built, drawing gags out of it.

The Marx Brothers Paramount films were just gags. In retrospect, Zeppo was useless and Chico was dull. Harpo was good only in small doses. Only Groucho and Margaret Dumont, his wonderful foil, were really amusing.

The success of Ruth Chatterton at Paramount followed by Jeanne Eagles in *Rain* convinced Zukor and Kent that the future of talking pictures was in Broadway stars. Zukor was back where he started, grabbing off talent from the stage. Ben Schulberg wanted to stand by the old stars and the movie-trained supporting actors whom talkies were shoving to the fore.

Kent was the real villain. Zukor was always flexible—one of the few top personalities in motion pictures who was willing to listen to someone else. Kent pointed to the success of Chevalier as an example.

"We pay Chevalier $1500 a week," Kent said, "and Dix gets $3000 a week, and he'll want more when his contract comes up for renewal. *Innocents of Paris* will

"Then-you'll-carry on?"

1199-131

Paramount illy served Richard Dix in his initial talking pictures. Here he is with O. P. Heggie in *The Wheel of Life*, a very poor picture that was panned by reviewers. *Copyright 1929 by Paramount-Famous-Lasky.*

gross double what Dix's best pictures will do. Bow, Daniels, Carroll—you name them. The public wants new faces. Faces that cost us less and make us more. I say, sweep them out."

This made sense, and plans were made to clean out the contract list. The authority for this being Kent's idea is Adolph Zukor. Zukor did not normally accuse others of mistakes in which he had a hand. This came in a wry remark after Kent left Paramount and picked up some of the very same stars for RKO that he helped cut away from Paramount.

Zukor said, "I wonder if he was getting his future star list ready then."

Bebe Daniels was the first to go, since her contract was expiring. Paramount did not even want to give her a voice test. According to her account, she and Clara Bow went together to Lasky to plead for voice tests. They got vague promises. Since Bow still had three years on her contract, she finally got her talkie debut. Bebe left to join ex-Paramount producer William LeBaron at RKO. He put her in *Rio Rita*, one of her biggest hits.

Later she said that Lasky asked her why she had not told him she could sing. She retorted, "You didn't ask me!"

Richard Dix was next for the chopping block. Dix had been one of Paramount's most popular stars during his six years with the studio. He never made an outstanding picture, although *The Vanishing American* came close. But Dix was something of a playboy. When Paramount closed the Long Island studio in 1927, Dix objected loudly to being transferred to the West Coast. He loved the glitter of New York. His objections offended Zukor. Then, when the Astoria studio was reopened in 1929 to make talking pictures, Dix again irritated the big brass by demanding to be transferred back to New York. This could not be done because the Astoria studio facilities were being used for Chevalier, the Marx Brothers, and others who could not leave New York because of stage contracts.

The word came down from up on high that Dix was expendable when his contract ran out. In 1929, his last year, he made one silent film and three talkies. *Redskin*, the silent, was supposed to be another *Vanishing American*. It merely vanished into the limbo that all silents dropped into that fateful year of change. His talkie debut was in *Nothing But the Truth*, the old stage and screen farce about a compulsive liar who was forced to tell the truth for 24 hours. Wynne Gibson was the girl his truthfulness almost lost him.

His next film, *The Wheel of Life*, was a tale of the British army in India. If there had been an Academy Award for the worst movie of the year, this would have been in the running. Dix, on Army leave, rescues Esther Ralston, a would-be suicide. They fall in love. But when he gets back to India, he discovers that she is the unhappy wife of his colonel, O. P. Heggie. But it all comes out okay. Heggie is killed saving Dix's life in an uprising. Dix gets Esther and "the Wheel of Life turns." Victor Schertzinger, who also directed *Redskin* and *Nothing But the Truth*, was behind the megaphone on this one. *Screen Book* said of it: "A mediocre movie. . . . Nobody in the cast seems particularly happy."

Dix's final picture for Paramount was *The Love Doctor*, who prescribed a romance for a patient and then fell in love with the "medicine" himself. Jean Arthur was the girl. It wasn't bad. Melville Brown, as director turned out a breezy farce, but Dix was gone after this. William LeBaron grabbed him for RKO and two years later put him in *Cimmarron*, a blockbuster and the best picture of his career.

Wallace Beery also got the ax. In 1926 his and Hatton's *Behind the Front* was Paramount's best grosser of the year. His other pictures did well. He was a critical success in *Beggars of Life*, and his ward heeler in *Chinatown Nights*, his talkie debut, was well received. This meant nothing. He did not fit in with the Broadway-oriented turn the company was taking. So he went to MGM where he made *The Big House* the next year. Then came *The Champ* and his pictures with Marie Dressler.

If Zukor and Lasky regretted losing these fine actors, nobody ever heard them say so. They were after a complete housecleaning to prepare for the new world of sound. These stars were dropped because it was the end of a contract period. Others were marked for the ax, including Clara Bow whose personal life was making Zukor nervous. He remembered Arbuckle, Taylor, and Reid.

As 1929 drew to a close, the world looked rosey at Paramount. The first scare that talking pictures brought had faded. Expenses soared due to the need for new cameras and sound stages, but lesser-priced stars and greatly increased box office prices were absorbing a lot of this.

The new gamble on casts was paying off. Cooper looked like a sure bet for a top star. William Powell was coming in strong after a decade of supporting others. It looked as though Bancroft would not make the grade, but he was offset by newcomers like Fredric March and Claudette Colbert from the stage. George Raft, a hoofer, was under consideration as a new type of gangster to replace the more uncouth Bancroft type.

Then came October 29, 1929.

The stock market, which was making everybody rich, faltered and plunged. Stocks lost as much as 40 points on Black Friday. Stunned brokers and investors saw the ticker running 90 minutes behind as frantic sellers tried to cut their losses. Fortunes melted away in minutes.

The source of the trouble was not in the fall of stocks. It was due to a system called buying on "margin." This meant that investors did not buy stocks outright. They put down as little as 10 percent. If the stock rose, they could sell at a profit. If the stock fell, they had to put up more "margin." The lower the stocks dropped, the more margin the brokers called for. Those who could not put up the additional margin were sold out and lost everything.

A report said that Mack Sennett dropped $5 million. Loew's stock—the controling interest in Metro-Goldwyn-Mayer—lost $30 million in value. Paramount stock had been selling for $137 a share. It finally leveled off at $7 a share.

Banks went broke. They had too many uncollectable loans. Bankruptcies ballooned. Breadlines were set up to feed the hungry. The Great Depression—the worst economic disaster in American history—was just beginning.

"You look quite upset, doctor."

Richard Dix's final Paramount picture was *The Love Doctor*. He
was supported by Jean Arthur and Gale Henry. *Copyright 1929
by Paramount-Famous-Lasky.*

10

The Big Shakedown

The stock market crash did not immediately affect the motion picture industry as much as it did other segments of society. Much of the stock losses were paper fortunes. That is, an investor put up $100,000 in margin on a $1 million stock purchase. When he was wiped out he screamed that he had lost "a million in the market." However, it had a depressing effect upon the economy that threw too many people out of work as companies struggled to cut costs. This had a domino effect upon the entire economy.

While the paper fortunes of the Hollywood stars and producers were wiped out, movies were still in demand. Paramount went into 1930, the first full year of the depression, with confidence in the future.

Word from Germany was that Sternberg's *The Blue Angel* with Paramount's newly signed Marlene Dietrich was a solid hit in its Berlin premiere on April 22, 1930. Immediately after the premiere, Von Sternberg and his new star sailed for the United States to go into *Morocco* with Gary Cooper and Adolphe Menjou. Kent thought the pairing of Dietrich with Cooper would have more box office appeal than Dietrich and Jannings. He suggested withholding *The Blue Angel* from U.S. exhibition until after

Dietrich was introduced to the American public with Cooper. Lasky agreed that the downbeat story of *The Blue Angel* was not the film to introduce Marlene.

The story of *Morocco* was hardly anything to get excited about. Dietrich was a cabaret singer in a Moroccan town where the French Foreign Legion was quartered. Cooper was a legionnaire. Just how a legionnaire who got paid in pennies a day could afford to go to cabarets was not explained. Anyway, Amy the singer had a rich suitor, Adolphe Menjou, who was as superb in this role as in most he played. In the end, Dietrich abandons Menjou to become a camp follower of Cooper, who really doesn't care much.

The poor story was offset by the electric personality of Dietrich and by Cooper in a role that fitted him perfectly. There are stories that Cooper was not happy with this film. He felt—correctly of course—that his director was more interested in projecting the female star than the male star. Von Sternberg claimed that Cooper had it put in his next contract that he would never have to work with Von Sternberg again.

Menjou also thought that Von Sternberg was giving

Morocco was a milestone film for both Gary Cooper and Marlene Dietrich. *Copyright 1930 by Paramount-Publix Corp.*

Tom Sawyer with Jackie Coogan and Mitzi Green drew good grosses despite the economic panic that followed the October 1929 stock market crash. *Copyright 1930 by Paramount-Publix Corp.*

Dietrich the best to the detriment of the others. But he was professional enough to smile and go his way, turning out the best performance of the three.

The picture was a success, but not the overwhelming financial blockbuster that some historians imply. The January 10, 1931, issue of *Motion Picture Herald* listed weekly gross receipts of Paramount pictures in Los Angeles. *The Right to Love* brought $30,000 that week. *Tom Sawyer*, with Jackie Coogan and Mitzi Green, took in $15,000, and *Morocco* hit $20,500. However, in Washington, D.C., on the same week, *Tom Sawyer* took in $25,500, outpulling *Morocco* by several thousand.

Tom Sawyer was one of the year's best pictures. Junior Durkin played Huck Finn. It was released in November 1930.

This first depression year also saw some new people who would become important box office stars in the near future. *Fast and Loose*, released November 8, 1930, had Miriam Hopkins and Carole Lombard. Fredric March, after his 1929 debut in *The Dummy*, was steadily rising. March, then 32, was the son of a prominent Wisconsin manufacturer. After serving as a lieutenant in World War I, he tried banking, but he soon turned to acting. He was in the George Kaufman-Edna Ferber hit *The Royal Family* in Los Angeles when Lasky signed him on B. P. Schulberg's recommendation.

Lasky also bought the play, but production was postponed. The play was a burlesque of the Barrymore family. Ethel Barrymore was furious, but her brother John told an interviewer, "I think the play was too harsh on Ethel, but I was just like that."

In *The Dummy*, March played the husband. Ruth Chatterton was his estranged wife. Their small daughter, Donzelle Darr, is kidnapped and recovered by Mickey Bennett, a juvenile who disguises himself as a mute to infiltrate the gang. He gives himself away by talking in his sleep. Jack Pickford played the mute role in the silent version. The danger to their daughter brings March and Chatterton together again.

March also played the stuffy professor who tries to cope with an unruly student, Clara Bow, in *The Wild Party*, Clara's first talkie. Other March roles were the murdered actor in *The Studio Murder Mystery* (1929), the man who shoots his wife's (Jeanne Eagles) former lover in *Jealousy* (1929), and an aid to harassed Mary Brian in caring for a group of children in *The Marriage Playground*. One of the children was a vaudeville kid billed as Little Mitzi. This was Mitzi Green in her film debut.

Then in 1930 March played a lawyer trying to prevent Ruth Chatterton from finding her son, who was adopted without her permission. The film was called *Sarah and Son*. He was then in *Ladies Love Brutes*, the George Bancroft picture, *True to the Navy* with Clara Bow, and *Laughter* with Nancy Carroll, and he closed out the year working on the film version of *The Royal Family*. It was released in January 1931 as *The Royal Family of Broadway*. The name was changed because Paramount did not want to run into trouble in Great Britain where the advertising might suggest a slur on the royal family there.

Henrietta Crosman from the stage, Ina Claire, and Mary Brian played the other Barrymore characters.

Some other 1930 films included Harold Lloyd in *Feet First*, William Powell in *Shadow of the Law* (a remake of Meighan's *City of Silent Men*), *Only the Brave* with Gary Cooper and Mary Brian, Clara Bow as a movie star in *Her Wedding Night* and a poor girl seeking a husband in *Love Among the Millionaires*, and Jack Holt with Richard Arlen in the Zane Grey story *The Border Legion*, which Antonio Moreno had done in the silents. Holt's time was running out at Paramount. After this film he went to Columbia where he lasted another decade. He was a true gentleman and a better actor than he is generally credited with being.

The big picture of the year was *Paramount on Parade*. It was a plotless revue that trotted out everybody on the lot for a sketch. In alphabetical order, the cast included Richard Arlen, Jean Arthur, William Austin, George Bancroft, Clara Bow, Evelyn Brent, Mary

Henrietta Crosman, Mary Brian, Ina Claire, and Fredric March
burlesque the Barrymore family in *The Royal Family of Broadway*.
Copyright 1931 by Paramount-Publix Corp.

Fredric March made his screen debut in *The Dummy* with Ruth Chatterton and Donzelle Darr. *Copyright 1929 by Paramount-Famous-Lasky.*

Harold Lloyd released his later films through Paramount. This is his second talkie, *Feet First.* Copyright 1930 by Harold Lloyd Corp.

Brian, Clive Brook, Virginia Bruce, Nancy Carroll, Ruth Chatterton, Maurice Chevalier, Gary Cooper, Leon Erroll, Stuart Erwin, Kay Francis, Skeets Gallagher, Harry Green, Mitzi Green, James Hall, Phillips Holmes, Helen Kane (the boop-boop-a-doop girl), Dennis King, Abe Lyman's band, Fredric March, Nino Martini, Mitzi Mayfair, David Newell, Jack Oakie, Zelma O'Neal, Warner Oland, William Powell, Charles "Buddy" Rogers, and Lillian Roth. With the exception of Claudette Colbert, this was just about the roster at Paramount right then.

There were 19 separate sketches. None can be called outstanding. Mitzi Green was cute imitating Maurice Chevalier. Clara Bow's singing "I'm True to the Navy Now" to Gallagher, Oakie, and a sailor chorus was enough of a hit to get it tagged as the title of her following feature. Nancy Carroll did "Dancing to Save My Soul" with a chorus and Abe Lyman's band backing her. Maurice Chevalier closed with "Sweeping the Clouds Away," backed by a chorus in different color costumes representing a rainbow arched above him.

The picture, directed by a group of directors, was not bad, nor did it do badly, but it was a disappointment. It came in on the tail of the flood of singing-dancing pictures. It might have done better if it had come out at the time of *Broadway Melody, Golddiggers of Broadway,* and the others that started the boom.

Some other 1930 Paramount films show the wide expanse of subject matter: *Young Eagles* with Buddy Rogers and Jean Arthur, portraying a World War I story built around flying and spying; *Young Man of Manhattan* with Claudette Colbert and Norman Foster, showing the trials of a sportswriter married to a movie columnist (Ginger Rogers is a dizzy socialite); *The Right to Love,* a film about life and love in a Midwest farm community with "the first

Only The Brave teamed Gary Cooper and Mary Brian. *Copyright 1930 by Paramount-Publix Corp.*

Not even Clara Bow's getting spanked helped the dismal box office record of *Her Wedding Night. Copyright 1930 by Paramount-Publix Corp.*

Clara Bow had a better role in *Love Among the Millionaires* with
Skeets Gallagher, Mitzi Green, Stu Erwin, and Charles Sellon.
Copyright 1930 by Paramount-Publix Corp.

lady of the screen" Ruth Chatterton (this film out-pulled *Morocco* in many places, attesting to Chatterton's popularity); *Monte Carlo*, in which a hairdresser is really a count in disguise so he can make love to Jeannette MacDonald and with Jack Buchanan in the Monsieur Beaucaire twist; *Sea Legs* with Jack Oakie and Eugene Pallette in the French Navy; and *The Return of Fu Manchu* continuing Warner Oland in the sinister role he created in the 1929 melodrama *The Mysterious Dr. Fu Manchu*.

Oland, a Swede, made a career playing Chinese parts. These extended from a Pearl White serial to Charlie Chan. When he very occasionally got to play another nationality, it was usually something like the Jewish cantor father in *The Jazz Singer*. If he ever got to play a Swede, we can find no record of it.

Overall, 1930 was a good year for Paramount. Clara Bow began making unpleasant headlines that climaxed in 1931 with the termination of her con-

tract, but this seemed to be the only dark cloud on the horizon.

So the company entered 1931 with high hopes. In January it released *The Blue Angel* to cash in on the success of *Morocco*. Maurice Chevalier made *The Smiling Lieutenant*. Jack Oakie made *Dude Ranch*. He played a member of a vaudeville troupe in trouble. Mitzi Green was a bright spot in the film.

Mitzi was an uncommonly able mimic. Her takeoff on George Arliss had to be seen to be believed. She had been on stage all her life and was an excellent comedienne. In later life she stopped the show singing "That's Why the Lady is a Tramp" in the Broadway production of *Babes in Arms*. She could have been another Judy Garland if handled right. Unfortunately Joe Keno, her father, had delusions of grandeur for his 11-year-old daughter. He pulled her out of Paramount in 1931, and her movie career went downhill from then on. Some of her other Paramount pictures were *Honey*, 1929; *The Sante Fe Trail*, 1930; and *Skippy* and *Forbidden Adventure in 1931*. She brightened every picture she was in.

Then suddenly the high promise for 1931 went sour. Warner Brothers made a raid on Paramount's

Jack Holt was king of Paramount's Westerns for nine years, but was nearing the end when he made *The Border Legion* with Richard Arlen in 1930. *Copyright 1930 by Paramount-Publix Corp.*

Two members of the giant cast of *Paramount on Parade* are Jack Oakie and Helen Kane, the boop-boop-a-doop girl, seen here in *Sweetie*, an earlier release. *Copyright 1929 by Paramount-Famous-Lasky.*

Clara Bow's own high speed was running down when she made
this skit with Skeets Gallagher and Jack Oakie for *Paramount on
Parade*. *Copyright 1930 by Paramount-Publix Corp.*

star list, helping itself to William Powell, Ruth Chatterton, and Kay Francis. All three contracts were up, and Warners' checkbook was liberal.

Since the beginning of talkies, the big studios had been getting rid of high-priced stars and bringing in Broadway actors at lower prices or upping featured players without increasing salaries.

Mitzi Green and Jack Oakie are the highlights of *Dude Ranch*. *Copyright 1931 by Paramount-Publix Corp.*

Motion Picture Herald magazine complained that Warner's action meant a return to high salaries again. A story in the January 28, 1931, issue said that Warners paid Ruth Chatterton and William Powell $7500 a week each to make the jump to its studio and that Kay Francis got "an impressive sum."

Another story said that producers, fearful of a disastrous "stars war," were trying to make peace between Jack Warner and Adolph Zukor. They thought Zukor planned a checkbook raid on Warner Brothers' star list. They feared this would drive up all salaries and hurt every producer.

Mitzi Green and Junior Durkin helped the wagon trains get through in *The Santa Fe Trail.Copyright 1930 by Paramount-Publix Corp.*

This proved to be an ill-founded rumor. Paramount did not have the money to raid anybody. It was suddenly on the brink of bankruptcy. The first intimation of trouble was a story that Paramount's top chiefs had a secret meeting about production wastes and rising costs in the West Coast studio, where Schulberg had been boss since 1925. Rumors indicated that he might be fired and replaced by Walter Wanger, who headed East Coast production.

Charles McCarthy of the Paramount legal staff put out a strong denial. Schulberg went on to push the career of Sylvia Sidney, in whom Schulberg had a personal interest. He put her into *City Streets* with Gary Cooper. Rouben Mamoulian was set to direct. He had done stage and opera direction and one previous film, *Applause*, a 1929 Paramount picture with Helen Morgan. Cooper was not too happy, but he was in no position to refuse. He had just turned down *Dishonored* with Marlene Dietrich because he refused to work with Von Sternberg again. Schulberg told him to take *City Streets* or be suspended.

The picture was a remake of Clara Bow's 1928 success, *Ladies of the Mob*. She was again slated to take the role but withdrew because of what the studio publicity department called a nervous breakdown.

This was the climax of a long series of troubles. She had become involved with Harry Richman, a New York dancer, and there were newspaper headlines that Clara tried to slash her wrists when Richman refused to marry her. In mid-1930 the wife of a doctor in Dallas, Texas, charged Clara with stealing her husband. Clara settled the threatened law suit out of court for $150,000.

Next she was accused of losing $13,000 in a Las Vegas gambling place and refusing to pay. But the biggest blow of all came in November 1930 when her secretary, Daisy Devoe, was charged with 37 counts of embezzlement. In the ensuing trial, Devoe told "all" about Clara's private life. It was sensational. Frederick H. Girnau, who specialized in gossip publications, immediately rushed out a pamphlet entitled *Clara's Secret Love-Life as told by Daisy*. It cost 5 cents a copy to publish and sold for a dollar—and it sold very well indeed.

With visions of another Arbuckle or Wallace Reid, Zukor and Lasky called on Schulberg to do something fast. They immediately released Clara's last two pictures, *No Limit* with Norman Foster and *Kick In* with Regis Toomey. Neither was a success.

Newcomer Sylvia Sidney took Clara Bow's role in *City Streets* with Gary Cooper. This was Rouben Mamoulian's second film. *Copyright 1931 by Paramount-Publix Corp.*

At this point Paramount and the "It Girl" parted company. Lasky said it was her idea and purely voluntary. Clara also said she demanded that Schulberg release her from the rest of her contract. Work on her new picture, *Manhandled*, was stopped, and the script of *City Streets*, planned as her next film, was given to Sylvia Sydney. Voluntary or not, Zukor was glad to see her go.

The rumors of Schulberg's departure increased. Said the *Motion Picture Herald*:

Clara Bow, shown here in *Dangerous Curves,* was the center of a messy scandal in 1930. *Copyright 1929 by Paramount-Publix Corp.*

Reports seeping through the industry since last November mentioned the existence of serious differences between Schulberg and Walter Wanger, the latter Eastern studio chief. Reported inability of the Hollywood lot to meet a lower production cost than the Eastern plant under Wanger is said to have launched a battle which caused Zukor to step in as peacemaker on at least two occasions. Schulberg was brought to New York, but contended that the Coast could not make films as cheaply as New York. This eventually brought an ultimatum from the home office insisting upon a slash in costs.

As the battle went on, Schulberg, in an effort to cut costs, worked his teams night and day. *City Streets* was filmed at night in large part because Schulberg had Cooper working on *I Take This Woman* in the daytime. Carole Lombard played an heiress who married cowboy Cooper just to spite her father for sending her down to the ranch. But true love triumphed as it did most of the time in Paramount films.

Cooper was not happy over this doubling up. But his refusal to take the Von Sternberg assignment and the fact that his currently released film, *Fighting Caravans*, was not doing so well made him reluctant to put up a fight. However, at the end of the double shooting he suddenly got sick. He did his recuperating on an European cruise with Countess Dorothy di Frasso.

In the meantime, Lasky was embarrassed by a financial debacle at a time when Zukor was pressing him hard to cut costs. Lasky had been greatly impressed by Sergei Eisenstein's *Potemkin*, a Russian-made film about the mutiny of a group of sailors and the bloody way the revolt was put down.

Lasky signed Eisenstein to a Paramount contract. The great Russian director then came to Hollywood to study American film methods. Eisenstein was a genius—most agree on that. But he was a Von Stroheim-type genius: money, time, and film meant nothing to him. The effect was the thing.

Lasky had bought Theodore Dreiser's sensational novel *An American Tragedy,* and this was handed to Eisenstein as his first American film. The story is tragic and grim. A working-class boy seduces a poor girl, who becomes pregnant. In a panic because he wants to marry a wealthy young woman, he plans to drown his girlfriend.

No Limit, with Norman Foster, was Clara Bow's next-to-last
Paramount picture. *Copyright 1931 by Paramount-Publix Corp.*

Tully Marshall and Ernest Torrance repeat their *The Covered Wagon* roles in *Fighting Caravans* with Gary Cooper. *Copyright 1931 by Paramount-Publix Corp.*

The story appealed to Eisenstein's brooding Russian temperament. He went to work on a script. The result was a probing of subtle human emotion that would have been a credit to Dostoevski, with a length that matched the *War and Peace* of Tolstoy. Lasky hurriedly canceled this project. He put Eisenstein on *Sutter's Gold,* a story of the discovery of gold that brought about the gold rush of 1849. Lasky saw it as a flag-waving epic of American history. Eisentein saw it as an epic of human greed and cruelty. The script he turned in was so monumental that Lasky's accountants estimated it would cost $10 million to film. And this was in 1931 when bread was a nickel a loaf and steak was 10 cents a pound.

Eisenstein was hastily released from his contract. Lasky then looked for some way to cut the losses. He decided for some obscure reason that Von Sternberg was just the man to pull *An American Tragedy* out of the loss column. So under pressure Jo put aside Dietrich for the moment and began work on the impossible task of making a grim story for an audience that wanted laughter in order to forget the depression.

At Schulberg's insistence the girl's role went to Sylvia Sidney. Phillips Holmes was the weak, unfortunate boy. He was the son of stage and silent picture star Taylor Holmes. He was in college when Frank Tuttle arrived on the campus with Charles "Buddy" Rogers to make location shots for *Varsity.* It was 1928. Holmes played a small part in the film and was good enough for Paramount to offer him a contract. "Flip"—as he was called—consulted his father, who said, "If you must, you must."

Holmes came to Hollywood, but as often happened, nobody knew what to do with him. He played bit parts until 1929 when he got the juvenile lead with Jean Arthur and Wallace Beery in the dreary silent Western *Stairs of Sand.* After six other pictures, he was loaned to Fox, Pathé and Warner Brothers before coming back to do *Stolen Heaven* and *Confessions of a Co-Ed* in 1931. Then he and Sylvia Sidney, his co-star from *Confessions,* went into *An American Tragedy.* Frances Dee played the wealthy woman Holmes wanted to marry.

The jinx that began when Eisensten was assigned to the picture held right to the end. Von Sternberg did not want to do the film. He was irritable and hard to work with. A story was whispered that Schulberg, who thought highly of Sidney, threatened to punch

"Jo" if he did not treat her more kindly. Then Theodore Dreiser, the author of the novel on which the film was based, blew up. He claimed that his concept had been twisted and his reputation defamed by the "butchery of Von Sternberg." The case came to court as the author tried to prevent its release. Dreiser lost, the judge decreeing that the picture was—considering the differences between the printed page and the screen—a faithful rendition of the novel.

The picture opened to good reviews. Both Sidney and Holmes were lauded for their roles. Holmes was especially good in the second half where he faced the court on a charge of murdering Sidney.

But even so, the film was a failure with the public. The bitter days of 1931 were no time for a downbeat picture. The people wanted to be cheered up. The film was remade twenty years later with Montgomery Clift in the role of the young man. Elizabeth Taylor had the wealthy young woman role, and Shelly

Phillips Holmes and Sylvia Sidney are the ill-fated lovers in Josef von Sternberg's *An American Tragedy. Copyright 1931 by Paramount-Publix Corp.*

Winters played the girl. Apparently Paramount was still smarting over the heavy loss from the original, for the film was given a new name, *A Place in the Sun*.

Holmes gave another good performance in Ernest Lubitsch's *Broken Lullaby*, released the next year. This was one of Lubitsch's few dramas for the American screen. It failed to draw and was retitled *The Man I Killed*. It still failed.

All things considered, 1931 was not too bad a year for Paramount's box office receipts, although they were falling off. But 1932 brought total disaster. The company's plight was kept quiet as long as possible to avoid further depressing its stock. But it is hard to keep up a pretense of prosperity when you drop 5,000 noncontract employees. Those on contract were being asked to take a voluntary cut in salary. Then Zukor

sold the half interest Paramount had in the Columbia Broadcasting Company for $5.2 million. The badly needed cash was sucked away in the flood of debts that engulfed the struggling company.

Zukor struggled to avoid bankruptcy, bombarding Lasky and Schulberg with demands for economy in production. But it was not the production side that was destroying them. The pictures for the most part were still drawing, and some exciting new personalities were being developed. One of these was an irresponsible crooner named Bing Crosby, who after some Mack Sennett shorts was signed by Paramount as the off-screen voice singing "Just One More Chance" in the dreary *Confessions of a Co-Ed* in 1931. This was followed in 1932 by *The Big Broadcast*. This solid hit had Crosby as a singer who helps Stu Erwin save George Burns' radio station by staging an all-star broadcast with Cab Calloway, Burns and Allen, Kate Smith, the Boswell Sisters, and others. Bing got second billing after Erwin.

Paramount's major trouble was caused by its theater division. Zukor had bought many theaters in the sincere belief that the company must control exhibition of its pictures in order to assure a market for its production.

This worked well until the depression deepened and stock prices failed to rebound as everyone at first thought. Financial panics were nothing new in the United States, but things usually improved in a year or so. When they did not, the theater divison of Para-

Broken Lullaby failed to draw. It was withdrawn and retitled *The Man I Killed*, but that did not help either. Phillips Holmes is the star. *Copyright 1931 by Paramount-Publix Corp.*

Bing Crosby is a crooning announcer in love with Leila Hyams in *The Big Broadcast. Copyright 1932 by Paramount-Publix Corp.*

184

mount dragged the rest of the company down with it.

Box office grosses dropped alarmingly, but even this was not at the root of the trouble. Warner Brothers and MGM were still afloat under the same conditions. The trouble was that Zukor had bought a lot of theaters with stock. This stock carried a guarantee for repurchase by Paramount in 18 months at not less than $85 a share. When this came due, the stock was selling for $7 or less on the market. This meant that Paramount's treasury lost at least $78 on every share it was forced to repurchase.

There was not enough cash to cover the stock. Zukor raised $13 million on a bank loan by pledging 23 feature pictures as collateral, but even so the company was running $1 million a month short in its cash needs.

Sam Katz came to the rescue. As head of the theater division of Paramount–Publix, he brought in financiers John Hertz, the taxicab king of Chicago, and William Wrigley, Jr., the chewing gum manufacturer. Hertz immediately took over as head of the Finance Committee, charged with the responsibility of putting Paramount on a sound financial base. He forced the resignation of Zukor's friends and relatives on the Paramount board and installed his own people.

Katz now started to meddle in production, infuriating Lasky and Sidney Kent. Kent suddenly agreed to terminate his contract for $200,000, which Hertz readily accepted. Kent had already agreed to head Fox, which had just gone into bankruptcy. He was sure that he could pull it out and asked Lasky to go with him as production head of the rival company.

"They're after your head," he told Lasky. "Get out while you can." Lasky refused to believe that he would be forced out of the company he helped found.

He wished Kent, whom he got on well with, good luck and settled down to weather the storm.

The continued prosperity that films had enjoyed while the rest of the country's economy floundered took a turn for the worse in 1932. Katz insisted that the company could still make a profit if the extraordinary waste, which he blamed on Schulberg and Lasky, could be eliminated.

Schulberg got the ax. Then on April 30, 1932, John Hertz, whose name is still attached to the Hertz rental cars, suggested to Lasky that he had been working too hard. "You need a few months rest," he said.

"But I have important business in Hollywood . . ." Lasky began.

"We would rather you stayed away from Hollywood," Hertz replied.

Lasky felt a cold chill. Kent's prediction had come true. He was being forced out. Later, in his autobiography, Lasky said that at long last he knew how Sam Goldwyn and Cecil B. DeMille had felt when they had been booted from the company they helped found. Lasky went with Kent to Fox, working as an independent producer.

Picturewise, the outlook was good as new stars

Sidney R. Kent, super film salesman, could not buck the Katz regime and left Paramount in 1932. *Copyright 1932 by Paramount-Publix Corp.*

185

started to twinkle. Fredric March, guided by the outstanding direction of Rouben Mamoulian, had an Academy Award role in *Dr. Jekyll and Mr. Hyde*. It surpassed John Barrymore's role in the 1920 film, which was hard to do. On the other hand, *Merrily We Go to Hell* with Sylvia Sidney and Fredric March was terrible despite a title that should have appealed to depression audiences.

On the sex symbol front, Jane Peters, a fugitive from Mack Sennett comedies, had become Carol (and then Carole) Lombard. After she burst on the screen, nobody at Paramount missed Clara Bow anymore.

Lombard came from a fairly well-to-do family in Indiana. After the death of her father, she traveled with her mother to Hollywood, where she got a small part in a Monte Blue picture in 1921. She was 12 years old and already a blooming beauty. Then it was

back to school until W. S. Van Dyke put her into some Buck Jones Westerns at Fox. Later she went to Mack Sennett until she impressed Joseph P. Kennedy, who brought her into Pathé in 1928, when she just turned 20.

Paramount put her into Victor Schertziner's *Safety in Numbers* in 1930. She was only ornamental background in this Buddy Rogers–Josephine Dunn quickie. After another support role she had the lead in *It Pays to Advertise* with Norman Foster and then had four solid roles in 1931. In *Man of the World* (Richard Wallace) and *Ladies' Man* (Lothar Mendes) she played the second woman in these William Powel films. Although she lost Powell on screen, off screen she did better. The suave, quiet Powell and the cussing jazz baby were an ill-matched pair. Their marriage lasted a couple of years and they parted, still friends.

In *No Man of Her Own* (Wesley Ruggles), Carole had Clark Gable as a co-star. Gable was hot after his great success with Norma Shearer in MGM's *A Free Soul*. Carole was equally on the rise. They made a steaming couple. The story concerned a con man who stopped in a small town while on the lam from New York. He meets and marries Carole, a librarian. They return to New York, where he must serve a three months' jail sentence. He tries to keep it from her, claiming he is going to South America on business. He arranges for souvenirs to be sent to her to keep up the deception.

Fredric March gave an Academy Award performance in *Dr. Jekyll and Mr. Hyde*, previously filmed by Paramount with John Barrymore in 1920. *Copyright 1932 by Paramount-Publix Corp.*

Carole Lombard and William Powell made such a good team in *Ladies Man* that they made an off-screen team as well. *Copyright 1931 by Paramount-Publix Corp.*

Paramount got Gable for this film in exchange for Bing Crosby. Marion Davies wanted Crosby for her *Going Hollywood* at MGM. In those days William Randolph Hearst's fabulous mistress still could get anything she wanted.

Cute little scenes, such as the ones where Carole is on a ladder getting a book and Gable tries to look up her dress, is one of the reasons for the later founding of the League of Decency.

Meanwhile, back at the ranch (as the subtitles used to say), things were getting worse and worse. Sam Katz was suddenly fired as head of Paramount's theater chain. He immediately sued for the remaining payment under his contract. Then some shareholders sued, charging Zukor, Lasky, and Kent with mismanagement. One of the charges was that they paid themselves enormous and unjustified bonuses. This was shown to be $887,500 each for Lasky and Zukor in 1929. Kent and Katz got $710,000 each. These enormous payments were in addition to their regular salaries. In purchasing power, these bonuses can be multiplied many times to get the equivalent in today's money.

One by one the founders had left. First it was Hodkinson. Then Goldwyn was pushed out. DeMille went next, and then Lasky. Finally it seemed that the last survivor, Adolph Zukor, had reached the end of the line.

But in true movie suspense fashion, Zukor escaped the ax. He emerged as one of the three court-appointed receivers to direct the company during its reorganization under the bankruptcy laws. How did Zukor accomplish this seeming miracle? The court took the view that he was an honest, diligent businessman harmed by extravagant and incompetent associates. Lasky, Katz, and Kent got the blame—which was not correct, except in the case of Katz. It was neither production (Lasky) nor sales (Kent). The theater-buying tactics of Katz and Zukor were at the root of the trouble. Also, the receivers needed somebody who knew something about the peculiar inner workings of the film industry. None knew this better than Zukor.

Although he kept a position in Paramount, Zukor was hard hit by the bankruptcy. His salary was cut to $23,000 a year. He lost his bonuses and had to repay his share of the more than $2 million the judge ordered Zukor, Eugene Zukor (his son), Jesse Lasky, Sam Katz, and Sidney Kent to repay from their exorbitant bonuses.

However, when the company was reorganized with money from Floyd Odlum's Atlas Corporation, John E. Otterson was made president. Zukor became chairman of the board with a salary of $156,000 a year and a percentage of the profits.

The problem now was to put Paramount back in the black. All that was available in real assets to do this were Gary Cooper, Marlene Dietrich, George Raft, Fredric March, and (real aces in the hole) newcomers Mae West and Bing Crosby.

Cooper and March were riding high. Raft was still untried. Crosby was just beginning, and nobody knew how he would hold up. West had created a sensation in her introductory film and was slated for her first starring part.

Carole Lombard hardly looks like a small town librarian with Clark Gable in *No Man of Her Own*, but that is what director Wesley Ruggles would have us believe. *Copyright 1932 by Paramount-Publix Corp.*

11

The Comeback

On the corporate side, 1932 was a miserable year for Paramount. Productionwise, it was a year of transition. Old stars were twinkling out. New ones were beginning to shine.

With a few exceptions, the Broadway invasion had not panned out. Nancy Carroll's career was being ruined by poor pictures. The Marx Brothers were slipping. Von Sternberg seemed to have lost his touch. *Shanghai Express* was the only really good picture he made after the highly successful *Morocco,* Dietrich's career at Paramount would dim with his. Sylvia Sidney had been a favorite with Ben Schulberg. When he left, the betting was that Sylvia would not do so well. She proved the betting wrong. She was a good and versatile actress, who deserves a better place in movie history than she is generally given.

But the brightest newcomer was Mae West. She came along just at the right moment. There had been a gradual loosening of the strict moral code that gripped the movie industry after the trauma of the 1921–1922 scandals. The public was ready for something a little rougher than Lubitsch's sophisticated digs at sex. And there was no denying that Mae was rougher. She once had been jailed for putting on a

Broadway show that even the tolerant New York police found too raw.

The *New York Times,* which contained more human interest stories in the old days than it does today, covered Mae's stay in the pokey in considerable detail. The paper reported that Mae accepted the rough jail uniforms but balked at the underwear. She insisted on wearing her own silk "teddies" or threatened to wear *nothing*—or so the papers reported.

Jesse Lasky had known Mae since 1911 when he booked her in one of his vaudeville shows. B. P. Schulberg had suggested her for a Paramount film in 1928. Lasky said, "Mr. Zukor would have all our heads!"

But after Lasky was gone, it was Zukor who okayed Mae's first starring role for Paramount. George Raft was the one who broke the ice for her. Archie Mayo, the director of *Night After Night,* was looking for someone to play Raft's ex-sweetie. He wanted Texas Guinan, the nightclub hostess. Texas had made some silent films as a cowgirl type before she became the toast of Broadway, where she welcomed patrons to her gangland-owned club with a raucous, "Hello, Sucker!"

Mae West (with George Raft and Alison Skipworth) said, "Goodness has nothing to do with it!" in *Night After Night* and thereby brought joy to Paramount's stockholders. *Copyright 1932 by Paramount-Publix Corp.*

Instead, Raft proposed Mae, whom he had known in his Broadway hoofing days. This was Raft's first starring picture, but he had gained a following after playing the coin-flipping killer in Howard Hughes' *Scarface*. The Hell's Kitchen boy, who once helped run prohibition beer, was headed for the big time. So Mayo reluctantly gave in.

The story of *Night After Night* was about a gambling czar who had aspirations to be a gentleman. He ran his business in a mansion formerly owned by Constance Cummings. Raft had designs upon Cummings and hired marvelous Alison Skipworth, a depression-hit society dowager, to teach him manners. Then, to Raft's embarrassment, in walks Maudie, his ex-mistress. Mae as Maudie made screen history with her entrance scene. When the hatcheck girl said admiringly, "Goodness! What beautiful diamonds!" Mae replied, "Goodness had nothing to do with it."

Night After Night's reception was one of the few bright spots in the closing months of 1932 for Paramount. There was general agreement that Mae West was a find, but no one knew exactly what to do with her. Mae herself suggested her Broadway success, *Diamond Lil*. After much soul-searching, the corporate okay was given. Zukor made the final decision. However, he insisted that the name be changed because he did not want to flag its association with the 1928 stage play. So Diamond Lil became Lady Lou. The title was changed to *He Done Her Wrong*, but it was finally released—due to Mae's insistence—as *She Done Him Wrong*.

It was a story of the Gay Nineties against a background of the white slave trade. Next door to the saloon where Mae presides is a religious mission run by a handsome captain of the Salvation Army by the name of Cummings, played by Cary Grant. Lou naturally tries to add the captain to her menagerie of conquests. After much sparring, he is revealed as an undercover policeman. He jails the white slave ring run by Gus Jordan (Noah Beery), but gives Lou a wedding ring instead of handcuffs.

The story was hardly a theatrical masterpiece, but Lowell Sherman staged it beautifully. Production values were high. The costumes were splendid, and there was Mae West tickling the audience with double entendre such as the screen had never heard before. This went far beyond the sexy naughtiness that Lubitsch touched them with.

When Grant said, "Haven't you ever met a man who could make you happy?"

Mae replied with a wiggle that got over her meaning clearly, "Sure, lots of times."

One of the Paramount legends is that Mae saw Cary Grant walking on the lot, eyed him speculatively, and said, "If he can talk, I'll take him."

Director Lowell Sherman tries to tell Mae West how to play a scene in *She Done Him Wrong* and ends up getting told. *Copyright 1933 by Paramount Productions Inc.*

This may have been true, but it was not Grant's film initiation, as many seem to think. He had already played leads with the likes of Tallulah Bankhead (*Devil and the Deep*), Marlene Dietrich (*Blonde Venus*), and Sylvia Sidney (*Madame Butterfly*). Earlier he had bits or supporting roles in four other pictures.

Alexander Archibald Leach—who became Cary Grant—was born in England in 1908. He got into theatrical work in his teens and came to the United States in the early 1920s as a juggler. Returning to England, he later came back to the United States and was in a number of Broadway plays. This led to his screen debut in 1932.

Dietrich, Bankhead, and Sidney all expressed the opinion that Cary had what it took to be a star, but Mae is the actress who gave him the opportunity.

After *She Done Him Wrong*, Grant was seen with Nancy Carroll in *The Woman Accused, The Eagle and the Hawk,* and *Gambling Ship* before being tagged by

Mae for *I'm No Angel*, in which West played a lion tamer.

Part of the West legend is that she saved Paramount from bankruptcy. Like most Hollywood legends, this one hardly stands up to critical analysis. *She Done Him Wrong* and *I'm No Angel* were box office successes, but their grosses were hardly enough to wipe out the millions that Paramount had lost—and was still losing—on its vast exhibition empire. Theaters were being closed all over the country. Prices were down to 35 cents top in many places. Dishes were being given away to attract customers. In one case, Paramount-Publix closed a deluxe house, taking a yearly loss of $187,000, because that was cheaper than trying to keep the place open.

Mae's success helped, but one must remember that Paramount was backed at this time by such box office champions as Gary Cooper, Carole Lombard, George Raft, Sylvia Sidney, rapidly rising Claudette Colbert, and Fredric March.

Carole Lombard made six films in 1932 and 1933, including *No One Man* (Lloyd Corrigan) with Ricardo Cortez and Paul Lukas; *No Man of Her Own* with Clark Gable; *From Hell to Heaven* (Erle C. Kenton) with Jack Oakie and David Manners; *Supernatural* (Victor Halperin) with Randolph Scott and old-timers H. B. Warner and William Farnum; *The*

Cary Grant was Lt. Pinkerton to Sylvia Sidney's Cho-cho-san in *Madame Butterfly. Copyright 1932 by Paramount-Publix Corp.*

Cary Grant, fresh from coming up to see Mae West sometime, joins Nancy Carroll in *The Woman Accused. Copyright 1933 by Paramount Productions Inc.*

Kent Taylor, Carole Lombard, and Charles Laughton were in
White Woman, a steamy tale of a singer who married a sadistic Malaysian planter. *Copyright 1933 by Paramount Productions Inc.*

Nero fed Christian virgins to lions. The more imaginative Cecil B. DeMille tied them to statues and turned gorillas loose. All of which proves that DeMille in *The Sign of the Cross* was the better showman of the two. *Copyright 1932 by Paramount-Publix Corp.*

Eagle and the Hawk (Stuart Walker) with Fredric March, Cary Grant, and Jack Oakie; and *White Woman,* a steamy tropic triangle with Charles Laughton and Charles Bickford. The ex-Jane Peters was doing her part to lift the Paramount mortgage.

With all due respect to the drawing power of Gary Cooper (in *A Farewell to Arms* with Helen Hayes), Carole Lombard, Mae West, George Raft, Cary Grant, and Fredric March, the greatest asset Paramount acquired in the beginning of the decade was the return of Cecil B. DeMille. In the long haul, DeMille's spectacles, with their interminable reissues, made more money for Paramount than did any star. This must be weighed against the value of the dollar at the time of release and not judged in light of today's inflated dollar.

It surprises a lot of people to learn that Mae West made only 12 pictures in her entire career, stretching from 1932 to 1978. Eight of these were for Paramount, one of which was a minor supporting role.

Money from DeMille, on the other hand, still rolls in. He had tough sledding after leaving Paramount in 1925. He made some fair pictures but had distribution difficulties with Fox, Loewe, and Paramount controling so many theaters. Sound finished his Producers Distributing Corporation. Then he went to MGM for three pictures. Both he and MGM were delighted to end the association.

B. P. Schulberg was the genius who started the "bring back C. B." campaign. It was his last service to Paramount before he was ousted. There was considerable opposition to DeMille's return. In the end, it was Adolph Zukor who held open the door. To the corporate opposition, Zukor said quietly, "Mr. DeMille makes pictures that make money."

This was not entirely true. DeMille's final film for MGM, *The Squaw Man* (third version), lost $150,000. Perhaps Zukor also was influenced by DeMille's desire to refilm *The Sign of the Cross,* a favorite play of Zukor's in which William Farnum starred in 1914.

In any event, DeMille was given a one-picture contract to do *The Sign of the Cross*. Fredric March was to play Marcus Superbus. Charles Laughton was Nero, with Claudette Colbert as his vicious queen. Elissa Landi was the Christian girl Mercia, for whose love Marcus went to the lions.

Whatever other qualities DeMille may have had, humbleness was not one of them. Emanuel (Manny) Cohen, who had taken over as production chief upon the exit of B. P. Schulberg, thought his position entitled him to humbleness on the part of the hired help, of whom Mr. DeMille was one. He told DeMille, "Remember, Cecil, you are on trial with this picture!"

DeMille in his autobiography does not record his reply to this observation. DeMille only wrote, "Perhaps Manny Cohen found me a trial too."

DeMille knew that his career was on the line. It had been almost three years since he had had a hit. The worsening depression and company finances made it most likely that he could never again get financing for a spectacle if this one failed.

Even so, DeMille did not try to buy success with stars. As he had for ten years, he used only featured players, depending upon himself as the "star." In the ad for his movie, he was the only one billed above the title. While his cast all became stars, they were still to reach the top when they appeared in *The Sign of the Cross*.

As for March, his only really good picture to this time was *Dr. Jekyll and Mr. Hyde* for Rouben Mamoulian. Claudette Colbert had been around since *The Hole in the Wall* in 1929, but her career did not reach stardom until later when she made *It Happened One Night* on loan to Columbia and Frank Capra. Charles Laughton was still so little known that Manny Cohen objected to wasting the role of Nero on him.

It is doubtful if any picture before or since was so coldly and calculatingly built—built, not filmed— to bring in audiences. DeMille had to have a success,

and he put everything he had learned in 18 years about screening sex, sin, and religion into this crucial film.

The king of bathtub scenes topped himself in this one. He had Claudette Colbert take her beauty bath in a pool of asses' milk. To prove that her bath was really milk, DeMille had two kittens lapping at the "water." Sadistic torture scenes, involving more shapely women than men, added additional spice. This was spectacle in its most lurid form.

He added a particularly lascivious dance by Joyzelle Joiner in the face of strong objections from the Hays office. In the overall film, this scene was not really important. DeMille did not really care if he were forced to cut the scene; it was designed for controversial headlines, and he got them.

The film was premiered in December 1932 but did not go into general release until February 1933. There was not a worse time in the history of the film industry to launch an expensive film. The country was economically at a total standstill. A vengeful Democratic congress was balking every attempt of President Herbert Hoover to cope with the paralyzing depression. Then the new president, Franklin D. Roosevelt, took office on March 4, 1933. He immediately closed all banks in the country. No one could withdraw a cent while the banks were reorganized to stop the catastrophic failures that were going on.

Mary Pickford blamed the failure of her *Secrets* on the bank holiday. Dozens of other pictures also were screened to empty houses. But *The Sign of the Cross* was not one of them. DeMille claimed that patrons gave IOUs at the box office to get in to see this gaudy spectacle of sex and religion.

The Sign of the Cross, for all the scorn heaped upon it by DeMille-hating critics, was a Paramount milestone. It brought DeMille back into the Paramount fold. It proved that a movie could draw even in the worst of economic conditions—and the United States had never been in worse condition than it was in February and March of 1933. It was a morale builder for the company. Perhaps most important of all, it strengthened Adolph Zukor's hand against his corporate enemies.

Kay Francis, Miriam Hopkins, and Herbert Marshall make up the triangle in *Trouble in Paradise,* one of Ernst Lubitsch's most delightful comedies. *Copyright 1932 by Paramount-Publix Corp.*

There had been some eyebrows raised when federal judge William Bondy appointed Zukor in January 1933 as one of the two receivers in equity of Paramount-Publix. The other receiver in the bankruptcy action was Charles D. Hilles, a member of the Republican National Committee. Creditors protested, and the judge appointed a third receiver, C. E. Richardson of the Chase National Bank.

As protests against Zukor mounted, receipts from *The Sign of the Cross* were cited as an example of his business acumen. He was lauded as the best possible man to lead the company out of its troubles. And this was probably true.

At the same time the fight continued over the huge bonuses previously paid to Zukor, Kent, Katz, and Lasky in 1929. The resulting lawsuits and reduced payments hit the four hard. Lasky lost his New York property. He moved his family to a beachhouse he owned in California. Zukor turned his palatial estate on Long Island into a country club and golf course. Lawyers for the four men huddled in a desperate fight to keep their clients from losing everything they had. The four may have been personal enemies due to three of them being forced out of Paramount, but they were again partners in the law courts.

Most pictures were losing money. *The Sign of the Cross* and *She Done Him Wrong* bucked the trend. Even such a delightful picture as Lubitsch's *Trouble in Paradise* (1932), one of the classic sophisticated comedies, had a rough time drawing theater attendance. Many deserving pictures failed to return their negative costs. Exhibitors, fighting to keep open, cut prices. Some first-run pictures could be seen for a dime. Things got so bad that often homeless people who could afford the money spent an entire day in a movie house just to keep warm in the winter.

Corporate officers and their banker backers laid blame for the mess on the production units: movies cost too much. The solution to evaporating profits was to cut production costs. All the studios asked their contract personnel to take a 50 percent cut in salaries for eight weeks. When this time was up, most refused to increase the salaries back again.

Congress passed the National Recovery Act, which provided a code for each industry to work under. The motion picture code was written by studio lawyers and supported block booking, ceilings on salaries, and agreements to stop talent raids. The act was declared unconstitutional.

Union members struck, closing the studios. They reopened after the unions agreed to salary cuts. Involved in this was George Browne of the International Alliance of Theater Stage Employees and Moving Picture Machine Operators union (IATSE) which controlled the projectionists who showed films in the theaters and studios. Browne and this union would shortly be involved in more sinister activities affecting the big studios. This was action that would send one of the most prominent producers in Hollywood to prison as a sacrificial lamb for the others involved, including some Paramount people.

Bitterness piled on bitterness. Both stars and studio technicians complained that the studios were taking advantage of them. They filmed for 18 to 20 hours a day, and in between shooting they were pressed into costume fittings, publicity gimmicks, and tests. In 1931 Gary Cooper was in *I Take This Woman* with Carole Lombard during the day and shot *City Streets* with Sylvia Sidney at night.

Cooper only got out of the night-and-day work by becoming ill. Manny Cohen, the production chief, was a rather excitable person at best. He became even more excited when he learned that Cooper had not checked into a hospital at all. Instead he was "recuperating" with a European cruise in the company of an American heiress who had acquired an Italian title by marrying and divorcing a count.

Cohen was all for suspending Cooper. Zukor refused. Cooper's contract had only a year to run, and any trouble would surely drive him to another studio. William Powell, Ruth Chatterton, and Kay Francis had fled Paramount's serfdom as quickly as they could. Cooper, despite his popularity, was still getting only $750 a week. Cutting that off now would save the company little money while jeopardizing a multi-million dollar property. So Cooper was left alone to frolic with the Countess di Frasso.

This adventure reduced his 1932 films to *Devil and the Deep* with Tallulah Bankhead, *A Farewell to Arms* with Helen Hayes, and one of the segments of the all-star *If I Had a Million*.

If I Had a Million does not occupy a large spot in the history of films. Millionaire Richard Bennett was dying. His predatory relatives were assembled, eagerly awaiting the end. One child put a record on a phonograph, playing, "I'll Be Glad When You're Dead, You Rascal You," a popular country tune of the day. Bennett, looking down sourly on them, said, "He's the only honest one of the bunch. I should leave him the money." But instead he selected names from the telephone book, willing a million to each.

In Cooper's segment, Cooper, Roscoe Karns, and Jack Oakie are Marines in the guardhouse. Cooper, thinking his check is a joke, gambles it away.

The best segment of all was Charles Laughton as a cringing clerk whom the mobile camera follows through door after door as he shuffles up to the boss's sanctum. With no change of expression, Laughton delivers a glorious Bronx cheer and turns away in his same browbeaten, shuffling manner.

Manny Cohen worked his stars hard in 1933. Cooper made *One Sunday Afternoon*, which is about a dentist who wondered whether he chose the right woman. Fay Wray (King Kong's future love) and Frances Fuller were the women. Ernst Lubitsch gave his touch to *Design for Living*, a bastardization of Noel Coward's sexy comedy. Fredric March, Miriam Hopkins, and Edward Everett Horton were very good. Gary Cooper was somewhat out of place in a drawing-room comedy. Claudette Colbert was seen in *Tonight Is Ours, Three-Cornered Moon,* and *Torch Singer.* In addition, the studio got an extra pound of flesh by loaning her to United Artists for *I Cover the Waterfront,* a prostitute role that served her better than anything she did for Paramount that year.

Some other pictures of 1933 were *Sitting Pretty,* with Ginger Rogers and Jack Haley in his first screen appearance. Jack Oakie and Haley were songwriters who joined with lunch-wagon waitress Rogers to storm Hollywood.

Cary Grant got a better role than usual with Fredric March (the star), Jack Oakie, and Carole Lombard in *The Eagle and the Hawk.* Written by John Monk Saunders, the ill-fated author of *Wings,* it was about a pilot who goes to pieces because too many of his observers are killed. Why did the Germans only kill the observers instead of the pilot? Author Saunders and director Stuart Walker kept this as their personal

Paramount failed to see promise in Ginger Rogers and Jack Haley after using them in *Sitting Pretty,* and they drifted on to other studios. *Copyright 1933 by Paramount Productions Inc.*

secret. Anyway, March kills himself out of remorse, and Cary Grant conceals the suicide by taking the dead man up and crashing the plane to make it appear he died honorably.

A 1933 novelty was Charlotte Henry in *Alice in Wonderland,* with Gary Cooper, W. C. Fields, Edna May Oliver, Charles Ruggles, Ned Sparks, Cary Grant, Leon Errol, Edward Everett Horton, Richard Arlen, May Robson, Ethel Griffes, Jack Oakie, Raymond Hatton, Louise Fazenda, and Sterling Holloway masked as the various characters. Norman McLeod directed. It was not a success.

So many players got their start in the first years of the 1930s that it is not possible to mention them all. One who never climbed to the top, but who had a long career, was "Buster" Crabbe. Paramount nabbed him after Johnny Weissmuller made a hit in MGM's *Tarzan the Apeman* in 1932. Larry Crabbe was also an Olympic swimming champ. So he was put into *King of the Jungle.* It was not a bad picture as jungle epics go, but Kaspa the Lion Man did not replace the ape man. Crabbe went on to make 39 Paramount films, mostly Westerns. He is best remembered for his Universal serials about Buck Rogers and Flash Gordon. He also did a Tarzan serial.

As one looks back on 1933, it is surprising to note the number of good people Paramount let get away. Some, like Ginger Rogers and Jack Haley, had their talents overlooked. But there was no excuse for mishandling Jeanette MacDonald and Maurice Chevalier. They left Paramount to make *The Merry Widow* for MGM in 1934—with another Paramount fugitive, Ernst Lubitsch, directing. It was a smash hit.

Paramount was betting on Gary Cooper, Cary Grant, George Raft, Fredric March, and rising Bing Crosby, among the men. Carole Lombard, Miriam Hopkins, Sylvia Sidney, and Claudette Colbert were among the women. With the exception of Sidney, all these women wanted to end their Paramount serfdom.

W. C. Fields was making a return, but only as a supporting character. Dumped in 1928 after Lasky said, "That voice would drive patrons out of the theater," Fields had to prove himself in some Mack Sennett shorts before Paramount—nobody else would

Gary Cooper's good looks are hidden as The White Knight in
Alice in Wonderland. Charlotte Henry is Alice. *Copyright 1933 by
Paramount Productions Inc.*

touch him—began slipping him into films like *International House* and (in 1934) *Mrs. Wiggs of the Cabbage Patch.* Paramount can take no credit for the talkie development of Fields. He pulled himself up almost alone, never hampered but rarely helped.

The difficulty was that there was no strong head of production to keep things moving. Lasky and Schulberg were both extraordinarily good talent scouts, and both understood story values. Lasky particularly did not interfere too much with his producers. Once he approved the story and budget, he had sense enough to keep out of the way until he sat in judgment on the finished film. Schulberg—although he sometimes was blinded by his personal feelings—understood filmmaking and what the public wanted.

Immanuel Cohen, who succeeded Shulberg, came up from heading the newsreel and short subject division of Paramount. He did not have the background seasoning of Schulberg and Lasky. In addition, he had neither of these two masters' ability to handle people. Even more important, Cohen was shoved into the production chief job at a time when everyone was jittery. The bankers were in control. The company had filed for bankruptcy. Zukor was fighting for his professional life. Pressure was on everyone to cut costs and make money at a time when very few people were making money.

Uneasiness gripped everyone. It was clear that if Paramount could not work out its financial troubles, the entire studio might close. Even those with contracts were nervous in 1933.

Under the circumstances, Paramount was not interested in taking any chances. Neither was it interested in breaking new ground. New directors with expanding ideas like George Cukor and Rouben Mamoulian spent their brief time with Paramount and looked for more fertile pastures. The symbolism of Mamoulian excited critics, but the Paramount public was not interested in anything but the sexuality of the stars.

The result was that Paramount, with only a few exceptions, no longer provided the "best show in town." The trend of the day was to work screwball comedies, gangster films, and—reviving after a lull—musicals. Warner Brothers went in for heavy prestige films with the likes of George Arliss and Paul Muni. Paramount's idea of prestige was a DeMille spectacle. Warner Brothers also pioneered social problem pictures with *I Am a Fugitive from a Chain Gang.* Paramount rarely ventured into such fields. In the 1935 film *Private Worlds,* mental troubles were touched on but not deeply explored.

As if producers did not have troubles enough, they were hit in 1933 by a concentrated church drive that threatened what they thought was films' greatest asset—the rawest kind of sex possible.

The belief in the power of sex at the box office has always been deeply engrained in producer psychology. Despite the fact that Will Rogers, Janet Gaynor, and—coming up the following year—Shirley Temple topped all the others in ticket-selling ability, one could not convince Hollywood as a whole that sex was not an essential ingredient for a successful film.

But the creation of the National Legion of Decency in 1933 forced a cleanup for a while. The industry as a whole had taken a cynical view of the previous production code which emerged after the 1921-1922 scandals. For example, when Hayes asked DeMille what he intended to do about the salacious dance in *The Sign of the Cross,* the great man replied, "Not a damned thing!"

This time the matter was more serious. The Catholic church asked its members to avoid films that received an objectionable rating from the Legion of Decency. The industry might have ignored the Legion, but Jewish and Protestant groups also joined in the condemnation. A new production code was hastily drafted up, and members of the Motion Picture Producers and Distributors of America—and that included all the important ones—agreed to abide by the code.

Paramount was especially nervous. Three of its best drawing cards were tied to sex: Carole Lombard, Mae West, and Lubitsch, whose "touch" was sexual innuendo.

Mae's *I'm No Angel,* with Cary Grant again, was rushed into release before the code was implemented in 1934. Mae was a lion tamer in a circus. Publicity told how ferocious the animals were and how men with guns stood outside the cage when the brave actress went through her paces. One story said the "head Paramount trainer had an arm torn off by the lions before Miss West entered the cage." Paramount had no "head trainer." The lions were handled, and Mae was doubled by Mabel Stark, one of the great animal trainers. Mabel had put in ten years in Ringling's center ring. She also handled the tiger in the escape scene in *The Greatest Show on Earth* for DeMille. Mae did some publicity stills with the lions. That was all.

The censorship question was so unsettled that Zukor decided to hold Mae for a while. She had no release in 1934 at all. Carole Lombard was toned down by teaming her wth Bing Crosby, whose image was clean. In 1933 Bing made *College Humor* with Mary Carlisle and Richard Arlen. Now DeMille's old *Male and Female* (from Barrie's *The Admirable Crichton*) was dusted off, sliced up, and repatched to make *We're Not Dressing.* The butler hero who dominated DeMille's picture became a yacht deckhand who took over after the shipwreck.

Carole had been used to strong lovemaking in her pictures, but with the code looking over their shoulders, lovemaking was done by proxy. Bing sang "She Reminds Me of You" to a trained bear instead of

Carole. He got an acceptable rating for a rather amusing picture that also had Ethel Merman, Leon Errol, and Burns and Allen.

Bing had another mild hit in 1934 with Miriam Hopkins and Elliot Nugent. *She Loves Me Not* was the story of a chorus girl fleeing from the police. She hid in a college student's room. This hokum gave

Richard Arlen and Bing Crosby have difficulties over Mary Carlisle in *College Humor. Copyright 1933 by Paramount Productions Inc.*

the world Jack Benny's future identifying song "Love in Bloom."

Paramount was not really doing Crosby justice in these programmers that followed his first hit in *The Big Broadcast*. But he was rising fast in radio, and his airwave popularity carried him through until he hit his stride in 1936. After that he never looked back.

While Manny Cohen was struggling to turn out films with angry stars, sullen directors, and apprehensive technicians, Zukor continued to fight for his professional life. A refinancing plan was worked out with New York bankers and Floyd Odlum's Atlas Corporation that would take Paramount out of bankruptcy. However, Judge Alfred Coxe, who now had jurisdiction over the bankruptcy proceedings, refused to approve any reorganization until the claims against Zukor and the other Paramount directors were resolved. This was settled when Zukor, Eugene Zukor (his son), Jesse Lasky, Sam Katz, Sidney R. Kent, and Jules Brulatour jointly returned $2,125,000 of

their bonuses. Attorneys for angry shareholders charged that this was only a tenth of what should have been repaid. However, they chose not to challenge the settlement further in court. Brulatour was a Paramount director and for years held a monopoly granted by Eastman to sell raw film stock to the studios.

The bankruptcy receivership was lifted in 1934. The new directors changed the name from Paramount-Publix to Paramount Pictures, Inc. An outsider, John E. Otterson, was brought in as president. Otterson came from the electrical manufacturing business and knew absolutely nothing about motion pictures. He asked Zukor to stay as chairman of the board. Both men were voted an annual salary of $156,000. In addition Zukor was to have a share of the profits as a bonus.

Zukor had successfully weathered the storm, but not without many anxious months of worry. At one time he was so discouraged that he considered quitting. At this point he received encouragement from an unlikely source. Cecil B. DeMille, getting word of Zukor's wavering, made a hasty trip to New York. He made quite a dramatic plea to Zukor, pointing out that nobody else could save the company.

Nice college boys do not harbor fleeing choris girls in their rooms. Bing Crosby did not know that and so Miriam Hopkins found a place to hide from the police in *She Loves Me Not*. The song hit from this picture was "Love in Bloom." *Copyright 1934 by Paramount-Publix Corp*.

Paramount borrowed Shirley Temple from Fox for *Little Miss Marker*. Pinning up her panties is that prince of actors Adolphe Menjou. *Copyright 1934 by Paramount Productions Inc*.

202

Carole Lombard and Gary Cooper both were upstaged by Shirley
Temple in *Now and Forever. Copyright 1934 by Paramount Productions Inc.*

Zukor, buoyed by DeMille's dramatics, agreed to stay on. Later, after the flop of DeMille's *Four Frightened People,* there was a top level drive to sack C. B. once again. Zukor stood staunchly behind DeMille this time and for the rest of DeMille's life. Zukor was often a hard man in his business dealings, but he paid his debts.

Films kept rolling out. Shirley Temple scored her first big hit in *Little Miss Marker,* based on the Damon

Kathleen Howard is fearful of Fredric March in *Death Takes a Holiday. Copyright 1934 by Paramount Productions Inc.*

Runyon story of a man who pawned his little daughter to a bookie (Adolphe Menjou) as security for a bet. Shirley was also in Paramount's *Now and Forever* with Gary Cooper and Carole Lombard before returning to her home lot at Fox to go on to screen immortality as one of the most popular child stars in history.

Two very noteworthy films of 1934 were *Bolero* with George Raft and Carole Lombard and *Death Takes a Holiday* with Fredric March. *Bolero's* story was hardly anything to set the screen on fire. It drew its power entirely from the chemistry of its stars. It was a cinematic milestone for both of them. Ray Milland and Frances Drake also did well in secondary roles.

It was the story of a French miner who wanted to be a dancer. He finally makes Paris as partner for Frances Drake. Raoul (Raft) discards Frances, who is becoming too romantically insistent, and takes Helen (Lombard) as his new partner. They agree that

Despite a tragic ending, *Bolero* with Geroge Raft and Carole Lombard was a big hit. *Copyright 1934 by Paramount Productions Inc.*

it is all business—no romance. Then World War I breaks out. He refuses to join the army, which causes Helen to break up the act to marry Englishman Ray Milland. This causes Raft to join the service, and he emerges at the end of the war with a weakened heart. He opens his nightclub, determined to dance. On opening night his new partner, Sally Rand, is drunk. Lombard is in the audience and agrees to dance the Bolero with him. She tells him that this will be their last dance together, and it was, because he dies in his dressing room after it is over.

Death Takes a Holiday is the story of Death, who takes the form of a handsome prince to mingle with the living. He meets a mystic, Evelyn Venable. In the end, when his holiday ends, he wraps his cloak about her and takes her back with him.

Fantasy rarely holds up on the screen, but this one—at least to the audiences of 1934—carried well. Frederic March was superb, and Evelyn Venable also was good.

The reorganization was not working, and the Paramount board hired Joseph P. Kennedy (Father of the future President of the United States) to make a survey of the company. It took two months and cost Paramount $50,000 for Kennedy's opinion. Earlier Kennedy had headed FBO and had financed Gloria Swanson's attempt at independent production.

As a result of Kennedy's investigation, there was another drive on production waste. Otterson's contract as president of Paramount was paid off to the tune of $200,000, and Barney Balaban took over. He was of the Balaban and Katz group. This was notice to the world that Paramount intended to make pictures aimed at the exhibitor—commercial products.

Zukor remained as chairman of the board, but the exhibition side was in the driver's seat. First to fall under the new regime was Manny Cohen as head of production. In his place they chose a man completely unsuited for such a job, Ernst Lubitsch. Why they chose him and why he accepted is a mystery. Perhaps they thought he could give the Lubitsch "touch" to all Paramount pictures.

This was a laudable goal, but Lubitsch was an individual filmmaker, not an administrative production head. Like DeMille, Paramount's first director-general, Lubitsch wanted to make pictures himself, not supervise others.

Barney Balaban became president of Paramount in 1934. He was formerly with the Balaban and Katz theater interests.

12

When the Gangs Came to Hollywood

The production end of Paramount was in difficulty in 1934, despite some successful pictures. Stars and technicians felt that they were not participating in the general national recovery. The studio was not restoring salary cuts made in 1933 as fast as employees thought necessary. Exhibitors were complaining that business was not increasing as much as the national recovery indicated it should. They blamed this on the pictures being turned out. Producers were bitter over what they felt was unwarranted interference from both Manny Cohen and New York. Two years before, DeMille had tried to form a directors union. Now both the Screen Actors Guild and the Screen Directors Guild were coming into force, as former peons decided they could do battle with their studio masters. Although the public seems to have the idea that directors are the controlling force in a picture, this had not been true since the rise of the producer system in the early 1920s.

The producer was the important person, choosing stories and cast and exercising artistic control—unless the studio happened to have a strong production head—in which case (David O. Selznick is a prime example) the producer often became no more than a

flunky. Irving Thalberg at MGM was another production head who exercised total control. Manny Cohen, beset by enormous difficulties, tried to be the same at Paramount.

At this point Manny was moved out, and Ernest Lubitsch was tagged for the job of getting pictures produced. It did not take long for the New York office to see that this was a mistake. Lubitsch was a filmmaker, not a production head. However, his contract was for a year, and Zukor and his banker bosses sat back to make the best of things.

Lubitsch was one of the glories of Paramount in the first years of the sound era. His silent film with Emil Jannings, *The Patriot,* was hailed as a masterpiece. *Monte Carlo* (1930) started Jeanette MacDonald on her rise to fame. Critics still enthuse over the closing sequence where MacDonald sings "Beyond the Blue Horizon" to the accompaniment of clicking train wheels, flying background, and assorted railway noises and support.

Then his *Love Parade* (1929) and *The Smiling Lieutenant* (1931) carried Maurice Chevalier to his peak. *One Hour with You* (1932) did not match these two, but it again gave Chevalier the Lubitsch touch.

All these films were notable for both critical and public acclaim—something that did not happen often at Paramount. His next film, *The Man I Killed (Broken Lullaby)*, failed because it was a downbeat picture at a time the public wanted screwball comedy to lighten its misery.

Then Lubitsch was back in form with *Trouble in Paradise* (1932) with Miriam Hopkins, Kay Francis, Herbert Marshall, Charles Ruggles, Edward Everett

The Patriot, with Emil Jannings as the mad czar, was the first picture Ernst Lubitsch directed for Paramount. *Copyright 1928 by Paramount-Famous-Lasky.*

Horton, and C. Aubrey Smith. This really had the Lubitsch touch and was one of Lubitsch's own favorites among his many films.

Trouble in Paradise is the story of Herbert Marshall and Miriam Hopkins, who team up to rob wealthy widow Kay Francis. Marshall then becomes infatuated with the lovely widow. When Hopkins goes ahead with the fleecing, Marshall decides she is for him after all. Critic Richard Watts acknowledged that *Trouble in Paradise* was a "less than novel tale" but that Lubitsch "by his great gift for subtly amusing treatment of sex problems, transforms it into a brilliant excursion into cinema light comedy."

Lubitsch's next film for Paramount was the less than successful *Design for Living*. He then followed Maurice Chevalier to MGM where he made *The Merry Widow* in 1934. He returned to Paramount in 1935 to take over production and did not direct any films himself in that year.

In his autobiography, Zukor does not go into detail on what was wrong with Lubitsch as a production head. He said only, "But as it happened our Hollywood production was not satisfactory." After Joseph P. Kennedy gave his gloomy assessment of Paramount's future, Zukor wrote, "I volunteered to go to Hollywood and see what I could do."

So although Lubitsch was production head in name, the chairman of the board was overseeing his every move. DeMille said that Lubitsch's trouble was that he hated to deal with other directors. He was embarrassed when one would come to him with problems.

It appears that there was more to it than that. He just did not care about the bulk of the products, but when something interested him, he became too much involved. It has been reported that Frank Borzage's *Desire,* with Gary Cooper trying to reform jewel thief Marlene Dietrich, was one he took too much interest in. The final result had neither the Lubitsch touch nor the Borzage sentiment.

On other fronts George Raft moved steadily upward, although he was quarrelsome about his parts.

Despite Maurice Chevalier's sober expression, he is really *The Smiling Lieutenant* in this early Lubitsch film with Miriam Hopkins and George Barbier. *Copyright 1930 by Paramount-Famous Lasky.*

Gary Cooper had a flop after being loaned out to Samuel Goldwyn for *The Wedding Night,* but back home he had two triumphs in the year of 1935. One was *Lives of a Bengal Lancer,* in which he was a rebellious British soldier in India. This was followed by *Peter Ibbetson.* Both films were directed by Henry Hathaway. *Peter Ibbetson* was a remake of *Forever,* the the 1922 film with Wallace Reid and Elsie Ferguson.

After skipping 1934, Mae West was back with *Goin' to Town.* Originally called *It Ain't No sin,* the title and a considerable amount of the story were changed in deference to the Legion of Decency. Mae inherits a ranch from an admirer and embarks upon a high life that involves her with Ivan Lebedoff, a gigolo, and Paul Cavanaugh.

Crosby continued to climb in public fancy without producing anything this year to really account for

Bing Crosby is "the singing killer," but it all turns out to be a publicity fraud thought up by showboat captain W.C. Fields in *Mississippi. Copyright 1935 by Paramount Pictures Inc.*

it. *Mississippi,* with W. C. Fields and Joan Bennett, had Bing as a showboat singer billed by Fields as "The Singing Killer." This reputation alienated Joan, who succumbed to him when she found out it was not true at all.

Bing also made *Two for Tonight,* perhaps one of the worst Crosby pictures ever made. Charles Laughton was quite different from Edward Everett Horton in *Ruggles of Red Gap* but did well in his own way in this amusing story of the uncouth Westerner who won an English butler in a card game and brought him back to America. Mary Boland and Charlie Ruggles supported Laughton.

All in all 1935 was not Paramount's best year, and Zukor had reason for hurrying out to Hollywood. Despite Raft and Lombard in *Rhumba,* attempting to duplicate the successful *Bolero* and the films of Gary Grant, Claudette Colbert, and others, the historic event of 1935 was the appearance of a low budget Western produced by an old-timer named Harry Sherman. Sherman had had this property for some time but had been unable to get anyone to back him. History does not record whether it was an outgoing Manny Cohen, an interim Lubitsch, or an interfering Zukor who agreed that Paramount release Sherman's *Hop-A-Long Cassidy.*

The film had old-timer William Boyd—now called Bill Boyd—as the limping hero from Clarence E. Mulford's Western books. The movie was a surprising success, leading to a series that carried through to 1941. After that Sherman moved the series to another studio. Then Boyd added five extra pictures of his own, moved to TV, and became a Western legend.

Some pictures released in 1936 were *Valiant Is the Word for Carrie* with Gladys George, *The Texas Rangers* with Fred MacMurray, and DeMille's *The Plainsman* with Jean Arthur and Gary Cooper as Calamity Jane and Wild Bill Hickok. The latter was about as far from the actual characters as Hollywood casting can get. But it was a success, as most of DeMille's pictures were. Bing and Ethel Merman made a hit of *Anything Goes.* Bing added to his popularity with another good one in *Rhythm on the Range* with rustic comedian Bob Burns, who would go on to become a minor asset to Paramount. Also debuting was Martha Raye, whose delightful comedy would brighten many dull pictures in the years to come.

Charles Laughton took the Edward Everett Horton role in the
remake of *Ruggles of Red Gap* with Charles Ruggles and Mary
Boland. *Copyright 1935 by Paramount Pictures Inc.*

Ethel Merman turns Chinese for a production number in *Anything Goes. Copyright 1935 by Paramount Pictures Inc.*

Publicity man Bing Crosby had troubles with pineapple queen
Shirley Ross in *Waikiki Wedding,* but it made money and pro-
duced two lovely songs, "Blue Hawaii" and "Sweet Leilani."
Copyright 1937 by Paramount Pictures Inc.

Martha and Bob would also highlight Bing's *Waikiki Wedding* the following year.

From the standpoint of future profit, the big star news at Paramount in 1936 came from a rather ridiculous story about an aviator who crashed in the jungle and met a *Jungle Princess*. The aviator was Ray Milland, an English gentleman who had labored rather fruitlessly in the Hollywood vineyard for several years. The girl was Dorothy Lamour, who taught the world how to pronounce the word sarong with a proper leer. As the popular joke of the day went, "What's sarong with Dotty?" There was nothing wrong at the box office, and both Milland and the sarong girl went on to cinema glory. Milland eventually became an Academy Award winner, and Dorothy went down a lot of "roads" with Bing and Bob Hope.

The Jungle Princess in 1936 introduced the famed Sarong Girl, Dorothy Lamour. Ray Milland was the wrecked aviator who found her. *Copyright 1936 by Paramount Pictures Inc.*

The big story, however, was not on the screens. It was being played in the executive suites of the big movie moguls. The gangsters whom the films had idealized on the screen came to Hollywood. Soon large sums of money were being carried around in brown bags, and cold-eyed men from Chicago called the turns.

It all began in Chicago in the depression years. George Browne and Willie Bioff gained control of a union that governed projectionists in Chicago theaters. They shook down Balaban and Katz (the future Paramount theater chain) for $20,000 to keep labor troubles from closing the chain's theaters.

Unfortunately Willie bragged about the shakedown to a woman he was involved with. He was overheard by a gentleman who reported to Frank Nitti, Al Capone's successor in the Chicago underworld. Nitti moved in. Browne and Bioff would continue to handle business, but they would get only one-third while Nitti would get two-thirds.

With Nitti supporting them, Brown and Bioff expanded their racket. By 1936 they were strong enough to demand $1 million from Metro-Goldwyn-Mayer to prevent closing down the studio with a strike. Bioff had become a very important person indeed. However, the million demand was a bluff. Bioff settled for $75,000. This was put up by different companies to avoid an industrywide strike. Paramount was one of them. Barney Balban had had experience with Bioff in Chicago and did not try to fight him.

Bioff grew increasingly arrogant. He demanded to be made film agent for the studios, drawing a $150,000 commission for his work. Once a Paramount gateman refused to let him enter the studio. Enraged at the slight, Bioff called off negotiations for a contract and threatened to close the studio.

Finally rumors of Bioff's shakedowns reached Westbrook Pegler, the Hearst columnist. Pegler's investigations sent Bioff to jail, broke the shakedown racket, and also brought a jail sentence for one of the producers involved in handing over the money. He was the fall guy for a lot of the others.

Also on the corporate level, Adolph Zukor—having gotten the studio running smoothly again—went back to New York. Y. Frank Freeman, who had been in theater exhibition in the southern part of the United States, took over as head of production. Freeman was not well liked, and his intelligence was maligned by some of Paramount's biggest names. However, he ran a tight ship, slick productions got filmed, and the company made money. Freeman and Balaban, the real ruler of Paramount, got along well because they both had exhibition backgrounds and made pictures for exhibitors—pictures cut and sewn with the box office as the primary goal. Prestige was left to MGM and Warner Brothers. Spectacle, except for DeMille, who had again become a law unto himself, was out.

Still, some very good pictures got made, although most of the first team who started the 1930s had gone. Claudette Colbert was still around, notably in *Bluebeard's Eighth Wife* (1938) with Gary Cooper and in Paramount's third remake of *Zaza* (1939). Bing Crosby, with newcomers Martha Raye and Bob Burns, had a solid hit in *Waikiki Wedding* (1937). Bing was a public relations man who had trouble with a pineapple queen contest winner (Shirley Ross). Bing, with great songs like *Sweet Leilani* and *Blue Hawaii,* and Raye and Burns carried the weak story. Mae West was still around, but her initial success was beginning to fade, and she would be gone before the end of the decade. Gary Cooper was now dividing his time between Paramount and Samuel Goldwyn.

This split assignment came about because Cooper made a verbal agreement to sign again with Paramount. Then Samuel Goldwyn came in with a better offer, and Cooper signed with him. Zukor, outraged, sued Goldwyn for $5 million for stealing Cooper. Considering how many stars Zukor had stolen, everyone thought his complaint odd. However, the two old enemies compromised instead of going to court. They agreed to divide Cooper's services between them.

Cooper's *Souls at Sea* with George Raft (1937) was only so-so. But the 1939 remake of *Beau Geste* was a solid hit. William Wellman practically duplicated

the 1926 Herbert Brenon film with Ronald Colman.

Both films followed the book's opening, a real attention grabber. A foreign legion detachment goes to aid beleaguered Fort Zinderneuf. They find the attacking Arabs gone. Legionnaires with pointed guns man the parapets, but all are dead and propped into position. A bugler is sent to climb the wall. They hear the sound of the bugler. Then the fort catches

In 1939 Paramount made *Zaza* for the third time. Claudette Colbert played the self-sacrificing French actress. Bert Lahr supported her. *Copyright 1939 by Paramount Pictures Inc.*

fire and he disappears. The film then flashes back to England to tell the romantic story.

The most important newcomer in the mid-1930s was Bob Hope, although nobody realized it then. He was picked up following his success in the stage musical *Roberta,* making a hit in *The Big Broadcast of 1938.* It took something to stand out in a picture that had Martha Raye, W. C. Fields, Dorothy Lamour, and other stars.

It seems that two ships were racing across the Atlantic. Hope is a radio announcer who is supposed to do a daily broadcast on the progress. His life is complicated by three ex-wives who have followed him because he is in arrears on their alimony. The rest is sort of confused. W. C. Fields sabotages the ship. Leif Ericson fixes it and wins Lamour. Martha Raye, considered a jinx, is thrown overboard, and Hope has to settle for his ex-wife Shirley Ross. Shirley and Bob reprise their early marriage in the song

"Thanks for the Memory," which has been identified with Hope ever since.

Paramount really did not know what to do with him. So he was reteamed with Shirley Ross in *Thanks for the Memory* (1938) and then with Paulette Goddard, who had been signed on the basis of her extraordinary publicity as Charlie Chaplin's maybe-and-maybe-not wife stories which aroused so much public interest.

At the end of the decade, the stars that began the 1930s were gone—Fredric March, William Powell, Ruth Chatterton, Buddy Rogers, Nancy Carroll, Miriam Hopkins, Marlene Dietrich, Richard Dix, Mae West, George Raft, and Gary Cooper (who was only half gone). Only Bing Crosby and Claudette Colbert, of the top names, were still around.

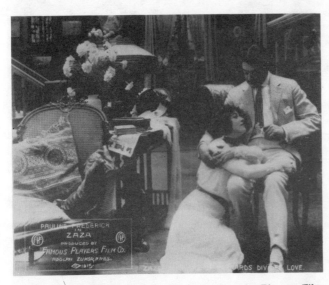

The first *Zaza* was made by Zukor's Famous Players Film Company in 1915. Pauline Frederick is Zaza and Julian L'Estrange is Bernard.

Gloria Swanson is *Zaza* in Allan Dwan's 1923 version for Paramount. *Copyright 1923 by Famous Players-Lasky Corp.*

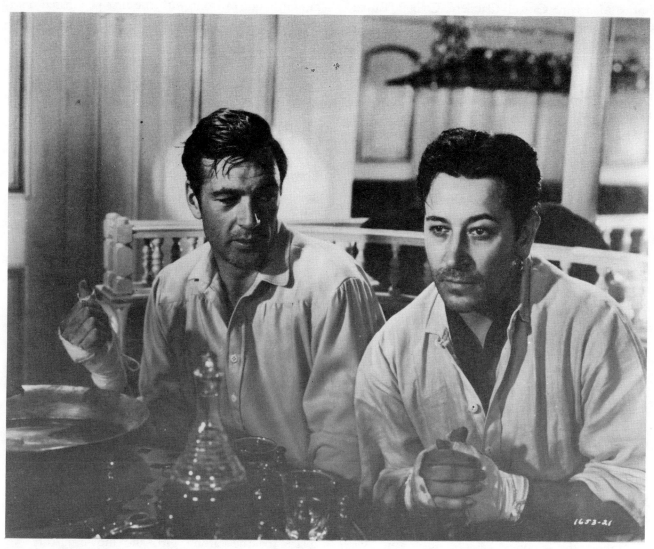

Raft, unhappy with his scripts, was closing his Paramount career
when he made *Souls at Sea* with Gary Cooper in 1937. *Copyright
1937 by Paramount Pictures Inc.*

Who were the replacements? The 1939–1940 press campaign book listed these names as "the freshest box office personalities: Eddie (Rochester) Anderson, Fay Bainter, George Bancroft, Jack Benny, Mary Boland, Bill Boyd, Olympe Bradna, Joe E. Brown, Bob Burns, Madelaine Carroll, Claudette Colbert, Ronald Colman, Gary Cooper, Jackie Cooper, Bing Crosby, Andy Devine, Melvyn Douglas, Leif Erikson, Doug Fairbanks, Jr., Frances Farmer, Preston Foster, William Frawley, Will Fyffe, Paulette Goddard, Tito Guizar, Bob Hope, John Howard, Allan Jones, Dorothy Lamour, Charles Laughton, Margaret Lockwood, Ida Lupino, Fred MacMurray, Ray Milland, Isa Miranda, Victor Moore, J. Carrol Naish, Lloyd Nolan, Pat O'Brien, Donald O'Conner, Lynne Overman, Elizabeth Patterson, Anthony Quinn, Martha Raye, Shirley Ross, Charles Ruggles, Akim Tamiroff, and Roland Young.

The majority of these were supporting players. Bancroft had long since ceased to be a star. Among the few real stars, Ronald Colman was around for only two films, *If I Were King* (1938) and *The Light That Failed* (1940). Cooper was no longer an exclusive Paramount star. During the 1940s he wandered in and out, generally for an occasional DeMille epic. DeMille now favored stars in his pictures.

While Y. Frank Freeman was production chief, the actual production direction was done by a string of managers, none of whom survived long. For the 1939–1940 season, it was William LeBaron, who returned after some years at RKO. In announcing the new season, LeBaron said, "I do not believe that any producing company in picture history has so completely and carefully used the knowledge and advice of exhibitors and salesmen to construct its program as Paramount has this year."

Among the pictures he promised were *Royal Canadian Mounted Police* (which became *The North West Mounted Police* when DeMille got through with it); *Jamaica Inn,* filmed in England by Alfred Hitchcock, with Charles Laughton as the squire who lead a cutthroat smuggling gang; and *Disputed Passage* with Dorothy Lamour as a half-caste girl. It was said that Paramount hired Anna May Wong to teach Dotty how to act like a Chinese. They would have done much better to have hired Anna May to play the part.

As a sinister peek at the future, the announcement lauded "*World on Parade* (tentative title)—Television is hot news this year. No longer a dream, but a reality, with tremendous public interest aroused, television now becomes excellent material for films. And Paramount is out in front with the first play based on a television plot!" The film finally was released as *The Television Spy.*

Bob Hope and the "much publicized Paulette Goddard," as Paramount's campaign book called her, were set for *The Cat and the Canary,* a remake of the Paul Leni 1927 Universal film with Laura La Plante and Creighton Hale. But the gem—the only one, incidentaly—in the entire announced lineup was *The Road to Singapore.*

When the sales convention was held, no one had any idea what this picture would be about. So the publicity department just said: "Ever since *Waikiki Wedding* tore the roof off box office records, the field has been clamoring for Bing in another picture with a South Seas background. And here it is! Bing sings in the crossroads of the world, with all its fascinating atmosphere. Teamed with Bing in this picture are Dorothy Lamour and Bob Hope, making a new, terrific box office trio."

The only true statement here is the final one. They did make a terrific box office trio. Bing did not sing in the crossroads of the world, as Singapore was called. They never got there. A lot of people have claimed credit for the idea of teaming these three, but it appears that Y. Frank Freeman was the genius. It seems that he saw Crosby and Hope together at a benefit and said, "The boys work well together. Why don't we team them?"

An old script about two wanderers was dusted off, tailored a bit to fit Bing's personality and to make a place for the sarong girl, and movie history was made—along with an enormous amount of dividends for the Paramount shareholders. The critics sneered at the story, blasted Bing, were snuffy about Dotty, and were noncommittal about Bob. But the box office called it a triumph.

Some very fine pictures were released in 1940 by various studios, including *Grapes of Wrath, The Bank Dick, Fantasia, Rebecca, The Great Dictator,* and others, but none have continued to pop up on late night television so often as *The Road to Singapore.*

If I Were King brought Ronald Colman back to Paramount for the first time since he made *Beau Geste* in 1926. Frances Dee supported Colman in this well known story. *Copyright 1938 by Paramount Pictures Inc.*

The year 1941 was the last before America went to war. It was a vintage year for films—but mostly for other studios, who gave us *How Green Was My Valley*, *The Little Foxes*, *Sergeant York*, *High Sierra*, and *Citizen Kane*, among others.

From Paramount we got *Nothing But the Truth*, the Bob Hope, Paulette Goddard remake of the old Richard Dix film; *The Road to Zanzibar*, which got Hope and Crosby tangled up with Dorothy Lamour

Charles Laughton was properly evil in *Jamaica Inn*. This film, which starred Maureen O'Hara, was filmed in England by Alfred Hitchcock. *Copyright 1939 by Paramount Pictures Inc.*

again; Eva Gabor and Richard Arlen in *Forced Landing;* Mary Martin, Oscar Levant, and Don Ameche in *Kiss the Boys Goodby*, which spoofed the search for *Scarlett O'Hara; and Lamour in Aloma of the South Seas*, a remake of the 1926 Maurice Tourneur film with Gilda Gray and Warner Baxter.

Definitely on the plus side for Paramount, Mitchell Leisen made *I Wanted Wings*, based upon the book by Bierne Lay, Jr., about learning to fly. It gave a career boost to William Holden, Ray Milland, and Constance Moore and introduced Veronica Lake in her first real part. Lake's trademark was her long blonde hair that fell enticingly over one eye. Leisen found her rather difficult during the filming of *I Wanted Wings*, and at one point she walked off the set. She also feuded with Constance Moore.

After the shaking experiences with Pola Negri and Gloria Swanson, Paramount developed a policy to dump temperamental actresses. But Arthur Hornblow, Jr., the producer, smoothed things over. Veronica went on to become a minor Hollywood legend.

Most brilliant of the new crop was Preston Sturges, who flashed like a rocket through Hollywood in the early forties and then quickly burned out. Sturges was restless after serving in World War I, like so many servicemen. Slender, mustachioed, and intense, he might have become an actor. Instead, he tried writing songs. Then he authored a hit play which brought him to Hollywood as a writer. He did *The Big Pond* script for Chevalier in 1930 and wrote others for directors William K. Howard, Rouben Mamoulian, and Mitchell Leisen.

Then he persuaded LeBaron to let him both write and direct. His first hit was a political satire, *The Great McGinty*, with Brian Donlevy and Muriel Angelus (1940). He followed it with *Christmas in July* (1941), in which a couple win a raffle. Then he really hit with the classic comedy *The Lady Eve* (1941). This film brought everlasting glory to Barbara Stanwyck and Henry Fonda.

Reduced to a plot outline, *The Lady Eve* does not show its brilliance. Barbara Stanwyck and her father, Handsome Harry (Charles Coburn), are cardsharps

Big screen TV was still science fiction when Paramount released *Television Spy* in 1939. Judith Barrett, Will Henry, and William Collier Jr. were in the cast. Anthony Quinn is the man in boots on the simulated TV screen. *Copyright 1939 by Paramount Pictures Inc.*

on an ocean liner. They set out to take rich, innocent Henry Fonda to the cleaners. Later disguising herself as Lady Eve, Stanwyck pursues Fonda to his estate in Connecticut, where she lands him. The dialogue, situations, and acting dovetailed so beautifully that what emerged is one of those rare pictures that everyone seemed to like.

Then in March 1942, the moviegoers got another and most unlikely hero, Alan Ladd. Quiet, cold, and hard–appearing, Ladd had been around Hollywood since 1932 without achieving any real foothold. Then Sue Carol, former star turned agent, took an interest in him that became personal as well as professional. A determined woman, Sue pushed her "Laddie" into stardom. It came with a bang in Frank Tuttle's *This Gun for Hire*. Ladd was Raven, a psychotic killer, who commits a murder for hire and then is double–crossed by being paid in counterfeit bills. In the course of

seeking revenge, he encounters Veronica Lake, and a new romantic team was born.

World War II, which involved America with the bombing of Pearl Harbor in December 1941, was good to Hollywood. While the studios had to face some shortages, the need for motion pictures to relieve the boredom of restricted life, both on the homefront and in the Army camps, caused Washington, DC, to look kindly on priorities for the movie industry. Paramount was fortunate in having leading stars who were mainly draft exempt. While the people of the starred mountain made an occasional film like John Farrow's *Wake Island* (1942) with Brian Donlevy, Robert Preston, Walter Abel, and Albert Dekker, mostly Paramount went in for pure escapism. Considering the times, this was all for the best.

Paramount's contributions to the war effort included *Caught in the Draft* (1941) with Bob Hope,

The road epics of Hope and Crosby began with *The Road to Singapore* in 1940, a milestone for the two actors and co-star Dorothy Lamour. Y. Frank Freeman is credited with inspiring this casting. *Copyright 1940 by Paramount Pictures Inc.*

Mary Martin from the New York stage was in Clare Boothe Luce's *Kiss the Boys Goodby*, directed by Victor Schertzinger. *Copyright 1941 by Paramount Pictures Inc.*

Dorothy Lamour starred in the 1941 remake on *Aloma of the South Seas*. Gilda Gray, the shimmy dancer, was in the first version in 1926. *Copyright 1941 by Paramount Pictures Inc.*

William Holden, Veronica Lake, Ray Milland, and Constance Moore were in Mitchell Leisen's *I Wanted Wings. Copyright 1941 by Paramount Pictures Inc.*

Lynne Overman, Eddie Bracken, and Dorothy Lamour; *True to the Army* (1942) with Judy Canova, Jerry Colona, and Allan Jones in the usual military comedy; *Priorities on Parade* (1942), a musical (or at least it was supposed to be); *I Love a Soldier* (1944), with Sonny Tufts and Paulette Goddard; and others of like caliber.

One of the better escape films was George Marshall's *Star Spangled Rhythm*. Marshall was a genuine old-timer, starting as an actor in 1912 and becoming a director in 1914. In his 57 active years in pictures, he never made a great picture, but he was always entertaining. He is best remembered for *Destry Rides Again* at Universal in 1939—a film that put Marlene Dietrich back in business after her career had been slaughtered by Paramount.

Star Spangled Rhythm had Victor Moore as a Paramount gateman whose sailor son, Eddie Bracken, thought he ran the studio. A crisis ensues when Bracken brings some sailor friends to visit. The plot then edges close to the basic idea of *Lady for a Day*. Betty Hutton arranges for Victor Moore to pose as the studio chief. When he protests that he does not know how, he is advised to answer every query with, "It stinks!" Then along came DeMille who asks what Moore thought of "my new picture, *Reap the Wild Wind?*" Moore mumbles, "It stinks!"

It all works out, however, and the studio sends down everybody who was loose to put on a grand finale show at the sailors' base. With practically everybody on the contract list present, the best thing in the show section was Paulette Goddard, Dorothy Lamour, and Veronica Lake singing "A Sweater, a Sarong, and a Peekaboo Bang." It was not these three sex symbols that brought down the house, but a replay of the song with Walter Catlett, Sterling Holloway, and Arthur Treacher taking the places of the girls.

Paulette Goddard, Dorothy Lamour, and Veronica Lake display their major talents in the "A Sweater, a Sarong, and a Peekaboo Bang" number in *Star Spangled Rhythm*. *Copyright 1942 by Paramount Pictures Inc.*

Preston Sturges' *The Lady Eve* is one of the classic film comedies. Charles Coburn, Barbara Stanwyck, and Henry Fonda gave splendid performances. *Copyright 1941 by Paramount Pictures Inc.*

Bing Crosby, Fred Astaire, Marjorie Reynolds, and Virginia Dale make *Holiday Inn* a memorable film. Bing introduced "White Christmas" in this picture. *Copyright 1942 by Paramount Pictures Inc.*

226

In the course of the flood of junk, some very good pictures got made—and most of these completely ignored the war. *So Proudly We Hail,* directed by Mark Sandrich in 1943, was an exception. It was the story of Army nurses in the Philippines during the Japanese attack. In this grim story, Veronica Lake sacrifices her life to try to permit the other nurses to escape.

Whispers from the set, however, claimed that Lake was not so cooperative with her co-stars, Paulette Goddard and Claudette Colbert. Hearing rumors of friction, a columnist asked Veronica how she got on with the other two. She replied that she liked Paulette best. "She is nearer my own age," she said. Rumors that Colbert detested Lake changed to a certainty after this.

The three stars who emerged as the best at the box office in the war years were Bing Crosby, Barbara Stanwyck, and Ray Milland. These were definitely Crosby's best years. *The Road to Zanzibar* and *The Road to Morocco,* with Hope and Lamour, were the usual farces, but *Going My Way* (1944) brought Crosby an Academy Award. The role of the young priest sent to aid an older one, Barry Fitzgerald, was ideal for Crosby, and Leo McCarey drew an exceptional performance from him.

Bing's greatest contribution to the war was *Holiday Inn,* directed by Mark Sandrich (1942). In it Crosby owned a night club which he only opened on holidays. The plot, with Crosby and Astaire rivals for Marjorie Reynolds, should be familiar to everyone, because it is revived each Christmas on TV. The punch for war audiences was Bing singing "White Christmas" in the December production number. Seen today, it is still a pleasant sequence. However, it is impossible for those who were not there in 1942–1943 to realize the emotional impact this had upon the audiences of the time. Those were the darkest days of the war. The outcome was still very much in doubt. Families were being ripped apart. Any moment a telegram might arrive that a loved one had been killed in the Pacific or European fronts. Thousands of young men were stuck in miserable places around the world. When Bing sang that he would be home for Christmas "if only in my dreams," he echoed the thoughts of everyone who was away from home. He also echoed the hopes and fears of the people left behind. Few movie sequences before or after expressed the hungers of so many people the way this did. The song itself sold 30 million records for Bing.

These were great years for Ray Milland, too. He had a hit in *The Major and the Minor,* Billy Wilder's first American film. (He codirected one film in Germany in 1934.) This was a lighthearted comedy in which Ginger Rogers poses as a child to save money on a train ticket. She becomes involved with Milland, a nearsighted major who runs a boy's military academy.

But it was Milland's performance in *The Lost Weekend* (1945) that proved he was more than a light comedian. Although a depressing tale of the miseries of an alcoholic, the picture was enormously successful. Milland richly deserved his Academy Award.

Wilder had been a scriptwriter in Germany. After coming to the United States, he joined Charles

Ray Milland gave an Academy Award performance in Billy Wilder's *The Lost Weekend. Copyright 1945 by Paramount Pictures Inc.*

Brackett as a writing team before becoming a director. After *The Major and the Minor*, he made *Five Graves to Cairo* (1944) in which Erich von Stroheim gave a highly regarded interpretation of what he thought Erich Rommel, the German panzer general, was like.

Wilder also directed *Double Indemnity*, based on the novel by hard-boiled author James M. Cain. In *Double Indemnity* Barbara Stanwyck took her place with the best screen actresses of that or any other time. Fred MacMurray, her co-star, showed that he had come a long way from the sax player in a band that he once was. In the weak insurance salesman who succumbs to the murderous entreaty of Stanwyck there is no resemblence to the bright young man we saw in *The Princess Comes Across* with Carole Lombard, *Coconut Grove* with Harriet Hilliard, and the fine *Trail of the Lonesome Pine*. MacMurray was revealed as a genuine actor of the finest caliber.

Barbara Stanwyck and Fred MacMurray were excellent in *Double Indemnity*, James M. Cain's hard-boiled novel of a murderous woman and a weak man. *Copyright 1944 by Paramount Pictures Inc.*

Harriet Hilliard was with Fred MacMurray in *Coconut Grove. Copyright 1938 by Paramount Pictures Inc.*

Stanwyck plays a vicious woman who seduces an insurance man into murdering her husband for his double indemnity insurance. Then things go wrong, and their growing desperation is beautifully brought out. The character contrast between Stanwyck, MacMurray, and Edward G. Robinson, as the insurance investigator, was superbly done by Wilder.

After this film and his next, *The Lost Weekend*, Billy Wilder took over from Preston Sturges as Paramount's resident genius. Sturges, erratic and often eccentric, reached his peak with *The Lady Eve*. After that he made *Sullivan's Travels* (1941), *The Palm Beach Story* (1942), *The Miracle of Morgan's Creek* (1944), *Hail the Conquering Hero* (1944), and *The Great Moment* (1946). Then he was through at Paramount, while Wilder would go on to make *A Foreign Affair* (1948) with Jean Arthur and Marlene Dietrich and *Sunset Boulevard* in 1950.

Barbara Stanwyck's reward for *Double Indemnity* was eight mediocre films for Warner Brothers, United Artists, and Paramount. Her Paramount films were *The Strange Love of Martha Ivers* (1946), with Lewis Milestone directing, and John Farrow's *California* (1946). She came back with a thunderclap in 1948, however, in Anatole Litvak's *Sorry, Wrong Number*. While some critics compared the film unfavorably to the radio drama (with Agnes Moorehead), no one faulted Stanwyck's performance as the hypochondriac wife who overhears a phone conversation plotting a murder. Burt Lancaster was good as the husband who wanted her dead.

As the decade closed, Stanwyck could look back on three outstanding performances: *The Lady Eve, Double Indemnity,* and *Sorry, Wrong Number*. Each part called for an entirely different characterization, and she came through splendidly. Looking back over her long career, we see that she played every kind of role from a teenage chorine to a worldly stripteaser to a 100-year-old woman in *The Great Man's Lady* (1942), and she was believable in every one of them—that is, an actress in every sense of the word.

The war ended in 1945, and exceptional movie business carried over into 1946, one of the best years financially in movie history to this time. Then trouble began. A studio strike tied up production. Great Britain slapped a 75 percent tax on foreign-made films. Rentals earned in France, Britain, and Japan were "blocked." This meant that money earned could not

The Trail of the Lonesome Pine, with Fred MacMurray and Sylvia Sidney, was the first outdoor picture made in the new Technicolor process. *Copyright 1936 by Paramount Pictures Inc.*

229

Barbara Stanwyck and Kirk Douglas were in Hal Wallis' production of *The Strange Love of Martha Ivers*. Copyright 1946 by *Paramount Pictures Inc.*

be exported to the United States but had to be spent in those countries.

Another calamity was the beginning of the communist witchhunt by the House Committee on Un-American Activities, which charged that communists had infiltrated the movie industry. This was to climax in the devastating McCarthy hearings of the early 1950s.

But worst of all for Paramount, the government resumed its antitrust actions to force separation of the production company and the theater division. Earlier in the decade, the government—after years of prodding by independents—outlawed block booking. This was a system under which an exhibitor was forced to take an entire block of films, sight unseen. This forced each theater owner or chain that was not a part of the studio's theater system to take a number of bad pictures in order to get the important ones.

The new law, however, did not do away with block booking entirely. It cut the number of films that could be included in a block to five. This the studios could live with, but the drive to divorce production and exhibition, forcing Paramount, RKO, and Fox to sell their theaters, would remove a sure market for studio films. The studios mounted a strong attack against the plan but lost when a final consent decree was signed in early 1951.

In the meantime, studio revenues dropped from a record in 1946 to a dismal situation in 1948. After the restriction of the war years, people were getting out more. Television was coming up fast and was being fought savagely by the movie industry. They refused to make films for the new medium, turned down offers to buy films, and threatened boycotts of actors and actresses who performed for the electronic media. Barney Balaban of Paramount was the sole executive in Hollywood who saw a future for TV. He bought a TV station in Chicago and later made Paramount the first major studio to set up a TV filming unit.

Despite the financial turndown, Paramount continued to turn out some good pictures as the decade came to an end—by good is meant financially successful. Among them were Cecil B. DeMille's sexy biblical epic *Samson and Delilah* with Victor Mature and Hedy Lamar; Fritz Lang's *Ministry of Fear* (1945) with Ray Milland as the bewildered man chased by Nazi spies who sought a film capsule hidden in a cake he bought; and *My Friend Irma*, based upon the Marie Wilson TV show, which introduced in 1949 the nightclub team of Jerry Lewis and Dean Martin. Shortly these two would become Paramount's biggest money-makers. Gary Cooper had an active decade, but only four films were at Paramount. These were *North West Mounted Police* (1940) for DeMille; *For Whom the Bell Tolls* (1943) for Sam Wood; *The Story of Dr. Wassell* (1944) for DeMille, which was as near to a failure as anything DeMille made after returning to Paramount; and *Unconquered,*

Burt Lancaster plots the death of Barbara Stanwyck in *Sorry, Wrong Number,* a film based upon a famous radio play. *Copyright 1948 by Paramount Pictures Inc.*

Ministry of Fear had Ray Milland and Marjorie Reynolds in conflict with a Nazi spy ring. Fritz Lang directed this thriller. *Copyright 1945 by Paramount Pictures Inc.*

another DeMille, in 1948. Bing, Bob and Dotty made *The Road to Rio* in 1948.

Two triumphs had Olivia DeHavilland as star. One was *To Each His Own,* which Mitch Leisen directed in 1946. The pure soap–opera plot had DeHavilland as the unwed mother whose lover, John Lund, is killed in World War I. She puts the child out for adoption. Then in World War II, the boy, now an American aviator, is in London. DeHavilland, not revealing their kinship, aids him in his romance with Virginia Welles. In the end, they are at a party, and Roland Culver–an old friend of DeHavilland–reveals the truth to Lund, who also plays the son, and Lund comes over to DeHavilland: "Mother, I think this is our dance."

A far better picture, but not as popular with the public, was *The Heiress,* directed by veteran William Wyler in 1949. The story was from Henry James' psychological novel *Washington Square.* The picture was beautifully mounted and superbly acted, catching the spirit of the 1890s beautifully.

Olivia is Catharine Stopper, the plain, unloved daughter of tyrannical Doctor Stopper, played by Ralph Richardson. Morris Townsend (Montgomery Clift) has run through his own money and sees this plain heiress as a means of recouping his shattered fortune. She is willing, but her father recognizes Clift for what he is, a fortune hunter. He threatens to dis-own her if she marries Clift. She does not care, but Clift does. He leaves.

Soon after, her father dies. She grows increasingly bitter. Miriam Hopkins accuses her of becoming hard. "Yes," she said, "I was taught by experts."

Seven years later, Clift returns. He begs forgive-ness and asks her to elope with him. She agrees, but when he comes for her, she has locked the door. She listens with a smile to his entreaties through the door. Then, taking her lamp, she goes up the stairs, pleased with her revenge.

Jerry Lewis shows Marie Wilson how he would play Groucho Marx in a bit of play on the *My Friend Irma* set. *Copyright 1949 by Paramount Pictures Inc.*

Olivia DeHavilland won her second Oscar for her role in *The Heiress*. Ralph Richardson played her stern father. Montgomery Clift, in the background, is her fortune hunting suitor. *Copyright 1949 by Paramount Pictures Inc.*

The big news on the production front was the transfer of Hal B. Wallis productions to Paramount at the close of 1946. Y. Frank Freeman had trouble keeping someone to oversee production. Buddy G. DeSylva, songwriter turned producer, stormed out in 1945. Wallis was offered the job, but turned it down. No one, it seemed, could get along with Y. Frank and Barney Balaban for long. Adolph Zukor, still chairman of the board, served only in an advisory capacity. Wallis moved his production unit to Paramount in 1946. Like DeMille, he operated independently, with Paramount exercising financial control.

Wallis came to Paramount with a remarkable production background. He started in Warner Brothers' publicity department in 1922, and after Darryl F. Zanuck quit in 1933, he became head of production, turning out the best films of Errol Flynn, Bette Davis, Paul Muni, and others. He gave up the production head job in 1944 and formed Hal B. Wallis Productions, which he soon moved to Paramount.

Wallis was responsible for bringing Burt Lancaster and Kirk Douglas to Paramount. Douglas had played some Broadway bits and summer stock when Lauren Bacall recommended him to Wallis. He played the weak man who let a domineering wife, Barbara Stanwyck, push him into a district attorney appointment and then into corruption in *The Strange Love of Martha Ivers*. After being loaned out a couple of times, he was back at Paramount in Wallis' *I Walk Alone*, in which he was teamed with Burt Lancaster.

Lancaster, a former circus acrobat, made his debut in Universal's *The Killers*. Then he came to Paramount for *Desert Fury*, which takes place in a desert gambling town. Lancaster was a young policeman in love with Lizabeth Scott, daughter of casino owner Mary Astor.

In *I Walk Alone* (1947), Lancaster and Douglas were rumrunners. When they are caught, Lancaster takes the rap. He returns after 14 years in prison to find Douglas running a nightclub. He expects his piece of the action, only to find Douglas is trying to kill him. With the help of Douglas' disillusioned girlfriend, Lizabeth Scott, Douglas is foiled.

Wallis had trouble with Douglas, who was released from his contract and did not return to Paramount until 1951. Lancaster, after some loan-out films, had the role of the murderous husband in Barbara Stanwyck's *Sorry, Wrong Number*. Here he showed a spark of the acting ability that would eventually lead him to an Oscar.

Hall Wallis joined Paramount as a producer in 1946. He is shown
here with director Curt Siodmak on the set of *The File on Thelma
Jordan. Copyright 1949 by Paramount Pictures Inc.*

13

The Desperate Decade

The big studios took a staggering blow in the final years of the 1940s. When Paramount lost control of its theater chain, it lost a large assured market for its films. Then television helped close a lot of other theaters, further reducing the film market. However, television was only one factor in reduced theater attendance. The Cold War in Europe and the need to rebuild war-shattered countries kept U.S. industry humming, except for an occasional, brief recession. People had money and were spending it on more sophisticated entertainment than movies.

But perhaps the most important factor of all in the decline of interest in films was that there was little in the films to pull the patrons in. On rare occasions, when the studios did turn out something the public wanted to see, there were returns to long lines at the box office.

Certainly C. B. DeMille had no trouble packing them in with his 1949 sex-and-religion epic, *Samson and Delilah*. Beefcaker Victor Mature was Samson, who fought lions single-handedly and pushed down temple columns. Hedy Lamar was a slinky Delilah. Together with DeMille, they may not have been biblical, but

they were certainly box office. One critic complained that "Samson got shorn, but the Bible got scalped."

Some fine pictures got made in 1950, such as Fox's *All About Eve*, Universal's *Harvey*, MGM's *The Asphalt Jungle*, United Artists' *The Men*, Columbia's *Born Yesterday*, and Paramount's *The Furies* with Barbara Stanwyck, Walter Huston, and Wendell Corey. But the one picture that is remembered above them all is *Sunset Boulevard*.

Why should *Sunset Boulevard* continue to be remembered over such decade films as *The Bridge on the River Kwai, On the Waterfront, Rebel Without a Cause, The Robe, From Here to Eternity*, and others? It may be because the picture seemed more real than all the others. And this was due entirely to the supreme artistry of Gloria Swanson.

The story was silly. A reigning star of the silent era lives in the reflections of her past glory. She is attended by a butler who was her former director and husband and has taken to herself a young and very bored writer as a gigolo. When her plans for a comeback are blasted and her lover leaves, she kills him. When the press and police arrive, her unbalanced

"Samson got shorn, but the Bible got scalped," one critic wrote about DeMille's *Samson and Delilah* with Victor Mature as the biblical strongman. *Copyright 1949 by Paramount Pictures Inc.*

mind goes back to the past, and she dramatically descends the steps every inch the queen of silent films.

The story by Charles Brackett and Billy Wilder, directed by Wilder, was totally artificial. There was never anybody on the Hollywood screen like the Norma Desmond of *Sunset Boulevard*, although Mae Murray in her last days did live in a dream world. The character is certainly not Gloria Swanson, but she has never been able to convince the world that it is not. When Norma Desmond said that she was still big and it was the movies that had gotten small, many who remembered the silent days were with her. Never before has such an artificial story carried such an air of realism. Wilder directed a triumph, but he probably could not have done it with any other star than Swanson. William Holden was good as the young writer, but Erich von Stroheim played a hammy role.

In 1951 George Stevens dusted off the old Von Sternberg film *An American Tragedy* under the remake title of *A Place in the Sun*. Montgomery Clift had the role of the boy who plots to drown his pregnant girlfriend (Shelley Winters) in order to marry a rich woman (Elizabeth Taylor).

The two films both followed the basic Theodore Dreiser story line, but there was more depth of characterization in the Stevens version. The picture was a definite career boost for its three stars. Raymond Burr was the prosecutor at the boy's trial, foreshadowing his long career in the courtroom as TV's Perry Mason.

The next year, 1952, brought back old favorites Bob Hope and Bing Crosby in *The Road to Bali* with Dorothy Lamour along as usual. This was the sixth of the popular road pictures. Like all the others, it made money, but Bing and Bob had been supplanted as Paramount's top comedy team. According to Adolph Zukor, Jerry Lewis and Dean Martin were Paramount's top grossers in the first half of the fifties.

Just why they were is hard to say. Lewis had an hysterical type of humor that grated on one's ears, and Martin was mediocre except when he sang. But the public liked them. The two continued to turn out picture after picture—with constant rumors of their jealousies and impending breakup. In 1953 they made *Scared Stiff*, based upon *The Ghost Breaker*, previously

made by H. B. Warner in 1914, Wallace Reid in 1922, and Bob Hope (with an "s" added to the title) in 1940. There was truth in the rumors of their disagreements, but they stuck together until 1956, when Martin pulled out to go his way alone. His first film away from Lewis was a flop, but Lewis had a solid hit in *The Delicate Delinquent* (1957).

The big studios were breaking up. Times were changing, but one thing remained unchanged: the

The argument here is for the film *The Stooge* (1953), but Dean Martin and Jerry Lewis carried their feud offscreen as well. *Copyright 1953 by Paramount Pictures Corp.*

Charlton Heston, Cornel Wilde, and James Stewart were among the cast of DeMille's *The Greatest Show on Earth,* a film that won the best picture Academy Award for 1952. *Copyright 1952 by Paramount Pictures Corp.*

institution known as Cecil B. DeMille. He produced in 1952 *The Greatest Show on Earth,* a film so monumental that even his critics were surprised into joining his side for a change. The cast included Cornell Wilde, Charlton Heston, James Stewart, Betty Hutton, Gloria Graham, Dorothy Lamour, and Julia Faye. Julia had a part in every DeMille picture since 1920.

In addition DeMille had the Ringling Bros. circus for background and Hopalong Cassidy Boyd as a bit player. Bing Crosby and Bob Hope were popcorn-eating spectators in the audience.

DeMille got complete cooperation from John Ringling North of the circus company. DeMille may have recalled the previous time he tried to get the Ringling circus for a film. This was in 1914 when Oscar Apfel made *The Circus Man* with Theodore Roberts. When Ringling representatives refused to let Apfel shoot on their lot, DeMille went down to argue with them. He was ignominiously put off the grounds and had to rent a broken-down, one-ring circus for Apfel.

Paramount's first circus picture was *The Circus Man* with Theodore Roberts and Florence Dagmar. DeMille had trouble getting the show's manager to cooperate with a lowly film company. *Copyright 1914 by Jesse L. Lasky Feature Play Co.*

Crosby's career was drawing to a close at Paramount. The old crooner was getting old. He did not draw as he once had. Also, his own production company coproduced, which further reduced Paramount's profits on his films.

Bing made *Riding High*. Frank Capra directed this remake in 1950 of his previous success *Broadway Bill*. Bing also made *Mr. Music* in 1950, *Here Comes the Groom* in 1951, and the *Road to Bali* in 1952. His only film for 1953 was the somber *Little Boy Lost* about a father who sought his lost son in France. Fortunately, in 1954 he joined with Danny Kaye and Rosemary Clooney in *White Christmas*, which put him back in the old groove. The film was a big grosser, probably riding in on the fame of the title song. But the critics pounded it heavily.

On the other hand, they were lavish in their praise of Bing's dramatics as the drunken star held up by the efforts of his self-sacrificing wife (Grace Kelly) in *The Country Girl* with William Holden. Crosby accepted the role of the alcoholic musical comedy star reluctantly but turned out a performance that rated him an Oscar nomination. (He lost to Marlon Brando.) While few will deny that he did an outstanding job of acting, he was not the Bing the public supported in past years.

He was back in character for *Anything Goes* (released in 1956) after a two-year absence from the screen. The only resemblance of this "remake" to the 1936 *Anything Goes* is the title. Mitzi Gaynor and Jeanmaire are the women. The ingredients were all there, but somehow the stew lacked flavor. And on this note Paramount and Crosby came to a parting of the ways. After 24 years, Crosby came down off the Paramount mountain.

His career was not finished by any means, but Paramount had now reached the point where it did not feel that the future warranted long-term starring contracts with expensive stars. The studio was moving more and more back to Hodkinson's original idea. Producers could put together packages, and Paramount

Bing Crosby (with Donald O'Connor) danced down the Paramount mountain for the last time in the 1956 remake of *Anything Goes*. This closed Crosby's 24 year career with the studio. *Copyright 1956 by Paramount Pictures Corp.*

Jane Russell and Roy Rogers join Bob Hope in *Son of Paleface*, a sequel to the highly successful *The Paleface* (1948). *Copyright 1952 by Paramount Pictures Corp.*

would finance them and make the releases. In this way ruinous overhead was sharply cut.

Bob Hope was still a draw, especially in films like *Son of Paleface*, sequel to *The Paleface* (1948), his most successful picture. He was again teamed with Jane Russell. Roy Rogers and his horse Trigger were thrown in for good measure. Hope did not do so well in biographical films such as *Beau James*, the story of ex-New York mayor Jimmy Walker, and *The Seven Little Foys*, based upon the life of Eddie Foy and his children. They were not the Hope character the public expected. He was more in character in *Son of Paleface* as the coward who teams with Roy Rogers to find a bandit, who turns out to be Jane Russell.

Falling box office receipts, government attacks on block booking, and theater ownership were major troubles of the 1950s. So were labor problems and the growing independence of stars. But the most worrisome matter was the resumption of attacks on Hollywood by the House Un-American Activities Committee and later by U.S. Senator Joseph McCarthy.

The attacks began in 1948 under committee chairman J. Parnell Thomas. In hearings in Hollywood, Thomas charged that communist sympathizers were inserting subversive propaganda into films. Frightened studios then issued the "Waldorf Statement," in which they pledged not to hire any person who was a member of the Communist Party.

Poor business, government regulation, labor troubles, and the star system were threats Hollywood had experience with and knew how to handle. The communist witch-hunt was something new and threw all the studios into a panic. Paramount, which took the beating in the 1921–1922 scandals, got off light this time. Under Balaban, Paramount had been almost entirely free of any concept beyond pure entertainment. With the exception of *Lost Weekend* in 1944, the company had found that films with social significance did not pay off at the box office.

The resumed hearings in 1951 were under Representative John Wood of Georgia. The previous hearing sent ten (the famous Hollywood Ten) Hollywood figures to jail for refusing to answer the committee's questions. Most of them were writers and directors. No top stars were involved, but the 1951 hearings brought an admission from Larry Parks (who had the lead in *The Jolson Story*) that he had been a party member. Then in April 1951, Edward Dmytryk, the director, who served a jail sentence as one of the Hollywood Ten, admitted that he had been a member of the Communist Party. This confession expiated him, and he went on to a long career. Dmytryk had been a Paramount editor in the early thirties. In 1964 he returned to direct *The Carpetbaggers*, Alan Ladd's last film.

Although not deeply involved, Paramount hastily took action to show its patriotism. A "message" picture was rushed out. It was *My Son John* (1952), directed by "safe" Leo McCarey. Helen Hayes was a

My Son John was made during the communist witchhunt. Here Robert Walker swears on a Bible to his mother Helen Hayes that he is not a communist. *Copyright 1952 by Paramount Pictures Corp.*

frantic mother who suspects her son, Robert Walker, of being a communist. The picture was sneered at by the critics and ignored by the public, but it served its purpose by showing which side Paramount was on. However, it would be a long time before Balaban would again okay another heavy message picture.

From a financial point of view he was certainly right. Paramount had just had an unpleasant financial experience with Billy Wilder's *Ace in the Hole*, a very uncharacteristic film for this able director. The story,

Ace in the Hole (retitled *The Big Carnival*) is an indictment of newspaper reporters and public morbidity. Kirk Douglas is the reporter willing to see a man die so he could get a good story. *Copyright 1951 by Paramount Pictures Corp.*

with Kirk Douglas, was suggested by the wild press coverage of the Floyd Collins tragedy in the 1920s. Collins had been trapped while exploring a cave and died when rescuers were unable to reach him. In Wilder's film, Douglas was a callous journalist who turned a similar situation into a carnival of morbid interest. It was a powerful indictment of both media irresponsibility and public fascination with the tragic misfortunes of others.

It was definitely not a Paramount-type picture, and it was approved by Freeman only because of Wilder's steady string of hits stretching almost ten years from *The Major and the Minor* to *Sunset Boulevard*. As could be expected from its theme, the picture bombed badly. It was recalled and reissued under a new title, *The Big Carnival*. This did not help either.

After this fiasco, Wilder got back in the groove with *Stalag 17* (1953) and *Sabrina* (1954). *Sabrina* had Audrey Hepburn and that fugitive from Warner Brothers' "tyrrany" Humphrey Bogart. Wilder, like most of the other talented people who got their start at Paramount, moved on to more fertile fields. This included such films as *The Seven-Year Itch*, *Witness for the Prosecution*, and *Irma La Douce*, all of which proved that Paramount needed Wilder more than Wilder needed Paramount.

Hal Wallis was the backbone of Paramount's film mill in these years. Wallis hedged his bets, offsetting *Come Back, Little Sheba* (1952) with Martin and Lewis in *Scared Stiff*. *Sheba* was a Prestige play by William Inge. Wallis brought Shirley Booth in to recreate her stage role of the aging wife who is driven into unreality by her middle-aged husband's drunkenness and impotence.

Burt Lancaster wanted the heavily dramatic role of the husband and argued with a doubtful Wallis about it. The critics thought him "inadequate." The role is a difficult one. When the couple take in a young and pretty boarder, Terry Moore, the sight of her and her boyfriend only increases Lancaster's dissatisfaction with his wife and causes him to drown his sexual inadequacy in more and more drink. Finally, in a drunken fit, he tries to kill his wife. When he recovers, he and Booth try to pick up the pieces of their shattered lives. She has been shocked into reality by his breakdown, and his feeling toward her seems renewed.

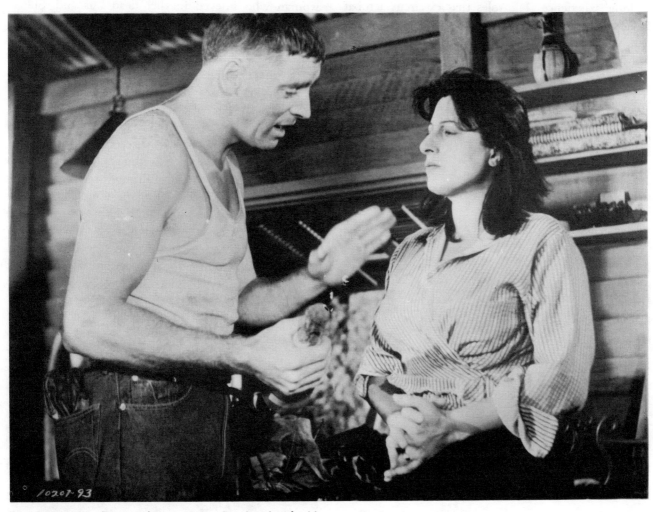

Burt Lancaster had matured as an actor when he played with
Anna Magnani in *The Rose Tattoo. Copyright 1955 by Paramount
Pictures Corp.*

Lancaster had shown great promise in his first film, *The Killers*, for Universal Studios. He did well as the murderous husband opposite Barbara Stanwyck in *Sorry, Wrong Number* (1948), but was still undeveloped as a dramatic actor. Good dramatic acting is the result of long experience. The roles that ex-circus acrobat Lancaster had been given between his better pictures hardly fitted him for the role of the tortured husband in *Sheba*.

Katharine Hepburn and Cameron Prud'Homme helped make *The Rainmaker* a success. *Copyright 1956 by Paramount Pictures Corp.*

Three years later, with more experience, he was better in *The Rose Tattoo*, which Daniel Mann directed for Hal Wallis in 1955. The film, based upon Tennessee Williams' play, starred Anna Magnani in her first American role. It was the story of an Italian-American woman who grieved for her dead husband. She is brought out of her sorrow by a lusty truckdriver (Lancaster), who by a coincidence also has a rose tattoo like her dead husband had. There was high critical praise for Lancaster in this role.

The following year he again played a man bringing light into the life of an unhappy woman when he teamed with Katharine Hepburn in another Hal Wallis production, *The Rainmaker*, directed by Joseph Anthony (1956). Lancaster is Starbuck, a con man, who promises to bring rain to a drought-stricken Kansas community for $100. This brings him into contact with Lizzie Curry, a plain spinster, whom he teaches to believe in her dreams. Katharine Hepburn, in her only Paramount film, was Lizzie. The role brought her another Oscar nomination and definitely proved that

Elvis Presley and Vic Morrow rough it up in *King Creole*. Jack Grimmage is in the background. *Copyright 1958 by Paramount Pictures Corp.*

Lancaster was an actor of the highest caliber. One test of an actor is versatility at playing different types of roles. One cannot hope to find such widely varying roles as Lancaster played in *The Rose Tattoo*, Columbia's *From Here to Eternity*, and *The Rainmaker* done any better.

Like a number of other stars of the 1950s, Lancaster wanted more artistic control–and money. He set up his own production company but did make one more film for Hal Wallis in 1957. This was the popular *Gunfight at the OK Corral* directed by John Sturges. He again teamed with Kirk Douglas. While it filled the theaters, critics compared it unfavorably to John Ford's version of the Earp-Clayton feud in *My Darling Clementine*.

Paramount's gradual rejection of the contract star system for reliance upon independent producers and free-lancers brought a number of famous people to the lot for a brief stop before they wandered on. Henry Fonda, along with Mel Ferrer and Audrey Hepburn, was in King Vidor's *War and Peace* (1956) and Anthony Mann's *Tin Star* (1957). William Holden, with Grace Kelly and Mickey Rooney, was in the Pearlberg-Seaton production of James Michener's novel *The Bridges at Toko-ri*, a story of Navy pilots in the Korean War. Then Hal Wallis presented the new singing sensation, swivel-hipped Elvis Presley in *King Creole*, based on Harold Robbins' *A Stone for Danny Fisher*.

Alfred Hitchcock, for the first time since *Jamaica Inn* in 1939, was back on the Paramount production roster. The picture was *Rear Window* (1954), a film worthy of the old master and its stars, James Stewart and Grace Kelly. It is the story of a photographer, confined to his room with a broken leg, who suspects a man he can see through a rear window as a wife murderer.

James Stewart also made *Strategic Air Command* in 1955 and an Alfred Hitchcock remake of *The Man Who Knew Too Much* in 1956. Then, after a two-year absence, Stewart returned to Paramount for Hitchcock's *Vertigo* in 1958 with Kim Novak. This was a curious, unbelievable story. Stewart plays a private detective hired to trail Tom Helmore's wife. He witnesses her suicidal fall from a tower and is crushed, because he has fallen in love with her. Then he sees another girl who reminds him of the dead girl (Kim Novak). Actually she is Kim. She had been hired to impersonate the dead woman so that her husband

could kill his wife in such a manner that the detective would be a witness to her "suicide."

Both Hitchcock and Novak came in for a critical ribbing on this one. However, Hitchcock was in rare form with his earlier Paramount release *To Catch a Thief* (1955) with Grace Kelly and Cary Grant, returning to Paramount for the first time since the 1930s. The story deals with a series of jewel robberies on the French Riviera. Suspicion falls on ex-burglar

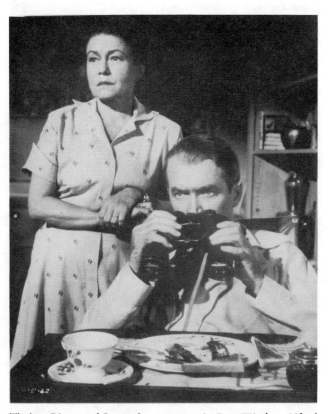

Thelma Ritter and James Stewart were in *Rear Window*, Alfred Hitchcock's first Paramount picture since 1939. *Copyright 1954 by Paramount Pictures Corp.*

Cary Grant, who must find the real thief to clear himself. In the course of doing this, he meets Grace Kelly, an American touring Europe with her rich mother. In light of today's permissiveness, it seems a trivial thing, but audiences in 1955 were delightfully shocked by the naughty double entendre Hitchcock introduced. Grace and Cary are having a picnic, complete with fried chicken. She asks if he wants a leg. He sighs and says that he would prefer a breast.

Vertigo had James Stewart and Kim Novak in one of Alfred Hitchcock's lesser efforts. *Copyright 1958 by Paramount Pictures Corp.*

Despite some very fine pictures, the 1950s were unfortunate years for the big studios. The old star system was breaking up. They tried to replace it with gimmicks. First came 3D, which promised the audience a lion in its lap. This phase died quickly because the need to use special glasses to unscramble the overlapping pictures and produce a three-dimensional effect caused eyestrain.

Next there was a rush to big screen effects, led by Fox's CinemaScope. Then came Cinerama, which used three projectors to envelop the audience in its screen image. Paramount was left at the starting gate in the big screen field, just as it was late in climbing on the talking picture bandwagon.

This was plain lack of foresight. Paramount had pioneered the wide screen effect in the 1920s, spending quite a bit on research. The Paramount system was introduced by Lasky at the premiere of *Old Ironsides*, the 1927 James Cruze film. It was a short sequence, but extremely dramatic, as the giant sailing ship completely filled the proscenium arch. After this demonstration, the system was rejected. Like the first Cinerama, it was not too sharp, and no one felt that it was needed. Regular films were filling the theaters. Why spend investment money on something that would not increase profits?

When it did reluctantly move into big screen films, Paramount turned away from CinemaScope, whose long frame was hard to compose when people were in the scene. Paramount's Panavision frame was higher and not so long.

While the big screen took its place in the industry, it was not the cure for box office troubles that the studios sought. Still believing that their troubles were caused by television rather than by pictures that bored audiences, the new trend was to those things which television could not give. Wide screen was the first step. The next was to fill the big screen with spectacle, something that was beyond TV both technically and financially.

This trend was right down Paramount's alley. Didn't the studio have the king of spectacle himself, Cecil B. DeMille? Those holding the corporate purse strings were now ready to listen when DeMille reintroduced an idea he wanted to do after *Samson and Delilah*. This was a spectacular remake of his 1923 triumph *The Ten Commandments*. Adolph Zukor no longer made the decisions, but his voice was loud in supporting DeMille,

Anthony Quinn grieves for his dead son in Hal Wallis' *Last Train From Gun Hill. Copyright 1958 by Paramount Pictures Corp.*

who obtained a $10 million budget—which he spent with a lavish hand.

Charlton Heston was given the choice role of Moses. Heston, born in 1924, got into acting after coming back from World War II. Hal Wallis spotted him in a TV show and brought Heston to Hollywood for a role in *The Dark City*, directed by William Dieterle in 1950. Three gamblers, Jack Webb, Ed Begley, and Heston, sucker Don Defore out of his money. He kills himself, and his insane brother (Mike Mazurki) kills Webb and Begley and almost Heston. Lizabeth Scott and Viveca Lindfors had the feminine roles.

According to Heston, he was driving past DeMille's office and was spotted by the great man, who thought he had the qualities for the circus manager in *The Greatest Show on Earth*. After making six other films, including *The Far Horizons* with Fred MacMurray, DeMille called him back in 1956 for the role of Moses.

The original *Ten Commandments* had a biblical prologue to a modern story of a man who was broken

Jerry Lewis and Peter Lorre add sparkle to *The Sad Sack*. *Copyright 1957 by Paramount Pictures Corp.*

himself because he tried to break the commandments. This time DeMille chose a dramatized biblical story throughout. Much of the film was made on location in Egypt and the Sinai. The parting of the Red Sea was done in Hollywood, following the basic plan developed by Roy Pomeroy in 1923, and supplemented by new techniques such as background projection. The actual parting of the water was made by discharging huge masses of water into a specially prepared tough. The filling was photographed and the film printed backward to make it appear that the water was separating instead of splashing together. The fleeing Israelites were added by masking and multiple exposures. In the 1923 version, Pomeroy combined five separate bits of scenes into the final scene on the screen.

DeMille suffered a collapse during the filming of the Exodus scene in Egypt, but he recovered to finish the picture. Asked his plans for the future, he replied tersely, "Another picture or another world."

And it was another world. He began a remake of *The Buccaneer* with Heston in the Fredric March role of Jean Lafitte but was unable to finish it. Anthony Quinn took over.

With rare exceptions in his later years, DeMille was sneered at by the critics, but the public overflowed the theaters where his films were shown. In his younger days he was an innovator and one of the best directors in films. After the failure of *The Whispering Chorus* and the near failure of *Joan the Woman*, DeMille said, "I stopped making pictures for critics. I make pictures for people." Regardless of what his enemies say about him and his films, DeMille was one of the greatest *showmen* Hollywood ever saw.

It may be argued that his arrogant, egotistical, and splashily flamboyant showmanship is not needed. That could well be true, because one of the best films of the 1950s was a Western with a plot as old as the genre itself. Yet, as we look back on the period, this film is more indelible in our minds than any of the others, with the possible exception of Gloria Swanson's queening it over *Sunset Boulevard*. This is simply because of the way George Stevens molded the trite ingredients with fresh vision. The picture is *Shane* (1953).

A "nester"—homesteader—and his wife and son are threatened by a cattle baron who wants their land. Van Heflin and Jean Arthur were the farmer and his wife, with Brandon de Wilde as their son. Emile Meyer was the ranch owner. In contrast to the usual

Western, Meyer tried to settle his differences peacefully and turned to gunmen only when this failed.

Into this explosive situation comes a lone rider (Alan Ladd), returning to the spirit of the character that made him famous. Ladd had fallen on poor days, and his popularity was slipping when *Shane* gave him the best role of his career. He stays to take up the homesteaders' fight.

What followed was storytelling of the highest order on film. Critics are often tempted to compare *Shane* with the other Western triumph of the 1950s, United Artists' *High Noon* with Gary Cooper as the lawman forced to fight alone. *High Noon* was the more popular film, and Cooper made the character live, but *Shane* was technically a better film. Suspense is increased as Shane moves to a gun battle showdown because the audience does not know if he is a gunfighter or not.

Director George Stevens' manipulation of the interplay between his characters was exceptional. This included the unspoken love of the wife for the stranger and her husband's realization of it as well as the hero worship of the child for Shane.

Some other pictures that closed out the decade, some good and some bad and noted just to show the range of films produced were Hal Wallis' *Last Train from Gun Hill* (1958), *The Sad Sack* (1957) with Jerry Lewis, *The Five Pennies* with Danny Kaye; and *Tarzan's Greatest Adventure* (1959) with Gordon Scott.

Sol Lesser, the longtime producers of Tarzan films which he released through MGM and RKO, sold his interest to Sy Weintraub. Weintraub's first jungle epic, which despite its name was not Tarzan's "greatest adventure" at all, was released through Paramount. Weintraub followed this with *Tarzan the Magnificent*, also a Paramount release, in 1960. Then he got himself a new Tarzan, Jock Mahoney, and moved to MGM.

Tarzan's Greatest Adventure brought the famed ape man to Paramount in 1959. Gordon Scott as Tarzan fights a crocodile in this scene from the jungle epic. *Copyright 1959 by Solar Film Productions Inc.*

The Five Pennies with Danny Kaye, Tuesday Weld, and Barbara Bel Geddes was a dull film based on the life of band leader Red Nichols. *Copyright 1959 by Paramount Pictures Corp.*

14

Sunset on the Mountain

The foundations of the big studios crumbled in the 1950s. The 1960s brought them crashing down. Twentieth Century–Fox was almost destroyed by the *Cleopatra* fiasco. RKO, battered by Howard Hughes' takeover and subsequent neglect, became a TV production house. Warner Brothers was sold and merged with Seven Arts. Mighty MGM was reeling, and the longtime bosses of Paramount found themselves under attack for the company's poor financial performance. Paramount, which had once released 104 pictures a year, now dropped to 16 releases. The profits from each successful film were eaten up by four or more failures.

Barney Balaban, who had been president of Paramount for 30 years, was kicked upstairs to the figurehead position of chairman of the board. Ninety-three-year-old Adolph Zukor became chairman of the board emeritus in the spring of 1965. George Weltner, who became president and operating executive, immediately found himself under attack by Cy Feuer and Ernest Martin, Broadway producers, who owned large blocks of Paramount stock. They teamed with Herbert Siegel, who was in the chemical business, to force the election of Martin and Siegel to the Paramount board of directors.

Siegel's company had a large interest in General Artists Corporation, a talent agency. Weltner claimed that this constituted a conflict of interest. Other talent agencies would not deal with Paramount because it would appear that General Artists had an inside track due to Siegel's participation on both sides. Siegel agreed to divest himself and his company of any stock in General Artists. When he did not do so, Weltner used this as an excuse to remove Martin and Siegel from the Paramount board. A lawsuit over the removals immediately followed, resulting in a victory for Siegel and Martin in a judgment handed down in January 1966.

Martin and Siegel, bolstered by the judge's decision that they had acted only in what they thought was the best interests of the company, filed notice with the Securities and Exchange Commission that they would seek proxies in an attempt to unseat the present Paramount management. The showdown was set for the May 31 shareholders meeting.

Then suddenly a new and unexpected element was

Where the Trail Divides, with Theodore Roberts, Robert Edeson, and Winifred Kingston, deals with interracial romance, a strong theme for 1914. *Copyright 1914 by Jess L. Lasky Feature Play Co.*

injected in the management fight. Charles Bluhdorn, chairman of the board of Gulf and Western Industries, a conglomerate, offered Martin and Siegel $83 a share for all their Paramount stock. The stock was then selling on the New York stock exchange at $73.50. The deal seems to have been arranged by Weltner. To everyone's surprise, the two dissidents agreed.

Then at the May 31 annual shareholders' meeting, a favorable vote of the majority merged Paramount with Gulf and Western. For the first time in its history, Paramount became a subsidiary of another company.

Present on the panel of directors and corporate officials at the meeting was Adolph Zukor. In announcing the results of the merger vote, Weltner introduced Zukor to the assembled shareholders, saying, "Mr. Zukor was here at the beginning of Paramount, and he is here at the end!" The audience rose and gave "Mr. Paramount" a standing ovation.

Thus the curtain fell on the old Paramount Pictures after an extended run of fifty-two years—fifty-four if one counts from the formation of Zukor's Famous Players Film Company instead of Hodkinson's Paramount Pictures.

One movie historian recently contended that Paramount Pictures' place in the industry was hard to assess. This is hardly true. In the first years of its existence Paramount dominated the industry. It was a leader in both the artistic and business sides of film-making. While individual producers sometimes turned out better films, as a company Paramount had the most consistent record until the rise of Metro-Goldwyn-Mayer. Selecting a few films at random to show outstanding critical and popular successes, there are: the first *Squaw Man,* the *Cheat, The Miracle Man, The Covered Wagon, The Ten Commandments, Peter Pan, Beau Geste, Wings, Underworld,* and *The Last Command.* In the sound era, however, Paramount was eclipsed by the competition.

Looking back over early reviews in the trade publications, it is clear that a surprising number of critics thought Paramount the top producer from about 1914 to 1925.

One reviewer for *Motion Picture News* said of *The Goose Girl*, directed by Fred Thompson for Lasky in 1915: "One would have to be blind not to see the outlines of a new art in motion pictures in many of the Lasky productions."

The *New York Dramatic Mirror* came out with a statement that would stun the latter-day critics who sneered at DeMille. Writing about *The Unafraid* (1915), the review said, "In picturizing a play or adapting a novel, Lasky is almost certain of logic, sequence, and—wherein lies the real art—drama. For it had Cecil B. DeMille, who was more than a director. He was a film architect who used, in this case, the rough plans outlined in the romantic novel of the same name. That he built so well is quite a fine feather in his cap."

At the other Paramount producer at this time, Famous Players, Mary Pickford was the most popular movie star in the world. After the merger of Famous Players and Lasky, the critical acclaim increased.

In this period Paramount was not afraid to tackle mature themes. In *Where the Trail Divides* (1914), Lasky presented a picture of the trials of an Indian man who marries a white woman. This picture with Robert Edeson and Winifred Kingston was strong drama for the time it was made. Audiences then were reluctant to accept stories of interracial romances where one of the partners was a white woman. *Where the Trail Divides* treated this sensitive subject with compassion.

Lasky struck other blows for integration. This review appeared in a 1916 issue of *Photoplay* magazine: "Lasky's rather uncertain impression this month is bettered by such a simple, logical and well-played

For Better For Worse, a Cecil B. DeMille film with Gloria Swanson, was one of the best pictures of 1919. *Copyright by Paramount Artcraft.*

piece as *Alien Souls*, the best note in whose motif is the underlying humanity of all peoples, whatever the pigment of their skins. We are interested to learn that the Japanese are not the peculiarly monstrous Mongolians of the arts in general." Hayakawa and his wife Tsuru Aoki were the Oriental princials, and Jack Holt was the American villain.

Frederick James Smith used to pick the best films of the year for *Motion Picture Classic* magazine. For the 1917–1918 season, his top ten selections were: (1) *Hearts of the World*, (2) *Revelation*, (3) *Prunella*, (4) *Barbary Sheep*, (5) *Les Miserables*, (6) *The Blue Bird*, (7) *Ruggles of Red Gap*, (8) *Believe Me, Xantippe*, (9) *Stella Maris*, and (10) *A Dog's Life*.

Smith listed an addition nine as runners up. They were (1) *Reaching for the Moon*, (2) *His Majesty, Bunker Bean*, (3) *The Adventurer*, (4) *Tom Sawyer*, (5) *The Rise of Jenny Cushing*, (6) *Up the Road with Sallie*, (7) *The Fall of the Romanoffs*, (8) *The Whispering Chorus*, (9) *The Land of Promise*.

Five of the first ten were Paramount: *Prunella* (Marguerite Clark), *Barbary Sheep* (Elsie Ferguson), *The Blue Bird*, (no stars), *Believe Me, Xantippe* (Wallace Reid), and *Stella Maris* (Mary Pickford). *The Blue Bird*, based upon Maurice Maeterlinck's fantasy, was the only commercial flop in the group.

Of the second group, *His Majesty, Bunker Bean* (Jack Pickford), *Tom Sawyer* (Jack Pickford), *The Rise of Jenny Cushing* (Elsie Ferguson), *Up the Road with Sallie* (Constance Talmadge), *The Whispering Chorus* (Raymond Hatton), and *The Land of Promise* were Paramount pictures.

For the 1918–1919 season, ending in August 1919, Smith's top ten were (1) *Broken Blossoms*, (2) *The Turn in the Road*, (3) *Shoulder Arms*, (4) *For Better For Worse*, (5) *Eyes of the Soul*, (6) *Don't Change Your Husband*, (7) *The Squaw Man*, (8) *The Girl Who Stayed at Home*, (9) *We Can't Have Everything*, (10) *The Avalanche*. Four of these were made by DeMille: *For Better for Worse*, *The Squaw Man* (remake), *Don't Change Your Husband*, and *We Can't Have Everything*.

From this point on Paramount's domination of the critics' lists began to fall as First National emerged as an increasingly important production company. Metro, despite continual financial problems, turned out some superb films, including Rex Ingram's *Prisoner of Zenda* and *The Four Horsemen of the Apocalypse*. United Artists with Mary Pickford, Douglas Fairbanks, Charles Chaplin, and D. W. Griffith added to the increasing competition.

Paramount continued to turn out profitable and pleasing films, but the company no longer dominated the lists of annual bests. Then competition from Metro-Goldwyn, beginning in 1924, hurt Paramount's dominant position still more.

Paramount films were mainly entertainment oriented. Occasionally someone like William C. DeMille would slip in a film like *Only 38* in which social criticism peeked through cracks in the plot. But the public was not interested in Lois Wilson as a young widow facing the disapproval of her children as she tried to make a new life.

Smith's list of the ten best for 1920–1921 were (1) *Passion*, (2) *Way Down East*, (3) *The Kid*, (4) *The Cabinet of Dr. Caligari*, (5) *Deception*, (6) *Sentimental Tommy*, (7) *The Golem*, (8) *Gypsy Blood*, (9) *The Jack Knife Man*, and (10) *The Four Horsemen of the Apocalypse*.

Only three of these were Paramount releases: *Deception* with Emil Jannings as Henry VIII; *Sentimental Tommy*, the James M. Barrie story, with Gareth Hughes and May McAvoy; and *The Golem* with Paul Wegener as the clay monster. Two of the three were German imports, leaving *Sentimental Tommy* as the only Paramount Hollywood film listed.

This was quite a comedown from the previous 1919–1920 season with seven Paramount films in the top ten. They were *The Miracle Man* with Thomas Meighan, Betty Compson, and Lon Chaney; *Why Change Your Wife?*, a DeMille society drama with Gloria Swanson; *On With the Dance* with Mae Murray; DeMille's *Male and Female*, with Swanson, Meighan,

Dr. Cyclops was a fantasy directed by Ernest B. Schoedsack, the man who directed *King Kong.* Albert Dekker is the mad scientist who shrinks Janice Logan, Thomas Coley, Charles Halton, and Victor Kilian to miniature size. *Copyright 1939 by Paramount Pictures Inc.*

and others; *Dr. Jekyll and Mr. Hyde*, John S. Robertson's excellent rendition of the Stevenson classic with John Barrymore in a marvelous performance; *23½ Hours Leave* with Douglas McLean taking that time to win the colonel's daughter; and Frank Borzage's fine *Humoresque*.

For the remainder of the 1920s pictures such as *The Covered Wagon*, *The Ten Commandments*, *Peter Pan*, *Beau Geste*, *The Patriot*, *Underworld*, *The Last Command*, and *Wings* were but mountain peaks rising above the ordinary plains. Two documentaries, which ordinarily get poor audience reaction, hit the bell for Paramount. They were *Grass*, the odyssey of a Persian tribe, and *Chang*, filmed in the jungles of Asia by Merian C. Cooper and Ernest B. Schoedsack. Both of these men are best remembered as producer and director of *King Kong*. Later the two worked on *The Four Feathers* (1929) for Paramount, and Schoedsack alone directed the fantasy *Dr. Cyclops* in 1939. In *The Four Feathers* Richard Arlen received a white feather from his fellow officers as a sign of his cowardice. Of course he is redeemed and shown a true hero in the end. *Dr. Cyclops* was a mad scientist played by Albert Dekker, who reduces Janice Logan, Thomas Coley, Charles Halton, and Victor Kilian to a tiny size and then tries to kill them. They save themselves by breaking his glasses so that he stumbles blindly into a well.

A very unusual picture that got high critical praise was directed by cameraman Karl Brown who shot *The Covered Wagon*. In 1927 Brown went to the Great Smokey Mountains of North Carolina and made *Stark Love* with a cast of nonprofessionals. James Forrest played a young man who loved a hill girl, Helen Mundy. After his drudge of a mother died, his mountaineer father tried to force the girl to marry him. The public did not agree with the critics, but the picture did not lose money. Brown made it cheaply.

Forrest and Helen Mundy got only $30 a week. Forrest was offered a Hollywood contract, but he refused. *Photoplay Magazine* called *Stark Love* one of the six best pictures of the month and gave high praise to the acting of Forrest and Mundy.

Paramount got into the talking picture race late but caught up fast. The company's big asset was Ernest Lubitsch, and his sly comedies poking fun at sex set the tone for Paramount in the 1930s. Mitchell Leisen's many films and Preston Sturges' *The Lady Eve*, while having the directors' individuality, were right in the Lubitsch mold.

In considering the pictures of the 1940s and 1950s, once one gets past *The Lady Eve, Lost Weekend, Sunset Boulevard, This Gun for Hire, Shane, The Ten Commandments* and the other DeMilles, *The Heiress*, and a few like these, it is hard to recall any particular Paramount picture other than the road epics. The pictures just were not memorable, and so the company's failing fortunes brought about the circumstances leading to its acquisition by Gulf and Western.

Looking back over Paramount's fifty-two years as an independent studio, one does not see Paramount going in for prestige pictures as Warner Brothers did. It did not strive for the perfection that made Metro-Goldwyn-Mayer "retake alley." But then Paramount never promised its audience social significance and educational values. The ads said, "If it's a Paramount Picture, it's the best show in town." The significance here is in the word "show." Paramount certainly–for the most part–did give us a *show*.

The story of Paramount under its new owners in this time of changing social and moral values is another story that is too detailed to relate here. The studio is not the studio of Lasky, Zukor, and DeMille, but neither are the other former great film factories what they once were. That type of film industry is gone forever.

Karl Brown filmed *Stark Love* with non-professionals Forrest
James and Helen Mundy as leads. *Copyright 1927 by Famous
Players—Lasky.*

But pictures still get made. We are told that each succeeding one "breaks all records." Unfortunately, movie records are kept in "grosses." The gross receipts are constantly being increased by inflation. A vice president of 20th Century-Fox, as this is written, has refused to compare his company's new film *Alien* with its champion grosser *Star Wars*. He said it could not be done because inflation had increased ticket prices since *Star Wars*.

DeMille's *Why Change Your Wife* cost $130,000 to film. It grossed $1 million. This is eight times its cost. A modern picture, such as *Apocalypse Now*, costing $40 million, must bring in $320 million to equal the popularity of the DeMille film, measured in profit percentage. So when we merely look at the grosses, it is not true that movies are more popular today than ever. Popularity can only be measured in the total tickets sold, and this must be adjusted for the large population increase of the past fifty years.

During the silent era and well into the sound period, movies were the major mass entertainment. Moreover, it was family entertainment. During the 1950s movie houses went broke by the scores, many closing their doors never to open again. The industry blamed the trouble on television, but it was actually downbeat pictures. Then along came MGM and put out *That's Entertainment* with ads that said, "And do we need it now!" Even so, a lot of producers still failed to get the word until *Star Wars*, which was nothing but pure entertainment, surprised a lot of people by becoming the biggest grosser of all time.

This caused Barry Diller, chairman of Paramount, to admit that films "of heavy import" were dying at the box office. "Eighteen months ago," he said in a newspaper interview, "Paramount made a decision to make only positive films."

By positive he meant entertainment pictures. This change of policy produced such successful films as *Saturday Night Fever*, *Grease*, and *Heaven Can Wait*. Each of these films was enough to bring smiles to the faces of Paramount's shareholders.

It would appear from this that Paramount had gotten the "message" from the best message picture it ever released. This was Preston Sturges' *Sullivan's Travels*. The picture had Joel McCrae as a producer who wanted to show the plight of the poor. So he dressed in rags and went out to learn about the subject at first hand. As he got to understand the people, he was most impressed by the way he saw them laughing at Mickey Mouse. For a short time this made them forget their misery. He realized then that the greatest gift he could give these people was to go back and create films to make them laugh. Most of the time the old Paramount tried to do this, and in doing so it often gave us "the best *show* in town."

Preston Sturges' *Sullivan's Travels* had a great message for moviemakers. This was that they should forget message pictures and devote themselves to making people laugh. Joel McCrae and Veronica Lake are the sign carriers in this scene. *Copyright 1941 by Paramount Pictures Inc.*

Afterword and Sources

Many years ago there was a set of books called *The Harvard Classics,* which were publicized as "Dr. Elliot's Five-Foot Shelf of Books." We fear that not even a library of similar size could begin to tell the full story of Paramount. So much happened and so many people were involved that no one book can do more than give an overview of this famous film factory. As a result, many people who deserved mention were squeezed out.

In particular, we neglected the directors. Except for a few like Cecil B. DeMille, George Melford, and Mitchell Leisen in later years, few of them could be called Paramount directors. They made a few pictures— some of them exceptional—and then moved on. They never stopped long enough to have their names associated with the studio, as people like DeMille, Bob Hope, Crosby, and a few others did.

Hitchcock dropped in occasionally for a picture. Victor Fleming made some fine pictures for Paramount, including *The Rough Riders* (1927). So did Herbert Brenon. And quite a few others could be mentioned, such as George Cukor, Rouben Mamou-

lian, and Leo McCarey. But with the exception of McCarey, each made his best pictures elsewhere. Lubitsch's *Trouble in Paradise* was a triumph, and his Chevalier pictures were a delight, but can any of them be put above *Ninotchka?*

In a like manner, many stars have been neglected. Pola Negri was an exceptional actress. Her German films showed this. However, Paramount did not do well by her. We suspect that *Imperial Hotel* (with James Hall), directed by Mauritz Stiller in 1927, was her best film in the United States. Despite all her publicity, she had little impact upon Paramount. Gloria Swanson, not nearly the actress Negri was, was far more important to the company. Paramount took her as a fugitive from Mack Sennett and developed her into one of the biggest stars of the day in a classic example of star building. It is doubtful if any other woman (except Mary Pickford, of course) had such an influence over the company's fortunes.

Also, we neglected Elizabeth Taylor's Paramount pictures and passed over Frank Sinatra. These and others were not truly Paramount stars. They just passed in and out.

Since this is the story of the company and its rises and falls, there was no room to pay proper tribute to the B players. Under the Realart banner in the early 1920s and then as Paramount feature players, they entertained us mightily. They deserve better than occasional mention. We hope someday that some writer will do them justice. Many had the talent to go on to better things, as Anthony Quinn did, but the breaks never came their way.

In sketching the rise and fall and rerise of Paramount, we have made use of most available sources.

The base was the Paramount collection in Margaret Herrick Library of the Academy of Motion Picture Arts and Sciences. This is the library's largest special collection. It consists of stills, press books, and script material. Samuel A. Gill has indexed and cataloged the collection in two thick volumes. These are invaluable to any person researching Paramount and its stars.

The collection is not complete. Some of the material was lost before Paramount donated it to the Academy library, but a great deal still remains.

In addition to the Paramount collection and the general files of the library, we gleaned the pages of *Motion Picture World, Motion Picture News, Photoplay, Motion Picture Classic,* and *Motion Picture* magazine, assembling a mass of notes and tapes. Most of this had to be discarded for lack of space. A lot of it, like the voluminous material on William S. Hart, was dropped because the star, while important, was not a major factor in the overall Paramount history.

In the course of many years in newspaper and freelance writing work, we have talked to many people connected with Paramount at one time or another. Of these, actors and actresses proved the poorest source of information. Their memories are faulty. They overemphasize their parts. And often all they tell you is rehashes of old stories invented by their press agents. Studio technicians are good sources. Cameramen, carpenters, grips, electricians, and office workers observe plenty in the course of their work. An especially good source, but difficult to get to talk, are people who work with the stars' financial advisers. Those who have retired and are willing to talk can tell us extremely interesting stories, since a manager's job is not just to invest a star's money, but to keep him or her out of trouble. Unfortunately, this kind of story had to be discarded also.

We would like also to express thanks to the memory of Jesse L. Lasky who was kind enough to talk to us years ago about the early days of Paramount and the Jesse L. Lasky Feature Play Company. In contrast to so many of the picture pioneers, what Jesse had to say is pretty well supported by the record.

We also had occasion to talk with Sam Goldwyn and came away with the impression that Goldwyn at that time (1956) still resented his former partners.

Index of Photos

266